THE FORMAL
MECHANICS
OF MIND

By the same author

Practical Reasoning in Natural Language

THE FORMAL
MECHANICS
OF MIND

Stephen N. Thomas

Cornell University Press

ITHACA, NEW YORK

Published 1978 by Cornell University Press.

Printed in the United States of America by Vail-Ballou Press, Inc.

Library of Congress Cataloging in Publication Data
(For library cataloging purposes only)

Thomas, Stephen N., 1942–
    The formal mechanics of mind.

    Includes bibliographical references and index.
    1. Knowledge, Theory of. I. Title.
BD161.T43   121   77-3128
ISBN 0-8014-1034-7

Acknowledgments

Much of the conceptual apparatus employed in this book is based on the pioneering work of such theoreticians as A. M. Turing, John von Neumann, Warren McCulloch, and Norbert Wiener. Much also is owed to Wittgenstein, whose philosophical instincts sensed the true locus of difficulties in the philosophy of mind, to Hilary Putnam, who first employed cybernetic concepts in epistemology, to Willard Van Orman Quine, for his liberating idea that a theory is ontologically committed to nothing more than the entities ranged over by its bound variables, and to Quine and Pierre Duhem for the insight that hypotheses or beliefs true by definition ("analytic truths") are not sharply distinguishable from those confirmable by empirical observation. In addition, I am indebted to Burton S. Dreben and Judith J. Thomson, who taught me philosophy, and to H. L. Teuber and Patrick Wall, who convinced me that present theoretical difficulties in the foundations of neuropsychology are identical to philosophy's traditional mind-body problem and cannot be solved by the methods of conceptual analysis alone. I am also grateful to Keith Donnellan, Jerry Fodor, and James Thomson, who read an earlier draft of some of these ideas in 1968, and to W. D. Hart, F. K. Lenherr, T. K. Stevenson, L. Guptil, C. A. Morrisey, J. Skaggs, B. C. Schwartzbaum, A. E. Stern, D. Stevens, M. Whisner, J. A. Zirbel, M. Almoslino, and P. J. Davick for their help and encouragement during the twelve years of preparation of this work.

STEPHEN N. THOMAS

Contents

A Note on Punctuation

Standard conventions govern my use of quotation marks. To talk about or describe nonlinguistic objects (e.g., roses, butterflies), linguistic expressions denoting these entities are used (for example, one says, "Butterflies are on the roses"). To talk about talk itself—that is, to discuss linguistic expressions such as words, phrases, or sentences—one must use linguistic expressions that refer to other linguistic expressions. The name of a linguistic expression is formed conventionally by enclosing that expression in single quotation marks. One says, for example, that the word 'roses' has five letters and is a noun, whereas roses have a lovely smell and color. So when a word, phrase, or other linguistic expression itself is the referent—in contrast to what this linguistic expression denotes—single quotes are used.

This distinction sometimes is described as the difference between *use* and *mention*. Words, phrases, predicates, and other linguistic expressions are said to be "used" when one is speaking in what is called "the material mode" or in "the object language" about their nonlinguistic referents; they are said to be "mentioned" (but not used) when they themselves are the subject matter of a discussion in "the formal mode" or in "a metalanguage." Thus, for example, when I say that apples contain seeds, I use the word 'apples', whereas if I say that 'apples' contains six letters, I mention (but do not use) the word 'apples'. When one wishes to refer not to instances of the fruit, but to its (general) name, the word must be mentioned; this is done by using its name, which is formed by enclosing the word in single quotes. In particular, when I refer in this book to the utterance produced by a speaker (where that utterance is conceived simply as a sequence of symbols, a noise, acoustic object, or inscription), that utterance is enclosed in single quotes.

Concomitantly, other conventions are observed also. When phrases are used by the author with reservations, or in a qualified or extended sense, or a statement is repeated from another source, the customary double quotation marks are used. Single quotes within double set off quotations within quotations. Linguistic expressions mentioned not merely as formal linguistic objects, but qua bearers of meaning, sometimes are enclosed in double quotes (rather than single as described above).

For the convenience of readers desiring a quick overview of this book's empirical content and experimental implications, a science abstract follows the appendices.

THE FORMAL
MECHANICS
OF MIND

Philosophy as
Intellectual Construction

A specific working hypothesis regarding the genesis, nature, and proper response to philosophic problems, particularly to those in the philosophy of mind, gives rise to this book. Although superficially resembling metaphilosophic presuppositions common to Wittgenstein, Rudolf Carnap, John Wisdom, and Peter Strawson, this hypothesis actually differs from these fundamentally. Since some sense of its basic assumptions will facilitate the comprehension and proper evaluation of this work by philosophers as well as by psychologists, neuropsychologists, psychophysiologists, neurocyberneticians, and others interested in the psychophysical relationship, I begin with a brief metaphilosophical apology.

This metaphilosophical working hypothesis entails that philosophy stands in a peculiar relationship to science; in particular, it implies that work in what traditionally is termed "philosophy of mind" is properly identical to research in the conceptual foundations of psychology and neuropsychology. This hypothesis is perhaps most succinctly explained with the unorthodox assistance of the following illustration from the genre of streamlined fact known as "biographical fiction": *Moving physical objects* (thrown sticks, falling leaves, clouds across the sky) presumably had been observed and talked about in the language of the age long before a great philosopher (whom I will call 'Aristotle') sought to comprehend these phenomena with a general theory. As a basic principle in his account of "why and what movement is," Aristotle plausibly generalized the seemingly universal observation that physical things move only insofar as and as long as something else pushes on them (e.g., to slide a heavy table across the floor, a force must be applied constantly to it). A few recalcitrant experiences prompted ingenious auxiliary hypotheses (e.g., how did thrown projectiles travel through the air?), but one theoretical difficulty exceeded all others: If each object moves only as long as something else pushes it, what about the object that is doing the pushing? To push, it, too, must move and so, according to the general principle, it must be pushed by something else in turn. Thus arises the following theoretical dilemma: Each moving physical object is being propelled by an infinite sequence of simultaneously acting pushers, or everything somehow moves in a circle, or all appearance of motion is illusory, or (last, but hardly more plausible) something exists that can move other objects without at the same time itself moving (a "prime mover unmoved"). For two thousand years or so, this was considered a major unsolved philosophic problem. Finally a group of theoreticians ('Newton', as I shall call them collectively) solved it. How? Did Newton establish that one of the apparent theoretical alternatives was in fact the correct one, or did he study the actual use of motion concepts in ordinary language? No. He *replaced* Aristotle's scheme with a different way of thinking about the same phenomena, a new system of principles that agreed with the same observations without generating the same problem. Roughly, Newton postulated that an object, once set in motion, continues to move uniformly in the same direction until acted on by something else that changes that movement. The same table that requires constant pushing to stay in motion across the floor would, if set in motion in isolated space, continue to move at the same velocity until acted upon by some other force. Sliding it across the floor requires constant pushing only because other forces (those of "friction") acting to retard its motion constantly need to be overcome. (So, for example, celestial bodies need no "prime mover" to continue their motion.) Because on this conception moving physical objects do not require constant pushing to stay in motion, Newton's way of thinking about motion did not generate the problem of the (contemporaneously acting) prime mover, and with its advent, *that* ancient predicament lost its status as an unsolved philosophic problem. The problem had been solved, in fact.

This paradigm suggests the following hypothesis about philosophic problems: Many such difficulties are simply the manifesta-

tion of the absence of satisfactory conceptualizing structures.[1]
That is, where philosophic difficulties exist or appear to exist, the
trouble actually is the lack of adequate theories, models, or other
conceptualizing devices (or equivalently, some defect in those
being used at the time to characterize the subject matter). If the
problem is the complete lack of any structure whatsoever for
conceptualizing some matter, then philosophy must start from
naught in an activity identical to innovative scientific theorizing.
(On this account, e.g., Thales is seen as an early physical chemist,
Plato as an early theoretical semanticist.) More commonly, however, philosophic problems arise in pre-existing conceptual contexts generated by some specific way of thinking about a matter.
For example, the structure used to conceptualize some class of
phenomena (e.g., moving physical objects, mental phenomena)
may represent its subject matter so as to entail an exhaustive
set of theoretical options, each implausible, unintelligible, or
intellectually repugnant in some way. One apparent theoretical
alternative may conflict with our empirical observations or cast
into doubt and disarray all our initial presuppositions about the
matter (e.g., entailing that nothing moves and hence all appearances of motion are delusory, or that changes of mental state and
bodily state are unconnected with each other), while another
leads to a theoretical *cul-de-sac*, an impasse, lacuna, or loop where
theory cannot be completed satisfactorily (e.g., an infinity of
pushers is required, or no mechanism can be described for causal
interaction between nonintersecting domains). Alternatively, a
philosophic problem may arise when different conceptualizing
structures, each used to characterize the same phenomena but in
dissimilar ways for diverse purposes, are so joined or related that
one's consequences apparently conflict with the other's presuppositions (e.g., the causal explanation of human behavior may
seem to have implications incompatible with requirements for
legal or moral responsibility). Or, no less disconcerting, an apparently natural and proper account of something may appear to
entail bizarre and disturbing consequences (e.g., a seemingly
plausible analysis of how subjects obtain knowledge of their
surrounding environment through their sense organs may appear
to lead to the conclusion that no such knowledge is attainable).
In each such case, the hypothesis conjectures, the "philosophic

1. The extension of the term 'conceptualizing structure' is more precisely delin-
eated in Appendix III.

problem" is actually only an artifact of the conceptualizing apparatus being employed. The appearance of a problem of the "philosophic" sort actually is a sign that something is wrong with the conceptualizing structure through which one is attempting to understand the matter in question.

To philosophers employing the faulty conceptualizing structure, however, the situation does not always appear thus. Viewed through its distortions, the philosophic problem may appear like any other, just deeper and more difficult to solve. To those who have internalized the problem's source, it may intellectually appear that one of the unpalatable alternatives *must* be true, or that an incomprehensible mystery is at hand, or that an entire conceptualizing structure that formerly served reliably must be abandoned, or that an amazing fact about the world has been discovered. Such appearances provide no obvious hint that the problem's continued existence actually is sustained only by the continued employment of the conceptualizing structure generating it. "A philosophic problem exists . . . !" is how the situation appears from within a defective conceptual frame of reference. In such a case, the insight "Something's wrong with how I'm thinking about this topic . . ." does not naturally occur, at least not initially. So one moral of this metaphilosophy is: When a philosophic problem arises, one should always ask oneself, "Could the way in which I am looking at the subject be causing the difficulty?"

Equally immediate is a second corollary. A philosophic problem generated by a conceptualizing structure can be "solved" (eliminated) only by getting rid of the conceptualizing structure that is generating it. So, for example, a philosophic dilemma is not to be resolved by choosing one of the competing horns, but rather (inconceivable as it may seem at the time) by restructuring its originating presuppositions so that it vanishes. To resolve a philosophic difficulty, the faulty conceptualizing structure must be located, isolated, and rebuilt, so that the problem no longer arises, or superseded by an altogether new one (for theoreticians always resist relinquishing a conceptualizing structure until provided with a superior replacement performing the same function); or when the problem is the complete lack of any such structure, one must be created from nothing. In any case, this metaphilosophical hypothesis entails that philosophers must synthesize conceptualizing structures to solve philosophic problems.

The hypothesis, then, implies that solving philosophic problems may require constructing or remodeling theories about physical events, models of the mind, or perhaps even principles of law and jurisprudence, political ideologies, or systems of ethics, as suits the problem at hand. But engaging in such an activity is identical to "theoretical research," "advanced studies," or "basic reform" in the discipline or practice associated with that conceptualizing structure. It follows, then, that to solve philosophical problems, philosophers not only legitimately may, but indeed must, engage in such activities as the formulation or revision of theories about the natural world, legal reform, political ideologizing, and ethical innovation. So, according to this hypothesis, the name 'philosophy' properly denotes not a separate discipline (defined perhaps by its own special methodology), but instead the general activity of creating new conceptualizing structures. In particular, on this view, the term 'philosophy of mind' is another name for research in the foundations of psychology and neuropsychology. The conclusion also follows that the *subject matter* of an area in philosophy is identical to that of the discipline associated with the conceptualizing structures with which it deals. Thus, for example, waves, fields, particles, and so on, are the subject matter of the philosophy of physics; psychological phenomena, their manifestations, related bodily processes, and so on, are the subject matter of the philosophy of mind; linguistic phenomena are the subject matter of the philosophy of language, and so on. Conceptualizing structures concern philosophy essentially, on this view, *not* as something to be characterized, but as something to be constructed; a philosopher's *subject matter* is the subject matter of the conceptualizing structure giving rise to the problem he is trying to solve.

The assertion *"philosophic activity = research in the foundations of the body of thought associated with the conceptualizing structure generating the philosophic problem being solved"* requires one qualification. Ordinary employments of current scientific conceptualizing structures (what Thomas S. Kuhn calls "normal science"[2]), of course, do not constitute philosophy. Even unexplained phenomena (e.g., how embryonic cells differentiate or how birds navigate) excite no special philosophic interest. Only

2. Thomas S. Kuhn, *The Structure of Scientific Revolutions* (Chicago and London: The University of Chicago Press, 1962).

if inconsistencies, paradoxes, unintelligibilities, unanswerable questions, or bizarre conclusions ensue, or the phenomena begin to appear not merely unexplained but unexplainable on existing conceptions, do theoreticians become philosophers. That is, only in its "abnormal" phase is science identical to philosophy.[3] (In this respect it is true that "philosophy is not one of the natural sciences." But very speculative science can be an instance of philosophy.) The same is true, of course, *mutatis mutandis*, of philosophy in relation to disciplines or bodies of thought and practice other than science.

My hypothesis is that many (perhaps all) philosophic problems actually manifest the lack of adequate ways of conceptualizing some matter and accordingly are resolvable only by construction of better conceptualizing structures that do not generate those problems, an activity indistinguishable from basic reform or innovation in the corresponding discipline. This view differs greatly from the metaphilosophies that have spurred and swayed the past half-century of Anglo-American analytic philosophy. Despite their many disagreements, all the metaphilosophers mentioned earlier shared certain basic presuppositions. Following Wittgenstein,[4] it was thought that the nonexistence of even acceptable candidates for answers to philosophic questions evidenced these questions' illegitimacy or logical impropriety, and that such questions *actually* manifested only confusions arising from unrigorous language or misunderstandings concerning the uses of words. The early Wittgenstein, the logical positivists, the ordinary-language philosophers, and the later Wittgenstein all accepted two basic metaphilosophic postulates: (1) Whatever doing philosophy consists in, it is (or should be) a very different activity from research in science or in any other discipline. (2) Philosophic problems manifest only linguistic or conceptual confusions, and accordingly are resolvable by an analysis of the concepts involved in the problem's statement or by linguistic clarification. Seldom openly and explicitly affirmed, more often today these two assumptions are presupposed implicitly by phi-

3. The commonplace that modern science arose because empirical observation replaced theoretical speculation is naively inaccurate. The renaissance of science involved the *conceptual constructions* of Copernicus, Kepler, Galileo, Newton, and other theoreticians.

4. Ludwig Wittgenstein, *Tractatus Logico-Philosophicus*, tr. D. F. Pears and B. F. McGuinness (1918; London: Routledge & Kegan Paul, 1961), secs. 6.5–6.5.1.

losophers who restrict themselves to a methodology and kind of analysis that received its initial justification from these meta-philosophical assumptions.[5] Wittgenstein, an originator of these ideas, changed many of his views during his lifetime, but never gave up these two assumptions. Both were explicitly affirmed in the *Tractatus*:

> Philosophy is not one of the natural sciences.
> (The word 'philosophy' must mean something whose place is above or below the natural sciences, not beside them.)[6]
> Philosophy aims at the logical clarification of thoughts.
> Philosophy is not a body of doctrine but an activity.
> A philosophical work consists essentially of elucidations.
> Philosophy does not result in 'philosophical propositions', but rather in the clarification of propositions.[7]

Similar claims about the nature of philosophy also appear in his later writings:

> ... the characteristic of a metaphysical question [is] that we express an unclarity about the grammar of words in the *form* of a scientific question.[8]
> The very word 'problem', one might say, is misapplied when used for our philosophical troubles.[9]

The close relationship between these two assumptions in Wittgenstein's thought is obvious in the *Blue Book*, where both find expression in the single formula: "Our problem, in other words, was not a scientific one; but a muddle felt as a problem."[10] In contrast, while agreeing that philosophic questions are unlike all others, that they have a unique origin, and that they cannot be answered like other questions but require an entirely different kind of response, I hypothesize that they appear unanswerable because no conceptualizing structure in terms of which an answer could be expressed exists at the time (and so, consequently, sentences answering the questions cannot be formed). Contrary to

5. So, if they have no other justification for their practices, then they have no justification for titling their activities "philosophy" or for observing the restrictions imposed by these doctrines.

6. *Tractatus*, sec. 4.111.

7. *Ibid.*, sec. 4.112.

8. Ludwig Wittgenstein, *The Blue and Brown Books* (New York: Harper & Row, 1958), p. 35.

9. *Ibid.*, p. 46.

10. *Ibid.*, p. 6.

the view of Wittgenstein and others, these philosophic problems are *not* the manifestations of "unrigorous language" or "misunderstandings of our forms of expression." In fact, they cannot even arise at a purely linguistic level; rather, their rarer, subtler origin is the use of abstract theories or conceptualizing structures to deal intellectually with the world. The divergence between my metaphilosophy and its competitors becomes even more obvious when their respective consequences are compared. Since according to the "linguistic pseudoproblem theory" only conceptual analysis or linguistic clarification can eliminate philosophic problems, this was thought to be the only proper response to them.[11] Accordingly, doing philosophy should differ radically from engaging in the activities proper to science or any other legitimate discipline. Above all else and in particular, Wittgenstein claimed, the correct response to philosophic problems is never theory construction—for either any theory constructed would be a scientific theory and hence, not philosophy, or else it would be unscientific and hence, cognitively vacuous, empty, a "pseudo-theory." Properly done, philosophy "leaves everything as it is," said Wittgenstein.[12] To meet philosophic questions with theories would only repeat the traditional error (of replacing one bad theory with another) rather than clearing up the linguistic muddle or confusion that actually is responsible for the problem. The "sole and whole function of philosophy," Gilbert Ryle declared, is "the detection of the sources in linguistic idioms of recurrent misconceptions and absurd theories."[13]

Some of the "problems" that occupied past philosophers perhaps were indeed spurious, and some of these even may have arisen from linguistic confusion. But why emphasize them? To characterize traditional philosophy as dealing only with pseudoproblems, while "science" always had the wisdom to handle only genuine problems, is a historical misrepresentation. When Thales raised the question, "What is everything made of?" and tried to answer it, was that the recorded beginning of philosophy or of

11. See, e.g., the exchange between Peter F. Strawson and Rudolf Carnap in *The Philosophy of Rudolf Carnap*, Library of Living Philosophers, ed. Paul A. Schilpp, XI (LaSalle, Ill: Open Court, 1963), 44–56, 503–518, 933–940.

12. Ludwig Wittgenstein, *Philosophical Investigations*, trans. G. E. M. Anscombe (New York: Macmillan, 1953), sec. 124.

13. Gilbert Ryle, "Systematically Misleading Expressions," *Proceedings of the Aristotelian Society*, 31 (1931–32); reprinted in *Essays on Logic and Language*, 1st ser., ed. Antony Flew (Oxford: Blackwell, 1963), p. 36.

chemistry? What about Democritus and his atomic theory? Or Locke's attempt to characterize "the ways whereby our understandings come to attain those notions of things we have"? How plausible is the suggestion that the problems with which these philosophers grappled were simply the manifestation of "misunderstandings concerning our forms of expression"?

While reviewing the model of philosophy underlying the alleged basic sharp distinction between a scientist's ponderings and a philosopher's speculations, the account of science presupposed by this dichotomy should be scrutinized also. How is science viewed by those who say that a philosophic problem is not a scientific one?

> It was true to say that our considerations could not be scientific ones . . . we may not advance any kind of theory. There must not be anything hypothetical in our considerations. We must do away with all *explanation*, and description alone must take its place.[14]

Is science not descriptive? What kind of "explanation" and "theory" is here being so sharply contrasted with "description"? Where does description leave off and explanation begin?[15] And how much of a theory really is "hypothetical"?

Also opposing the suggestion that philosophy properly involves theory construction are other misconceptions of the nature of science. The point certainly will seem obscure to those who take, e.g., "All ravens are black" (concluded inductively perhaps after observing many black ravens) as their paradigm of scientific method and theory. Without attempting to explain how theories go beyond observational data to provide a deeper understanding of phenomena, nevertheless it can be emphasized that they do so. Early astronomers who watched the motions of the heavenly bodies in the night sky perhaps simply could have summarized

14. *Philosophical Investigations*, sec. 109.
15. Berkeley objected that Newton's account of planetary motions was not really an *explanation* because the postulated laws were only "rules . . . observed in the production of natural effects, the efficient and final causes of which are not of mechanical consideration. Certainly, if the explaining a phenomenon be to assign its proper efficient and final cause, it should seem the mechanical philosophers never explained anything; their province being only to discover the laws of nature, that is, the general rules and methods of motion; and to account for particular phenomena by reducing them under, or shewing their conformity to, such general rules" (George Berkeley, *Works*, ed. Alexander Campbell Fraser, III, *Siris* (Oxford: Clarendon Press, 1901), sec. 231).

their observations in general descriptions of the data (e.g., "Body Y always moves in such-and-such a path through the celestial dome"), but in fact, they did more. The Ptolemaic and Copernican theories, for example, provided models yielding whole new ways of thinking about the same familiar phenomena (e.g., proposing arrangements in space of the bodies that would account for their motions as seen from Earth). The observed motions of the celestial objects were *explained* by these theories (i.e., made intelligible and comprehensible) in a way that no mere generalization of the observed data could accomplish.

Wittgenstein speaks as if a difference between science and philosophy is that science is concered with finding causal connections and discovering new facts, while philosophy properly operates "not by giving new information but by arranging what we have always known."[16]

> [Our investigation] takes its rise, not from an interest in the facts of nature, nor from a need to grasp causal connections; but from an urge to understand the basis, or essence, of everything empirical. Not, however, as if to this end we had to hunt out new facts; it is rather of the essence of our investigation that we do not seek to learn anything *new* by it. We want to *understand* something that is already in plain view.[17]

But with reference to moving physical objects, Aristotle and Newton both wanted to understand something with which, in another sense, they already were familiar. What causal connections did Copernicus's theory postulate? For Copernicus, the problem quite literally was "understanding something that is already in plain view," yet undeniably that was science. On which side of Wittgenstein's sharp "explanation-description" distinction does the Copernican model go?

In opposition to Wittgenstein's injunctions, my metaphilosophical theory entails that a philosophic problem should be met by isolating the faulty conceptualizing structure generating it and replacing it with a better one—a proper response thus includes theory construction, the very thing Wittgenstein admonishes against. And therefore (as explained earlier) far from being separate and distinct from other disciplines of thought, philosophy may include scientific theory building, legal reform, ethical

16. *Philosophical Investigations*, sec. 109.
17. *Ibid.*, sec. 89.

innovation, formal research, etc. (If everything were left as found, as Wittgenstein urged, the philosophic problems too would remain.) So in sum, as contrasted with Wittgensteinian views, my hypothesis postulates: (1) Many philosophic problems actually manifest difficulties within established ways of thinking about some phenomenon (and not linguistic confusions). (2) In order to "solve" these problems, it may be necessary to *replace* the defective conceptualizing structure with another way of looking at the matter. In other words, a proper response to the discovery of bad theories is not abstaining from all theorizing, but rather building good theories to replace them. (3) This activity may be indistinguishable from scientific theory construction; indeed, it may result in science.

The story of Newton illustrates these metaphilosophic ideas.[18] For the traditional philosophic problem of the prime mover obviously was built right into the Aristotelian assumptions (natural as they seemed) so that once those assumptions were accepted, the problem became inescapable. To the intellects halted at this theoretical impasse, however, that fact was hidden; the problem's peculiar "philosophic" quality was its only sign or evidence. Moreover, since the problem was created and sustained by a particular way of thinking about the subject matter, it could be solved (i.e., eliminated) only by *replacing* this conceptualizing structure with another that did not generate it. This Newton accomplished by developing a different framework that could accommodate all the same facts (about locomotion) as Aristotle's without leading to the same difficulties. (Another famous philosopher-scientist's subsequent correction of certain defects in Newton's system again instantiates my metaphilosophical hypothesis.) Newton's solution, elaborated and built upon, provided the foundations for much fruitful theory. It constituted "science," which in that word's strict sense means simply *knowledge* (supposedly the aim and goal of philosophy's pursuit).

Science and philosophy both originate in what Socrates called "a desire to attain knowledge of the nature of things." Reflective minds seek ways to describe and explain, to order and relate, the

---

18. A tidier case fit for fastidious philosophers is the conceptual difficulty over infinitesimals encountered by the calculus's early developers, Berkeley's critique in *The Analyst*, and the Cauchy-Weierstrass resolution of this philosophic problem; this example, however, is too complicated to develop here. (Berkeley's interesting attack is reprinted in part in *The World of Mathematics*, ed. James R. Newman [New York: Simon and Schuster, 1956], I, 286–293.)

world they encounter. From this desire theory springs. Many of what today are belittled as "pseudoscientific philosophic theories" were simply misstarts in our attempts to get a conceptual grasp on reality. Although they may have begun with mistaken assumptions, embodied great confusions, generated paradoxes, and so on, many of these theories *attempted* to do what came to be called "science" when finally done successfully. What come down to us today as "philosophical theories" include these misstarts; the successful attempts appear, among other places, in the textbooks of science. Science is not an organon alternative to speculative theorizing; it is a *product* of speculative theorizing.

"But if Aristotle and Newton both were engaged in similar efforts with the same goal, why is Aristotle called a *philosopher* and Newton a *scientist?*" In point of fact, Newton called himself a "natural philosopher."[19] We apply this distinction in historical retrospect, for one reason, because Newton succeeded where Aristotle did not. Science is philosophy that made good.[20]

This metaphilosophical hypothesis entails that what appear to us as "philosophic problems" about mental phenomena, our knowledge of them, their relationship to physical events and processes in the body, and so on, actually arise from defective models or conceptualizing structures employed (possibly without even realizing it) in our thinking about these phenomena. (Thus, consistent with this hypothesis, Chapter 1 postulates that the main source of problems in the philosophy of mind is the revered, familiar, and natural "inward observation" or "clasical introspectionist" model of the epistemological relationship between subjects and their own subjective mental phenomena.) This metaphilosophic hypothesis also entails that these problems can be solved (or perhaps better, "dissolved") only by replacing the defective model engendering them with an alternative conception that does not do so. This means that extensive theory construction may be required with open importation into the philosophy of mind of the "hypothetico-deductive method" used elsewhere in science: if some new model or conception (a) makes better sense of familiar facts, (b) fits (rather than conflicts) with other wellgrounded beliefs and theories, (c) explains previous mysteries or incomprehensible aspects of the phenomena, (d) has intuitively

19. As accorded with the terminology of the time.
20. W. D. Hart (personal communication).

plausible implications regarding traditional theories and posits in the philosophy of mind, and (e) entails surprising empirical predictions (different from those expected on classical accounts) that are experimentally confirmed—if so, then one is justified in rejecting the old conception, accepting the new model, and regarding the traditional problems as solved.[21] By similar reasoning, actually to find a defective model of the sort predicted and to replace it with another that fits the same facts without generating the same problems and lays theoretical foundations in the science of its subject matter (if this can be accomplished) would confirm this guiding metaphilosophy in the most direct way possible. If these problems successfully are eliminated by this approach, to that extent this general metaphilosophy will be confirmed.

Since this hypothesis entails that solving a philosophic problem may involve constructing extensively developed theory, the solution is *not* expected to come in the form of some isolated sentence or single short formula such as, "Sensations are brain processes," "The mental and the physical are two aspects of the same reality," or "Pain is a functional state of a probabilistic automaton." Without a detailed theory to give them meaning, such slogans are devoid of cognitive content. (A single sentence, of course, might encapsulate a developed theory, but in that case, the entire developed theory gives it content.) Indeed, to resolve satisfactorily a philosophic problem may require building a great dome or vast suspension bridge of theory. The basic units accepted or rejected as knowledge often are entire conceptualizing structures as wholes, rather than individual specific statements or axioms in their formulations.

"Are you saying, then, that an effort will contribute to the philosophy of mind to whatever extent it advances the frontiers of the scientific study of mind?" No. Rather, the suggestion is that solving problems in the philosophy of mind necessarily involves reconstructing theoretical *foundations* for the scientific study of mind.

"What conditions of adequacy must be met by a successful undertaking of the sort you propose?" One necessary condition,

21. One must realize, however, for the same reasons, that the hypothesis or model that finally clears away the difficulties may, as frequently is the case in physics and elsewhere in science, prove so abstract and remote from observation as to be, to some extent, comprehensible and confirmable only indirectly via deductions of theoretic consequences and empirical predictions.

obviously, is that upon viewing the phenomena in question in terms of the new conceptualizing structure, the philosophic problem no longer exists or appears to exist. In addition, when theories are involved, they must fit with all observations and data, ordinary or laboratory, and with other justified theories; lead to new insights, fruitful results, novel predictions; and be simple, clear, perspicuous, and elegant. Furthermore, of course, they must be true. In short, an adequate solution should have a respectful. quota of those virtues which, according to the philosophy of science (as "the theory of theories"), all good theories ought to have.

"Your identification of philosophy with conceptual engineering or cognitive model building is tempting, but does it not leave out, for example in the philosophy of science, such standard issues as the nature of explanation, the difference between laws and accidental universals, and the ontological status of theoretical entities? Your identification seems to cover problems involving concepts used in talking about the world, including those of mathematics and logic, but not concepts used in discussing talk about the world or mathematics." On the contrary, the hypothesis perfectly fits the philosophy of science and the philosophy of mathematics. The *subject matter* (i.e., the "object-to-be-studied-and-characterized") of the philosophy of science, presumably, is the practice and activity of science, its theories, definitions, methods, etc. (different approaches, of course, may take different aspects of scientific activity as basic in their representations). Attempts are made in the philosophy of science to construct "conceptualizing structures" (e.g., theories of the nature of scientific explanation, formal models of natural laws, accounts of the ontological commitments of scientific statements, etc.) that will provide a better understanding of the nature of science. And here, too, as elsewhere in philosophy, defective representations of the subject matter can result in conceptual conflicts, confusions, and paradoxes. The philosophy of mathematics similarly fits my hypothesis perfectly (indeed, my model explains the special relationship between metamathematics and this domain of philosophy better than any other metaphilosophy).

This hypothesis is applied in detail to problems in the philosophy of mind in the following chapters.

CHAPTER 1

The Epistemological Problem for Mental Phenomena

Suppose a person is depressed, or happy, or has a pain or an afterimage, or intends to do something, or has a dream, and tells us so. How should we view the epistemological situation?

1. Background of the Problem

Most classical or traditional theories of mind are based upon a particular way of thinking about the epistemological relationship between a mental phenomenon and the person experiencing it. In these theories, a subject's knowledge of his own mind is conceived or understood on the model of sense perception, that is, each person is assumed to come to know the contents of his own mind, his thoughts, feelings, sensations, etc., through a kind of inner awareness or inward observation. On this model, the person who says that he has a pain, for example, inwardly has noted or apprehended a certain state of affairs, and is now reporting its existence and nature.[1] Since each person can experience only his own pain and never another's, the conclusion seems to follow that each person stands in a unique and privileged epistemological relationship to his own "mental contents." A typical recent expression of this assumption is J. J. C. Smart's:

> Suppose that I report that I am having an orange-yellow roundish after-image. Or suppose again that I report that I have a pain. . . . There seems to be some element of 'pure inner experience' which

---

1. The theoreticians who have presupposed this model, from Locke onward, are too numerous to cite.

is being reported, and to which only I have direct access. You can observe my behaviour, but only I can be aware of my own after-image or my own pain.[2]

This view of the epistemological relationship between a subject and his own mental phenomena sometimes is called "the doctrine of inner recognition" or "the introspectionist view."[3] Ryle describes it as follows:

> The technical term 'introspection' has been used to denote a supposed species of perception. It was supposed that much as a person may at a particular moment be listening to a flute, savouring a wine, or regarding a waterfall, so he may be 'regarding', in a non-optical sense, some current mental state or process of his own. The state or process is being deliberately and attentively scrutinised and so can be listed among the objects of his observation. On the other hand, introspection is described as being unlike sense observation in important respects. Things looked at, or listened to, are public objects, in principle observable by any suitably placed observer, whereas only the owner of a mental state or process is supposed to be able introspectively to scrutinise it. Sense perception, again, involves the functioning of bodily organs, such as the eyes, ears, or the tongue, whereas introspection involves the functioning of no bodily organ.[4]

Different classical theories give various accounts of the alleged introspective faculty, but most involve the same underlying model. The assumption of the appropriateness of such an analysis is so natural and widespread that in traditional accounts its presupposition is seldom even explicitly noted.

This initial assumption has notorious consequences: it generates the great traditional problems in the philosophy of mind including the problem of other minds, the classical mind-body problem, and at least one version of the problem of the external world.

How the problem of other minds arises from the introspectionist

2. J. J. C. Smart, *Philosophy and Scientific Realism* (London: Routledge & Kegan Paul, 1963). p. 89.

3. This name is somewhat misleading, however, for one can repudiate the model in question without denying that "introspection," as the word *ordinarily* is used, sometimes occurs. Some philosophers, moreover, hold that such knowledge of mental particulars is the *only* direct knowledge we can ever have, so for them there is not the contrast between internal and external observation that the term 'introspection' suggests.

4. Gilbert Ryle, *The Concept of Mind* (London: Hutchinson, 1949), p. 163.

model will be reconstructed rigorously in Section 3, but general outlines are familiar. According to this model, each person is in a privileged position to observe his own mental phenomena. Apparently, then, since others do not share a subject's special epistemological position, they can learn the contents of his mind only by inferring them from his behavior or accepting his report. But how is this possible? All they observe is the subject's behavior (including his verbal behavior). What possible justification could they have, then, for concluding from these observations that a certain mental phenomenon, which they cannot observe, exists in him? Is it not possible that some entirely different mental phenomenon exists in him, or even none at all, and that he is merely a body devoid of mental contents that happens to be exhibiting this behavior? And even if what he says can be regarded as a genuine report of a subjective experience, what justification have they for assuming that the subject is honest and reliable in his introspective reports? What reason is there to think that the subject is not lying and has not made a mistake? And even assuming others knew that mental phenomena do exist in the subject and that he is honest and reliable in his judgments, what reason is there to assume that he uses words of mental description in the same way they do? Is it not altogether possible (perhaps even likely) that the verbal expression used by the subject to describe his experience is understood by me to refer to a different kind of experience because that is how I use it in reference to myself? Could, for example, what he calls a "sensation of redness" be what I would call a "sensation of greenness" if I could have his sensation? If different color sensations were produced in each of us by looking at the same objects, how could such a difference ever be detected, and if it could not be detected, what reason have we to think that it does not exist? Such considerations seem to point to the conclusion that no one is entitled ever to claim knowledge of another's mental phenomena. Yet such claims are made regularly, and with apparent justification. How is this paradox to be resolved?

It is also easy to see how the traditional mind-body problem arises on this model. The model implies that mental phenomena do not exist in the shared public world (since if they did, others could also observe them and they would not be "private"). If they exist at all, therefore, they must exist somewhere else than in the public world. (Once the introspectionist model with this consequence is accepted, a philosopher consistently can deny the existence of this other realm only if he claims never to be aware of any thoughts, feelings, sensations, etc., in himself.) But then, what is the nature of these nonpublic phenomena, and what is their relationship to events in the public physical world, including events in the body of the person who has them? How, for example, do phenomena in the two realms interact or influence each other (as it appears they do since bodily changes seem to produce mental changes, and vice versa)? As everyone knows, this problem proves difficult to solve. Once the fundamental bifurcation of reality is made, no theory seems capable of intelligibly reuniting the two worlds.

The introspectionist assumption also raises grave problems for any general theory of knowledge. Suppose, for example, one accepts the reasonable premise that much knowledge about the physical world is gained through sense experience, and assumes, moreover, as the introspectionist does, that we can perceive our own sensations directly. Since when I, for instance, view an object I do not seem to see two separate things, the sensation and the object, but only one, and since in sensory hallucination (when supposedly only visual impressions are perceived) everything appears the same as in presumed veridical perception, it is difficult to avoid concluding from the assumption that I perceive my own sense impressions, that they are the *only* things I ever directly perceive, and that, if the external world is perceived at all, it is somehow perceived only indirectly or mediately via my sense impressions. Thus one arrives at traditional epistemological idealism and a host of doubts about the possibility of knowledge of the external world.

This treatise manifests the conviction that characterizing a subject's knowledge of his *own* mental phenomena, "the first-person epistemological situation," is presently the most fundamental problem existing in philosophic psychology. Although the introspectionist account has considerable initial plausibility (which doubtless is a reason why it has found widespread acceptance), the scope and seriousness of the problems it generates suggest that perhaps some alternative model of mental self-knowledge should be sought. Such is an aim of this book. It will spend little time discussing the connection between the introspectionist model and other problems in the philosophy of mind, or the history of this model in philosophy, but will instead concentrate on attempting to characterize the epistemological relationship between a subject and his mental phenomena in a way that eliminates the difficulties surrounding this topic.

Many contemporary philosophers share the conviction that the first-person epistemological problem is fundamental.[5] Wittgenstein perhaps was the first to question the introspectionist view; he gave, however, no clear explanation of precisely what he wanted to reject, and he certainly gave no complete or detailed positive account of mental self-knowledge. Following Wittgenstein, many other philosophers also have rejected the introspectionist model, and after rejecting it, have offered their own accounts of mental phenomena and our knowledge of such phenomena. These accounts include (1) behaviorisms that interpret a subject as deriving mental descriptions of himself from observations of his own behavior; (2) criteriological views that appear to maintain that the mental phenomenon is distinct from the behavior that manifests it but nevertheless is linked to it by some quasi-logical "criterial" relationship; and (3) mind-body identity theories which posit the identity of mental states with neural states yet to be discovered. These are perhaps not as much accounts as promissory notes on possible accounts, or very general sketches of projected theories, for none yields enough knowledge or is sufficiently detailed properly to be called a theory, but suffice it to say that the theory to be developed in this work is identical to none of these.

Like traditional philosophers, neurocyberneticians also have encountered theoretical difficulties after presupposing an introspectionist account of psychological self-knowledge. In the first section of a recent paper, after recounting the success of cybernetics in describing human brains and their behavioral functions

5. For further introductory background to the problem readers may consult the following: Bruce Aune, "Feelings, Moods, and Introspection," *Mind*, 72 (April 1963), 187–207; R. C. Buck, "Non Other Minds," in *Analytical Philosophy*, ed. R. J. Butler, I (New York: Barnes & Noble, 1962), 187–210; Douglas Gasking, "Avowals," in *ibid.*, pp. 154–169, esp. pp. 161–162; Norman Malcolm, "Knowledge of Other Minds," *Journal of Philosophy*, 55 (November 1958), 969–978; Joseph Margolis, "Certainty about Sensation," *Philosophy and Phenomenological Research.*, 25 (December 1964), 242–247; D. Mitchell, "Privileged Utterances," *Mind*, 62 (July 1953), 355–366; Ryle, *Concept of Mind*, esp. chap VII; J. J. C. Smart, "Sensations and Brain Processes," *Philosophical Review.*, 68 (1959), 141–144; Peter F. Strawson, *Individuals* (London: Methuen, 1959), chap. III; Ludwig Wittgenstein, *Philosophical Investigations*, trans. G. E. M. Anscombe (New York: Macmillan, 1953), sec. 243f.

from an external objective standpoint, the distinguished cyber-
netician and brain theorist W. Ross Ashby naturally and automatically presumes an introspectionist model when he considers
the *subjective* aspect of mental phenomena:

> Turning to consideration of the subjective, of the facts given to
> a person by his own introspection, we can see that we are making
> a fundamental change from the point of view held in the first
> section. There we discussed the general theory of systems, but
> always from the point of view of an observer *outside* the system.
> Now we are considering the general theory of the system that
> 'observes' itself internally. Such a branch of general system
> theory has hardly been started, though D. M. MacKay has in-
> sisted on the great importance of the distinction.[6]

As Ashby explains, he means 'internally' in an epistemological,
not a spatial or physical sense:

> In this connection I must clarify the confusion that sometimes
> arises when experiments, on animals perhaps, study the animals'
> changes between somnolence and alertness. Such studies, in our
> present context, are purely objective, as objective as the study of
> the different responsivenesses shown by a portable radio set
> when connected, or not connected, to its battery.[7]

After assuming that the system or person obtains subjective self-
knowledge by "observing" itself internally, Ashby confesses that
he finds this operation cybernetically unfathomable:

> So far as mind shows in objective behavior . . . we have today
> an *exact* understanding, for the modern logic of mechanism is
> complete in itself. But what of the subjective aspect, the inward
> self-awareness that is an inseparable part of the whole concept
> of mind? I can do little more here than record my conviction
> that cybernetics, while providing a brilliant light for the objec-
> tive, has thrown absolutely no light on the subjective—has only
> made us even more acutely aware of how different are the objec-
> tive and the subjective, and how different are their relations to
> the classic scientific methods.[8]

By what mechanism, after all, could a computer introspect?
Accordingly, he bequeaths the problem to a future generation of

6. "What Is Mind? Objective and Subjective Aspects in Cybernetics," in *Theo-*
ries of the Mind, ed. Jordan M. Scher (New York: Free Press, 1962), p. 310.
    7. *Ibid.*
    8. *Ibid.*

neurocyberneticians:

> While cybernetics can speak to some point on the objective
> aspects of human behavior, it has only one thing to say on the
> subjective aspects, and that is—that it has nothing to say. It is
> true that the cybernetician can chat around the topics, perhaps
> interestingly, but the question is still open to what extent such
> chat is, or can be, relevant. This generation has largely solved
> the main problems of the brain so far as its objective behavior
> is concerned; the nature of its subjective aspects may be left to
> the next generation, if only to reassure them that there are still
> major scientific worlds left to conquer![9]

To this problem we now turn, and if successful, a cybernetically
comprehensible model of mental self-knowledge will begin to
emerge by the end of this chapter.

In the next section I will formulate the schematic framework
of what I call the "Transition Model." This model characterizes
common situations in which someone observes and describes
some object. Using this framework, the "doctrine of inner recognition" is reconstructed in its most basic form, shorn of embellishments or addenda that distinguish different versions of it. This
reconstruction is denoted "Application I" of the model. Together
with a plausible additional assumption, it leads to the problem
of other minds as well as other philosophic problems, and hence
is rejected. Other possible psychological applications of the same
model are similarly examined, showing how many contemporary
philosophers and psychologists who reject the doctrine of inner
recognition nevertheless have retained its basic idea in the "alternative" accounts they give of mental self-knowledge. Finally,
I conjecture that no adequate account of the first-person epistemological situation can be given within the framework of this
model, and hence in the last section, I begin construction of
an entirely different model providing an account of mental self-
knowledge that avoids the traditional problems and leads to
new insights into the nature of psychological phenomena.

2. The Transition Model of Identification and Description

This section introduces "the Transition Model" and also explains some of the formal machinery used throughout this book.

9. *Ibid.*, p. 313.

This model is given in two parts. The first, called the *"general characterization,"* is a compound relation, or set of relations, expressed by a conjunction of open sentences. These are simply sentential frameworks or sentence forms that can be made into complete sentences by inserting logically proper names or other designating terms (such as definite descriptions) in place of the free variables. (But since some readers of this book may be unacquainted with the formal concept of a variable, it is hoped that logicians among the readership will overlook the author's initial use of the unusual typographical device of indexed empty blank spaces to represent free variables. This spares logically knowledgeable readers the possible boredom of reading elementary logical pedagogy and expedites the exposition by making the meaning and nature of open sentences graphically obvious to nonlogicians. Before the end of this chapter, more standard notation for logical variables will supplant this simple pedagogical device.) Since open sentences are incomplete and hence assert nothing, the general characterization is neither true nor false in itself. It is merely an open formal framework. The second part of the model is a specification of what goes into the empty blanks. Each specification yields what I call an *"application"* of the general characterization.

The general characterization of the Transition Model abstractly delineates a set of relations present in a certain class of cases in which someone observes, identifies, and describes something—for example, when a birdwatcher looks at a bird and identifies it as a goldfinch. This general characterization is *not* an attempt to define the *meanings* of the terms that appear in it nor of any words referred to in its applications. (The concern here is with characterizing a certain concrete epistemological situation rather than with semantic analysis.) The words and phrases in the characterization are taken as primitives and reasonable agreement over their use is assumed; they receive no further definition.

This general characterization will be used to formulate the introspectionist model or "doctrine of inner recognition." Although more complex formulations would yield essentially the same result, the simple one below suffices. The addition of further details would serve no purpose here and even might obscure the main point. This general characterization is printed with the phrases 'observer-identifier,' 'object-for-description' (or interchangeably 'object-of-identification'), and 'the description' in parentheses beneath the blanks; these show how subsequent substitutions will go. The following is a conjunction of open sentences containing empty blanks:

TRANSITION MODEL

General Characterization

1. _____ examines or inspects[10]
   (*The observer-identifier*)
   _____ and on the basis of this applies
   (*the object-for-description*)
   _____ to it.
   (*the description*)

2. _____ may or may not be true of ____
   (*The description*)   (*the*
   _____. If _____ that ____
   object-for-description)   (*the description*)   (*the*
   _____ affirms truly applies to _____
   observer-identifier)   (*the object-for-*
   _____, that affirmation is correct; if not, it is
   description)
   incorrect.[11]

Instances satisfying this general characterization later will be referred to as cases in which "the observer-identifier makes a transition from an object-of-description to a description of it" or more briefly as situations in which someone "derives a description" from something. The term 'transition' suggests passing from one thing (the object-for-description) to another (the description), which is what the observer-identifier does. Since it is unnecessary to give a maximally economical formulation, it will not matter if some principles in the characterization are entailed by others.

10. The term 'inspects' here is being used in its ordinary general sense of "scrutinize," "view closely," "attend to," "observe," etc.; its use is not here restricted as in C. D. Broad's special technical application of this term.

11. Thus correctness or incorrectness of identificatory judgment is a function of two variables: (a) what the object-for-description really is, and (b) what the observer-identifier takes it to be. This function takes the values 'correct' or 'incorrect' according as the object is what he judges it to be or not.

Accordingly, each needed principle is here written out separately. The following, therefore, also will be considered part of the characterization:

3. For anyone, in order that he may be said to know

that _____ is an instance of ____
    (the object-for-description)   *(the*
_____, this description must truly apply to it.
description)
4. Someone knows "firsthand" what the _____
                                        (object-for-
_____ is if and only if he has examined or inspected
description)
it personally and knows from this what it is.

5. Anyone who has not examined or inspected ____
                                            (the
_____ but knows what it is through the
object-for-description)
testimony of someone who has firsthand knowledge, knows

this "secondhand."

This general characterization is *"applied"* to a particular case by specifying who or what in that situation is "the observer-identifier," "the object-for-description," and "the description." This can be done by inserting terms denoting these entities in the appropriate blanks in the general characterization (e.g., 'John P. Smith' for '*the observer-identifier*'). If the application of some primitive term in the characterization (e.g., 'examines or inspects') is unclear in the particular situation to which the characterization is applied, an explanation of how the term is to be understood in that case must also be included. In short, the conjunction of open sentences 1–5 expresses a three-place predicate or triadic relation, R_Txyz, which holds, e.g., between entities a, b, and c when b is an object or event which person a observes and identifies as an instance of some description or predicate, c, in the manner described by sentences 1–5; if this triadic relation obtains between a, b, and c, then the closed sentence 'R_Tabc' is true.

To illustrate, imagine some occasion on which, say, John Smith, a birdwatcher, observed a feathered biped on a twig and identified it saying, "A goldfinch!" (or "It's a goldfinch"). To apply the general characterization to this simple case (which it seems to fit), put the birdwatcher's name ('John Smith') for *'the observer-identifier'*; put a term designating the bird for *'the object-for-description'*; put " is a goldfinch" (or simply "Goldfinch") for *'the description'*; and suppose Smith has a friend who will be one instance of "anyone." Moreover, let "examining or inspecting" be understood to include observation by means of binoculars. Since the birdwatcher's performance has taken place already, the characterization is rewritten in the past tense. This application asserts that:

> John Smith examined or inspected the bird and on the basis of this, applied the description 'goldfinch' to it. This description may or may not have been true of the bird. If the description that he affirmed truly applied to the bird, that affirmation is correct; if not, it is incorrect. For anyone, in order that he may be said to know that the bird is an instance of 'goldfinch', this description must truly apply to it. Someone knows "firsthand" what the bird is if and only if he has examined or inspected it personally and knows from this what it is. The birdwatcher's friend who has not examined or inspected the bird but knows what it is through the testimony of someone who has first-hand knowledge, knows this "secondhand."

If all these sentences are true, then the characterization applies to this instance of Smith's identifying a bird.

The characterization should be thought of as applying, or failing to apply, to individual concrete situations—such as a particular Mr. Smith who on a specific historic occasion went through a certain sequence of motions.[12] It either fits or fails to fit what happened on that occasion. Naturally, however, since my concern is with *general* questions relating to *types* of applications, instead of citing actual events, I will use imaginary cases as illustrations. But the characterization should be understood as applying or failing to apply to actual concrete cases.

12. With antecedent clauses and quantifiers, its application over whole classes of concrete cases also can be asserted.

For reasons soon evident, the "general characterization" is distinguished from its "applications." The same general characterization may have many different applications (e.g., to geologists identifying rocks, travelers recognizing rivers, children describing rainbows, and so on[13]). Sometimes a characterization may be applied to the *same* case in several *different* ways. An example will be seen shortly.[14]

When the characterization is applied to a particular case, I speak of this as "giving a model" of that case (or, in reference to the particular characterization above, as "construing that case on the Transition Model"). The term 'model' is used here somewhat loosely without worrying about whether it is the interpreted formalism, the uninterpreted formalism, or some paradigm case or application that is "the model." The term 'model' is not here used in the formal logician's sense.[15] Rather, my usage of the term 'model' corresponds more nearly to its use in natural science, as when one speaks of "the Copernican model of the solar system."

3. Application I of the Transition Model

Suppose that Smith has a pain and tells us so. Consider the following attempted application of the Transition Model to this case: Let Smith be *the observer-identifier*; let "his sensation" be *the object-for-description*; and let 'is a pain' or simply 'pain' be *the description*. And suppose that "feeling it" or "introspection" or something similar is assumed to be a means by which sensations

13. No limit (outside any necessitated by the characterization) has been placed on what can count as an "object-for-description." It need not be what is ordinarily called an "object"; it could be, e.g., an event.

14. There is an ambiguity in the term 'apply'. If someone "applies" the characterization to a case it does not fit, does the characterization "apply" to that case? Let us adopt the following convention: 'apply' as an intransitive verb (with the name of the characterization as its subject) asserts that the characterization does fit the case—that is, that it "(truly) applies." But as a transitive verb with the name of the model as its direct object, it merely asserts that someone has attempted to "apply" it. An "application" of the model is the result of someone's attempting to apply it in this latter sense and may be spoken of even when the model does not apply to the case.

15. The two can be connected, however. Take the open schemata corresponding to the open sentences of the general characterization, conjoin them, and form their existential closure. Now any system of objects to which the characterization applies constitutes a "model" of this schema in the logician's sense. Its existence shows the logical consistency of this closed schema (and derivatively, at least under certain kinds of inference, of the open sentences constituting the general characterization).

can be examined or inspected. Thus applied, the characterization reads:

Smith examines or inspects his sensation and on the basis of this applies the description 'is a pain' to it. This description may or may not be true of his sensation. If the description that Smith affirms truly applies to the sensation, that affirmation is correct; if not, it is incorrect. For anyone, in order that he may be said to know that Smith's sensation is an instance of 'pain' this description must truly apply to it. Someone knows "firsthand" what the sensation is if and only if he has examined or inspected it personally and knows from this what it is. Anyone who has not examined or inspected it but knows what it is through the testimony of someone who has firsthand knowledge knows this "secondhand."

This will be called *"Application I"* of the Transition Model.

Application I is a reconstruction of the underlying model of the doctrine of inner recognition.[16] In respects the general characterization makes explicit, it portrays the epistemological relationship between the subject and his sensation as analogous to the epistemological relation between the birdwatcher and the bird in the previous example. It represents the subject as standing in a relation of observer-identifier to one of his sensations, somehow taking note of it, and identifying it as a pain.

Remark: Application I's account of the epistemological relationship between a person and his sensations is independent of whether sensations are viewed as objects, events, processes, states of the mind, modes of consciousness, or mental processes to which the subject has this access.[17] Someone who held one of these particular views possibly might prefer to interpret the variables in a slightly different way (e.g., substitute 'the mind' for the object-for-description), but no issue presently under investigation would be affected by this change. Different philosophers also have offered various theories of the nature of the faculty by which mental contents allegedly are noted inwardly, and accordingly have used different terminology. Some say that a subject "perceives" the contents of his mind, others that he "apprehends" them, others that he

16. Or, what does as well, it is entailed by that doctrine.
17. In particular, Application I does not entail or presuppose an "object theory of pains"—that is, a theory that explains "having" a pain in terms of some relation between a further object (a pain) and the subject.

"inspects" them, and so on. But because Application I attempts to express a basic idea common to all these theories (i.e., that mental facts are known by something like inner observation), these possible additions to, or embellishments on, Application I are not important here. Since the *general* nature of the epistemological relation between a subject and his mental phenomena is our present interest, we can proceed most expeditiously by operating on the most abstract level, for if the basic underlying conception is wrong, there is no need to consider its more detailed possible developments.

Application I has the consequences of traditional philosophic views. Consider what happens when the following further assumption is added:

Additional Assumption 1:   *No one else can examine or inspect a subject's sensations.*

This assumption has seemed plausible to many theoreticians. For, in order to examine or inspect another person's pain, they reason, I would have to experience it; but I cannot experience a pain that I do not have (because experiencing a pain is the same as having it); hence, any pain I experience is mine; therefore, it is impossible for me to perceive, examine, or inspect the pain another person has. But once this additional assumption is adopted, it follows immediately (see Principles 4 and 5 of the model above) that no one but the subject himself can have firsthand knowledge of what his sensations are. Others who go by the subject's reports have at best secondhand knowledge. This was John Austin's view:

> In the usual case, we accept this statement [i.e., the person's own statement as to what his feelings are] without question and we then say that we know—as it were, 'at second hand'—what his feelings are; though, of course, 'at second hand' here could not be used to imply that anybody but he could know 'at first hand'.[18]

According to the introspectionist model plus the additional assumption, the epistemological situation of others with respect to the subject's own sensations is analogous to the situation of the birdwatcher's friend who has not himself observed the bird in question. One important difference, however, is that in the sensation case, it appears to be impossible for another person ever to

18. John L. Austin, "Other Minds," in *Logic and Language*, ed. Antony Flew, II (Oxford: Blackwell, 1961), 156.

examine the thing for himself to confirm the report. Thus other's knowledge of the subject's sensation is irredeemably secondhand. Many philosophers have accepted this conclusion.

This generates the "problem of other minds." If I never can observe the entity in question, but only can see the subject's behavior and hear his reports, how confident can my beliefs about his mental life be? Perhaps something quite different from what he reports actually is going on. In fact, since on this account I never observe his mental occurrences, for all I know, is it not possible that none take place in him, that what I think is a person is merely a body devoid of mental contents exhibiting certain verbal and other behavior? Is there any reason to think that this is not so? For *if* I have *no* reason at all for excluding these possibilities and accepting his report, how can I claim even to have secondhand knowledge? If the acceptance of the speaker's report is unjustified, how can I claim "knowledge" at all? Another problem also arises. Even assuming that the subject has mental experience and is sincere in his report, how can I be certain that I properly understand what he means or intends to assert with his words in describing his mental phenomena? Is it not possible that he uses terms of mental description to denote different kinds of entities from what I use the same words to denote? Perhaps what he calls a 'pain' I would call a 'tickle', or what he calls a 'sensation of redness' I would call a 'sensation of greenness', if I could experience it. If so, how could such misunderstandings ever be discovered or rectified? Apparently not by examining or inspecting the entity of which he affirms the description, since this possibility is precluded by the Additional Assumption. (Nor could I check his usage indirectly by correlating it with his and my overt behavior, since then the first problem is encountered: What reason is there to assume that the kind of sensation correlated with certain behavior in him is the same as the kind correlated with similar behavior in me?) This difficulty exceeds the earlier one. For now it appears that even if the subject were known to have mental experiences and to be honest and generally reliable in his judgments, still others might not know what sensation he has, since the way he uses terms of mental description might be different from the way they take him to be using them. Thus, if the introspectionist account is accepted, it becomes questionable whether anyone could ever be said to have knowledge of another's mental phenomena.

The combination of Application I and the Additional Assumption leads to other difficulties as well. Just giving a further characterization of something which could satisfy the conditions or description already proposed is a problem. What other properties would something forever accessible to one and only one person have? Suppose we call any object (or event) that is observable, in principle, by one and only one person or subject a "private object (or event)"—as contrasted with "public objects," which are entities that are, in principle, equally observable by several persons. According to this definition, then, a private object (or event) is one which it is impossible in principle for anyone other than a certain subject or person (or "self") to observe. Thus, a painful sensation as experienced by the person who has it, or a visual image or a thought, would be a "private object" according to the proposed model (viz., Application I plus the Additional Assumption). A clock, a bird, a star would be "public" entities. Notice, incidentally, that this definition does not require that a "public" object ever *actually* have been observed by more than one person, but only that it be equally observable by more than one person. Since others *could* observe it also, a freshly unearthed rock in my garden is, in this sense, a public object, even though I am the only living creature ever actually to perceive it. The entity denoted by the description "the highest mountain on the planet Pluto" (assuming such a peak exists) likewise is a "public" object, although (presumably) *no one* has ever actually observed it (due to the lack of the requisite technological means), for it is, in principle, still *equally observable* by anyone. Someone need only travel to its location in space (under conditions of adequate illumination, etc.) to perceive it. Even electrons and other atomic particles qualify as "public" objects by this definition, for although no one in fact can observe directly a single electron with his unaided bodily sense organs, electrons are *equally* observable by everyone, insofar as they can be observed at all. Everyone has, in principle, equal observational access to the indirect evidence that exists for the presence of these entities, and when electrons move in large ensembles through space (as in a Crookes tube or a lightning flash) the visible result is equally observable by all. In fact, every object or event in physical space-time seems, in principle at least, to be equally observable by everyone (for which reason, physical space sometimes is called "shared," "common," or "public" space). It is very difficult to understand how private objects or events could be located in physical space, or how something located in physical space could be, in principle, observable by one and only one person. Everyone certainly can readily understand how entities might exist in physical space that are (directly) observable by *no one*—for example, because of their small size (as with elementary particles), or because everyone lacks the requisite sensitivity (as with radio waves or cosmic rays), or for other reasons (as with "dark holes" in space). But it is extremely difficult to understand how there could exist something located in physical space which *one* person could observe directly perfectly well, but no other person could observe directly.[19] How could something in physical space be observable, in principle, by one and only one person? For if the entity is located in "shared," "common" space, how would others be prevented from going to its spatial location and there observing it? All brain and other bodily processes likewise are "public" by this definition, since they are, in principle, equally observable by everyone (with the aid, perhaps, of a surgeon to expose them). If this is so, however, and if Application I plus the Additional Assumption are accepted, it follows logically that sensations (and all other mental phenomena treated on the same model) are *not* identical to any brain or other bodily processes, and moreover that they exist somewhere other than in physical space. The dualistic hypothesis that mental phenomena do not occur in physical space at all, but instead occur in some domain or realm outside physical space thus becomes inescapable. But if mental events do not take place in physical space, while all events in one's *body* do happen in physical space, what then is the connection or relationship between the happenings or phenomena in the two realms? Universal observations indicate an intimate relationship and close interdependency between phenomena in the physical body and "psychological" phenomena. Stepping on a tack, for example, regularly is followed by

19. "The idea that something should be going on in such and such a [spatial] place and yet that one person should occupy an intrinsically privileged epistemological position vis-à-vis that occurrence is prima facie absurd," premises Robert C. Coburn in his critique, "Shaffer on the Identity of Mental States and Brain Processes," *Journal of Philosophy*, 60 (1963), 91. Unfortunately, however, Coburn's formula obscures or misses a crucial distinction: as Chapter 3 will demonstrate, under certain conditions, it is quite possible for one person to occupy a unique and intrinsically privileged "epistemological position" vis-à-vis an occurrence going on in a place in physical space. What *is* difficult or impossible to understand is how something taking place at a location in physical space could be, in principle, *observable* by one and only one person.

a painful sensation, and deliberating and deciding to perform a certain act usually is followed by corresponding bodily movements. These observations might seem to suggest that a causal relationship exists between mental and physical events, but it is very difficult to conceive of any mechanism whereby an object or event which is *not* in physical space could interact with something that is. The problem thus arises of explaining the apparently intimate (causal?) relationship between a group of objects or events existing outside space (a collection constituting, perhaps, Jones's "mind" and/or its "contents") and Jones's body, a physical object having a particular location in space. This is the traditional "mind-body problem" in its classical form. Infamous difficulties await anyone who accepts this dualism and tries to develop it. If (as seems a reasonable postulate) everything in physical space is, in principle, equally observable by anyone, then the two proposed postulates, (1) that we gain mental self-knowledge by direct inner observation (Application I of the Transition Model—"introspectionism") and (2) that no one else can, even in principle, directly observe the contents of another's mind or the objects of another's inner subjective experience (the Additional Assumption—"the doctrine of privacy"), appear to entail that mental or psychological phenomena, or "minds," exist somewhere other than in physical space (and therefore are incorporeal or immaterial in nature). If sensations, feelings, thoughts, etc., are not public, then it seems they must exist elsewhere than in the shared public world. They must be nonspatial and nonphysical. In that case, however, it is difficult to understand how they could depend upon or influence events in the material body of the person who has them.

In addition to the problem of other minds and the mind-body problem in its classical formulation, Application I of the Transition Model also generates a version of the "problem of the external world." One of the various ways this problem can arise from introspectionism is as follows. The introspectionist model implies that each of us can directly observe, perceive, or perceptually feel our own painful sensations. Suppose I have *visual* sensations, too. Can I also observe these? Of the many sensations one experiences, surely it would be arbitrary to single out only pain sensations as perceivable or observable. If my pain sensations are directly observable, surely all my other sensations likewise are observable. (Strictly speaking, the consequence below does not require assuming the foregoing conditional since the supposition that subjects also can examine or inspect, e.g., their visual sensations is merely another application of the Transition Model of the same kind as Application I.) Presumably, then, on this account, I also can examine or inspect, observe and perceive, my own *visual* sensations. But how do I "examine" or "inspect" my visual sensations? When (if ever) do I "perceive" my visual sensations? This question traditionally receives something like the following answer:

> At any time they are present, you quite easily can observe or perceive your visual sensations or "visual impressions." To do so, simply attend to the subjective content of your visual experience—that is, to what you directly see, considered as your own subjective image. Your visual sensations or impressions constitute your visual image. They are what you would continue to see or experience if you had a visual hallucination or other delusory visual experience.

Suppose a white plastic disk is placed against a black velvet backdrop before me under normal illumination. Suppose that "what I see" (that is, what C. D. Broad and others have called the "objective constituent" of my perceptual situation) is truly describable as "something round and white against a black field or background." Suppose that when I "attend to the content of my subjective visual experience," all that I see or seem to see, all that I sense in this visual experience, is something white and round against a black field. Is this—i.e., this "other" or "it" which I seem to see, this objective constituent of the perceptual situation whose subjective constituent I am—is *it* the "visual sensation"? Is "the white circular something against a black background that I see" identical to my "subjective visual sensation(s)"? If so, and the field filled with visible entities that I see or seem to see is only my own subjective visual image, then surely this is *all* I ever perceive (directly, at least); for I am quite certain (in the indicated example) that I see just this one thing and nothing else. If the white circular something against a black background that I see is my "visual sensation," "visual impression," or my "subjective visual image," then this must be *all* that I ever directly perceive. For in my visual experience, I am quite certain that I see only *one* "white circular entity against a black background" (I am not, for example, having double vision). Therefore, *if* the one "white circular thing" that I see is *not* the external physical plastic disk but *merely an image* in my subjective visual field, then it must be the case that *I do not directly see* the external plastic disk at all.[20] It thus follows that the external physical object is *not* the entity I directly see, i.e., it is not the objective constituent of my perceptual situation. I perceive, at best, an image that resembles a corresponding external physical object, an inner subjective phenomenal replica of the outer object (the "representative theory of perception"). Something like this conclusion has been accepted as obviously correct by countless philosophers (both Eastern and Western) who have maintained that, contrary to ordinary opinion, the *only* things each person *ever* directly perceives, or sensuously apprehends, are his own subjective mental phenomena, "the contents of his own mind" (a hypothesis soon to be rejected in this chapter). The introspectionist model thus ultimately leads to the conclusion that the objects or events with which a subject of sensory experience is in direct cognitive contact are never the external physical clocks, roses, and stars ordinarily supposed, but always, at best, merely the subject's own subjective sensory images of them—that is, the conclusion seems to follow that each person directly perceives only his own private mental phenomena. From this conclusion, of course, arises the infamous "problem of the external world" and the epistemological predicament of a knowing subject (or "self") which, limited to the domain of its own mental contents (or "ideas"), finds it difficult, if not impossible, to determine whether there exists a world of physical objects existing outside its mind and independently of its experience of them, or to justify belief in such an external reality. [The same difficulty still arises even if it is claimed that I can take either of two different mental stances or attitudes toward the "objective constituents" of my (visual) perceptual situations: a part of the visual field that is "sensed and selected (i.e., attended to)" by me, says one traditional epistemologist, for example, *either* can be "used for perceiving a certain physical object and for learning about its physical characteristics" *or* can "become an object of inspection by me with a view to learning accurately *its own* ap-

20. Berkeley uses a somewhat similar argument in "Three Dialogues between Hylas and Philonous" (1713), reprinted in *Berkeley's Philosophical Writings*, ed. David M. Armstrong (New York: Macmillan, 1965), p. 140.

parent characteristics."[21] But even supposing that areas in this postulated subjective visual field can *either* be used as a means of perception by me *or* inspected and attended to as objects-of-study in themselves, the basic philosophic difficulty still remains, because the entity to which I allegedly stand in this basic "sensing" relationship, the "it" I directly sense, nevertheless, in either mode or stance, on this account, is only my private subjective visual image.] All these consequences ensue from the seemingly plausible initial supposition that I can inwardly examine and inspect the pains and other mental phenomena I experience. Once it is assumed, e.g., that my *pain sensation* can be perceived by me, consistency seems to require assuming that I also can perceive all my other sensations; but if it is true that I can (and sometimes do) observe or perceive my visual sensations, for example, then it is very difficult not to conclude that my visual and other sensory impressions are the *only* things that I ever directly perceive. Thus, one is pushed toward a representative theory of perception, skepticism, the problem of the external world, and even finally perhaps to a total denial of the existence of matter (some form of subjective idealism, e.g.). This general line of development is familiar to all students of philosophy.[22] Some of these similar conclusions and difficulties can be generated perhaps in other ways than by the model under consideration, but it is one widespread and powerful source of the problems.

What, therefore, is to be done about the introspectionist account? The fact that it generates problems and leads to counterintuitive conclusions is certainly some ground for rejecting it. But can any decisive argument be given against it? The general characterization itself must be logically self-consistent since, as has been observed, it can fit the birdwatcher case. Hence the only possible objection is that Application I fails to accord with the facts. But then any argument against it must be premised on some independent claim about what the facts are, and a proponent of

21. C. D. Broad, *The Mind and Its Place in Nature* (1925; London: Routledge & Kegan Paul, 1968), p. 297.

22. Through step-by-step argumentation from the initial assumption that pains are "immediately perceived" and hence, "sensible things," plus additional assumptions, Philonous, the idealist, eventually compels Hylas, the (recanting) materialist, altogether "to give up the notion of an unthinking substance exterior to the mind" and, agreeing that "there is no other substance, in a strict sense, than *Spirit*," to accept a complete philosophical "immaterialism" (*Berkeley's Philosophical Writings*, p. 224). Of course, Berkeley's route from Application I to idealism or mentalism is strewn with many other assumptions as well.

Application I could simply reject any such claim. For example: if, in opposition to Application I it were denied that a person can in any way examine or inspect his sensations, an introspectionist simply could reject this claim without thereby being inconsistent. (This fact is important because it proves that no one logically can be compelled to give up Application I.[23])

Perhaps, then, a refutation could be premised on some universally accepted fact. Recent contemporary efforts in this direction attempt to base a rejection of the introspectionist model on the alleged incorrigibility of first-person mental reports. The argument goes like this. Principle 2 of the Transition Model states: "The description may or may not be true of the object-for-description. If the description that he affirms truly applies to the object-for-description, that affirmation is correct; if not, it is incorrect." Thus on the Transition Model, it is logically possible that the subject misjudge what the object-for-description is. That is, it would be logically possible for the subject sincerely to affirm a description that is false of the object-for-description. For example, he might judge a pain to be a tickle. But, the argument continues, it is *not* logically possible for a subject's sincere beliefs regarding the nature of his own mental experience to be mistaken.[24] Although it is logically possible for someone to have a goldcrest before him and mistakenly believe it to be a goldfinch, it is logically impossible for someone to have a pain and mistakenly believe it to be, say, a tickle. Necessarily, if a speaker believes he has a pain (and understands the meaning of that word), then he has a pain. Hence, Application I is false.

One weakness in this line of attack lies in the incorrigibility thesis itself. As stated above, at least, it seems open to endless counterexamples.[25] For instance, suppose a man is hypnotized and told that when he awakens he will believe he has a pain and will so report.[26] Brought out of the trance he says, "I have a pain." We ask, "Do you really believe this?" and he answers, sincerely, "Yes." We say, "Does it hurt?" and again he answers affirma-

23. No one is compelled to accept it either; it is only a hypothesis.

24. Many philosophers make this assertion. See, for example, Norman Malcolm, *Knowledge and Certainty* (Englewood Cliffs, N.J.: Prentice-Hall, 1963), pp. 84–85; Sydney Shoemaker, *Self-Knowledge and Self-Identity* (Ithaca: Cornell University Press, 1963), p. 168; Coburn, "Shaffer on the Identity of Mental States," p. 91.

25. Bruce Aune gives a counterexample more complex than mine. See his *Knowledge, Mind, and Nature* (New York: Random House, 1967), pp. 34–35.

26. Malcolm discusses such a case but does not show that it fails to refute the incorrigibility thesis. See *Knowledge and Certainty*, pp. 113–114.

tively. Then we ask, "Where does it hurt?" and he looks puzzled. "Describe your pain in more detail," we demand, and he becomes more confused. (The hypnotist gave him no answers to these questions.) Finally, after a long pause, he says, "I thought I had a pain, but now I'm not sure that I did." A moment later he affirms he did not. This looks like a case in which someone did not have a pain but for a period of time believed that he did. If it is, then the claim that "It is not possible for a person to believe he has a pain when he does not" is false. And if this is not a counterexample to the incorrigibility thesis, why not?[27]

While the incorrigibility principle may approximate an important truth,[28] at this point, at least, I am inclined to think that it cannot be stated sharply enough to cut decisively against Application I without being subject to possible counterexamples. So, since I know of no other argument that conclusively disproves it, I cannot "decisively" refute Application I. In fact, I am inclined to think that no logically decisive refutation is possible.[29] No matter what claims are adduced in opposition to this model, its proponents always can reject them; no matter what unsolvable problems are raised or paradoxes generated, the doctrine's supporters can always maintain that these are just mysteries which we may never understand. To wait, then, for a "conclusive" refutation only would forestall progress, and, accordingly, I will do what is done elsewhere in science. I will simply reject this model on nonconclusive grounds and seek a better replacement. Application I has, admittedly, considerable initial plausibility, but it raises too many unsolvable problems and has too many counterintuitive consequences to be acceptable. If another account of the same phenomena can be found that does not lead to the same (or other) difficulties, is at least equally intelligible, and

27. In "Is Ultimate Epistemic Authority a Distinguishing Characteristic of the Psychological?" *American Philosophical Quarterly*, 8 (July 1971), 294, Harold Morick replies that 'I have a pain' as said by this formerly hypnotized man "fails to display the correct use of this sentence for avowing pain." This is true, but it does not help the incorrigibility thesis. Generally, any affirmation of a falsehood "fails to display the correct use of that sentence," but this does not entail that it displays a misunderstanding of the *meaning* of the words or the sentence, as the argument must show. A speaker can understand the meanings of the words he uses and yet assert a falsehood. So this answer does not save the incorrigibility thesis.

28. This develops in Chapter 3.

29. In saying this, the inconclusiveness of Wittgensteinian and post-Wittgensteinian arguments against the possibility of a private language is presupposed. Were those arguments sound, rejection of introspectionism might receive stronger justification.

leads perhaps to additional fruitful insights, I will consider acceptance of the new model and rejection of the present one entirely justified.

Let us now consider whether more acceptable results could be obtained from some *other* application of the *same* model.

4. Application II of the Transition Model

Consider the following application of the Transition Model. Let Smith be the *object-for-description*; let *the description* be 'has a pain', a predicate true or false of different persons at various times; and let someone other than the person who is object-for-description, say Mr. Jones, be *the observer-identifier*. (Notice that the case of someone who *says of himself* that he has a pain is *not* covered by this application.) Let visually observing someone count as a way of "examining or inspecting" him. This will be called "*Application II*" of the Transition Model. According to it, the following happens:

> Jones examines or inspects Smith and on the basis of this applies the description 'has a pain' to him. This description may or may not be true of Smith. If the description that Jones affirms truly applies to Smith, that affirmation is correct; if not, it is incorrect. For anyone, in order that he may be said to know that Smith has a pain, this description must truly apply to Smith. Someone knows "firsthand" that Smith has a pain if and only if he personally has examined or inspected Smith and knows from this that Smith has a pain. Anyone who has not examined or inspected Smith but knows that he has a pain through the testimony of someone who has firsthand knowledge, knows this "secondhand."

If this is true, Application II describes the case.

Again, embellishments could be added to this account to provide a more extensive and detailed characterization, but since the present concern is a basic type of account (of which this is merely a simple illustration), and its underlying structure, there would be no point in doing so here. Accounts like Application II differ from ones like Application I in construing mental predication as a form of description of *persons* rather than of introspectively observable concrete particular mental objects or events. Application II represents the identificatory task as that of recognizing that someone is in a certain state or has a certain property, whereas Application I represented the identificatory task as that of recognizing that some sensation is an entity of a certain kind. So while Application I talked of someone observing his sensation and concluding that it was a pain, Application II talks of observing someone and concluding that he has a pain. Thus Application I is an expression of the doctrine of inner recognition, while Application II is not.

Strawson's analysis of knowledge of mental facts entails Application II:

> There is a kind of predicate which is unambiguously and adequately ascribable *both* on the basis of observation of the subject of the predicate *and* not on this basis, i.e. independently of observation of the subject: the second case is the case where the ascriber is also the subject.[30]

Strawson lists 'is in pain' among these predicates.[31] (Although Strawson denies that the domain of observer-identifiers in Application II properly can be extended to include the subject himself,[32] he offers no positive account of how persons *do* accurately predicate mental descriptions of themselves, a question I shall take up momentarily.)

Conjoining the Additional Assumption:

Additional Assumption 1: *No one else can examine or inspect a subject's sensations*

to Application II leads to none of the same problems as it did when conjoined with Application I. For since the object-for-description on Application II is a *person*, asserting that no one other than this person can have access to this person's sensations logically or formally entails no limits on the possibility of firsthand knowledge, nor does it lead to the other problems generated by Application I. (This provides some reason to think that the source of the philosophic difficulties was indeed Application I, and not the

---

30. Strawson, *Individuals*, p. 108.
31. *Ibid.*, p. 104.
32. For such mental predicates, Strawson says on p. 107, "when one ascribes them *to oneself*, one does not do·so on the strength of observation of those behavioral criteria on the strength of which one ascribes them to others."

Additional Assumption.) Indeed, as far as Application II is concerned, this assumption can be broadened to:

> *No one (including the subject himself) can examine or inspect a subject's sensations*

That is, Application II is consistent with denying that "sensations" are things of the sort that can be observed by anyone, including the subject himself. Proponents of Application II can (as I shall) deny that the word 'sensation' functions to denote an entity at all, treating it instead simply as a verbal constituent of more complex expressions (like 'has-an-intense-sensation') predicable of persons. (Cp. the function of the noun 'build' in the sentence 'Henry has a medium build'.[33])

Several other points deserve mention. (1) Application II does not assert the equivalence of mental descriptions to sets of hypothetical, semihypothetical, or dispositional statements; in particular, as far as Application II is concerned the phenomena described by mental predicates may be episodic in nature.[34] (2) Application II does not deny that it may be impossible to tell a person's mental state from observing him, nor does it deny that someone can hide or disguise his feelings and that in this sense, mental phenomena may be "private." (3) Nothing in Application II is incompatible with sense yet being given to the idea that mental phenomena have a distinctive "inner" or subjective aspect.

While apparently engendering no philosophic difficulties, Application II leaves the original problem completely unsolved since it offers no characterization of the first-person epistemological situation. Ryle might suggest remedying this omission simply by extending the domain of observer-identifiers to include the subject himself—that is, postulating that each subject arrives at his own mental self-description by examining or inspecting himself in the same way others do, and that on the basis of this, he applies the description to himself. (This I shall call Application III of the

33. See J. W. Cook, "Wittgenstein on Privacy," *Philosophical Review*, 74 (1965), 281–314.

34. To avoid the problems generated by Application I, Ryle thought he had to deny the episodic nature of mental phenomena. "The imputed episodes seemed to be impenetrably 'internal' because they were genuinely unwitnessable. But they were genuinely unwitnessable because they were mythical" (*Concept of Mind*, p. 318). As will be seen later, to avoid these problems it is not necessary to deny the episodic nature of mental phenomena, but only to deny the representation of these phenomena as objects of private access. The episodes only seemed "impenetrably" internal because of the model given of our knowledge of them.

Transition Model.) For Ryle says, "The sorts of things that I can find out about myself are the same as the sorts of things I can find out about other people and the methods of finding them out are much the same."[35] That is, "Our knowledge of other people and of ourselves depends on noticing how they and we behave."[36] According to Application III, then, each person finds out that he is in a certain mental state by using the same procedure he uses for everyone else, namely, by observing himself and his own behavior in various circumstances and concluding from this that he himself is in a certain mental state.

Again, although I cannot conclusively refute it, this representation seems to me clearly unsatisfactory.[37] It might perhaps characterize how a person finds out that he is good at long division or fit the case of someone who determines that he had a pain earlier by subsequently watching films taken of himself at that time. But it does not seem to fit the ordinary case, e.g., in which a person reports a pain or tells her thoughts. A person does not normally observe her behavior and on this basis declare that she has a pain or certain thoughts. Indeed, in this respect Application I almost seems more plausible. What I do in arriving at a pain description of myself seems (to me at least) more like attending to and describing some further entity (e.g., something unpleasant located in my foot) than like observing and describing my behavior or outward demeanor. I do not, for example, need to look at myself or hear myself groan to learn that I have a pain. Somehow I seem to know it in some other, more direct and immediate way.

If Application II of the Transition Model cannot be extended plausibly to the first-person case, how then is it to be understood? Let us review some salient facts. A person in pain may produce pain descriptions true of himself, and his doing so seems to be rational behavior. His utterance expresses a meaningful statement that can be treated linguistically in the same way as other statements he produces. Others can learn the existing state of affairs with regard to his condition by interpreting his utterance linguistically and extracting from it the information it contains (they need not, for example, treat it as mere behavioral evidence).

35. *Ibid.*, p. 155.
36. *Ibid.*, p. 181.
37. A secure incorrigibility principle *would* decisively refute this account. For on Application III, the subject could be mistaken in his judgment that he has a pain, and this is incompatible with the incorrigibility claim. But we possess no such principle. See pp. 48–49.

If what the subject says is meaningful and true, and bears information, and he understands it and is not basing it on poor or inadequate grounds, then it would seem strange to deny that he has knowledge that he has a pain.[38] But if so, *how* does he know this? How does he obtain this information if not by observing his sensation (Application I) or by observing himself (Application III)?

Let us move to diagnosis. We know that any difficulties that oppose extending Application II to the first-person case do not come from the fact that the subject here would be applying a description to himself. For no special difficulty would arise, for example, if the goldfinch of Section 2, having decided himself to take up birdwatching, should, after reading an ornithologist's guidebook, look at himself and say, "Why, I'm a goldfinch!" Here (as the possibility of his misidentifying himself shows) the fact known and his knowledge of it would remain separate and distinguishable. Instead, the obstacle to characterizing first-person knowledge of mental states with the Transition Model seems to be the peculiar relationship between the fact known and the subject's knowledge of it. The state of knowledge of the subject (i.e., that state of him as a result of which he is able to provide this information) seems not to come about as a *result of observing* that he is in a certain mental state, but rather it seems automatically to come with that mental state. Thus in the usual case when I *have a pain* at the same time I *know* that I have a pain. It seems as though (a) the state of knowledge of the subject qua describer and (b) the state of himself qua object-of-description in virtue of which the mental description is true are *both* part of the same state. But if so, then the whole Transition Model is inappropriate to the situation because it fits only cases where the two states (the state of the object-for-description in virtue of which the description applies and the observer's state of knowledge) are separate. For otherwise he could not pass from (observing something's being in) the one to (being in) the other. If this is correct, it follows that no adequate account of the first-person epistemological situation can be formulated within the framework of the Transition Model. Some entirely different characterization of the relations between state of affairs described, describer, and description must be found.

38. Wittgenstein did deny this, but his reasons are unclear. (See *Philosophical Investigations*, sec. 246.) And in any case, his denial does not solve the problem of characterizing the first-person epistemological situation.

If not by deriving them from observation of the facts described, how then does a subject arrive at accurate mental descriptions of himself? The next section offers a model of mental self-description that seems to meet this problem with a solution that does not generate the familiar philosophical troubles and that eventually leads to a wholly different view of the nature of mental phenomena.

Application II has been tentatively accepted, but much more still is needed.

5. Foundations for a Model of Nontransitional Self-description

This section initiates construction of an account of mental self-knowledge and self-description that escapes problems associated with the foregoing attempts. To this end, first, the *mode of representation* used with this model, an unusual generalization and psychological application of the concept of a *"(possibly incomplete) probabilistic automation" description*, is explained.[39] (This form of representation is employed because it clearly and easily applies to humans and other organisms, it is realizable by neurological networks possessing nothing more than presently known properties of the vertebrate nervous system, it entails no dubious or unneeded additional postulated entities, it has a straightforward and unambiguous concrete interpretation, and, in the end, finally, because it works out correctly—in short, considerations of perspicuity, simplicity, comprehensiveness, economy, consistency with known fact, and ontological parsimony motivate its choice. Readers previously unacquainted with automata theory will enjoy perhaps, for this reason, the advantage of comprehending the present special psychological and neuropsychological adaptation of this mode of representation with initial ease and clarity, for the topic of the relationship of applied to formal automata theory is a subject on which mathematics is probably more confused today than it has been since the days of Berkeley's attacks on the differential and integral calculus.) Assume that a system, *M*, possesses the following properties. At

---

39. Incomplete sequential machines explicitly first appear in G. H. Mealy, "A Method for Synthesizing Sequential Circuits," *Bell System Technical Journal*, 34 (1955), 1045–1079. For a formal treatment of probabilistic automata, see Michael O. Rabin, "Probabilistic Automata," in *Sequential Machines*, ed. Edward F. Moore (Reading, Mass.: Addison-Wesley, 1964), pp. 98–114.

any time, M can be in no more than one of the states S_1, S_2, ..., S_n (or possibly in an indeterminate state that may be different from any of these). (Although throughout my exposition these states generally are assumed finite in number, since nothing[40] in the theory actually depends on this restriction, readers so wishing need not actually suppose this restriction in force.) In some (or possibly, all) of these states, M will or would respond to the "input" of an item of one of the mutually exclusive kinds i_1, i_2, ..., i_p by producing as "output" behavior of one of the kinds o_1, o_2, ..., o_m *and* also possibly by changing state. The output M produces depends (at least probabilistically) both on the *kind of input* received and on the *state* of M when the input is received; a function, called the "output function," describes this dependency. Furthermore, in at least some of its possible states, M will or would react to the presence of an input of a listed kind either by changing state or by staying in the same state, and another function, called the "next-state function," specifies the state into which M will pass from the given state after confrontation with an input of this kind. Thus, both the output which M will produce, and also the next state into which it will pass, are assumed to depend on the input that confronts it and also on its state at the time confronted. The special convention is stipulated and understood throughout, however, that inputs in the list and states may exist for which the next-state function and output function are undefined. In other words, for some listed inputs and states, the value of the output and next-state functions may be unspecified; that is, the representation of system M by these functions is permitted to be "incomplete." It also is assumed that passages between states and productions of outputs may occur with probabilities less than one. Such a system is characterizable by a "*state table*," such as Table 1–1. (N.B. Throughout this analysis, state tables are regarded not as the mysterious equivalents of platonic abstract or ideal machines, but rather as formal objects, matrices constructed from linguistic symbols describing [in some degree of incompleteness] possible *concrete* [rather than abstract] systems. These state tables, in other words, are regarded formalistically [somewhat as Hilbertian metamathematics would view the sentences of arithmetic]. Also it will be seen that despite the apparently discrete form of these state tables, passages between

40. Except where indicated otherwise (as in the derivation in Section 4 of Appendix II, which also assumes the state table's completeness).

states and productions of outputs nevertheless may be continuous
in the concrete systems they describe.)

States

Inputs	S_1	S_2	S_3	$\ldots$
i_1	$S_2(o_4)$	$S_6(o_{12})$	$S_3(o_3)$	$\ldots$
i_2	$S_9(o_{12})$	$S_1(o_5)$	(o_2)	$\ldots$
i_3	$prob[S_7(o_3)] = .80$	$S_4(\Lambda)$	.	$\ldots$
	$prob[S_3(o_1)] = .10$			
.	.	.	.	$\ldots$
.	.	.	.	$\ldots$
.	.	.	.	$\ldots$
i_p				

Table 1–1.

Table 1–1 says, in particular detail, for example, that when M
is in state S_1 and receives an instance of i_1 as an input, it does o_4
and passes into S_2. When in S_2 and confronted, say, with an
instance of i_3, M performs no action or behavior ('Λ' represents
the "null output") and passes into state S_4. If in state S_3 and
receiving an instance of i_1, it *remains* in state S_3, but performs
behavior of the kind o_3. For an input of kind i_2 when in state S_3,
the next-state function is undefined, as indicated (conventionally)
by an empty space in the table. This entry may be read as, "When
in state S_3, after the input of an instance of i_2, the system passes
into a state whose properties are uncharacterized." Later we will
say in such a case, e.g., that the input of an i_2 in state S_3 "takes
the system out of the given state table." The entry for an i_3 input
to the system when in state S_1 schematically illustrates the
possibility of a system (in a given situation) reacting with any
one of several different outputs and next states. This entry says
that the probability that system M, in this situation, will pass
into state S_7 and output an o_3 is .80, that it will pass into state S_3
and output an o_1 is .10, and (by implication) the probability is .10
that it will pass into an unspecified state. Probabilities less than
unity may be associated with all, some, or none of the entries in
a state table; probabilities not otherwise specified in a table will
be assumed, by convention, equal to unity.

All terms denoting or describing inputs and outputs in tables
throughout this book are understood to be general names or
descriptive predicates. For example, input descriptions might be

"A token of the zero symbol," "A red apple," or "A stormy sea-scape."[41] As output descriptions, "Erase scanned square, print a token of the symbol '1' on the tape, and move it one frame to the right," "Utter, 'Yes'," or "Raise right arm" might be included in a table. A system, then, is conceived as receiving as inputs, and producing as outputs, concrete scenes, entities, or items of behavior that instantiate the input and output descriptions appearing in the table. (As it might be, for example, in a certain state and shown a red apple, the system utters 'Yes'.) This use of general terms (having themselves the ultimate status of logical predicates) to characterize inputs and outputs exploits the well-known ability of such terms to partition a continuum into discrete parts so that concrete systems with continuously varying responses to continuously varying stimuli nevertheless can satisfy (and not merely as a finite approximation, but *genuinely*) state tables ostensibly having a discrete linguistic form. (Appendix I exhibits many examples.) Tables having different general names or descriptions in exactly corresponding places (i.e., isomorphic tables), of course, are considered nonidentical.

Several other points deserve mention. First, notice that instances of the *same kind* of output behavior can be evoked from *different* states. For example, Table 1–1 shows an action of the kind o_{12} produced both in response to an i_2 when in state S_1 and in response to an i_1 when in state S_2. Notice, too, a point frequently overlooked by early formulations of behaviorist psychological theories: the same kind of stimulus or input can elicit different kinds of responses or outputs from a system, depending on the system's *state* when confronted with that stimulus. For example, Table 1–1 shows that an instance of i_1 will elicit behavior o_4 from the system when it is in state S_1, but instead will elicit behavior o_{12} from the system if it is in state S_2 when confronted. Notice also that columns in a state table show not only what the system will do in response to the input that actually is presented, but also (counterfactually) how the system *would have reacted* to possible inputs of various other kinds, had they been presented

41. The pioneering analysis of how *neural networks* could realize state tables of this sort is due to Walter Pitts and Warren McCulloch, "How We Know Universals: The Perception of Auditory and Visual Forms," *Bulletin of Mathematical Biophysics*, 9 (Chicago: University of Chicago Press, 1947), 127–147; reprinted in Warren S. McCulloch, *Embodiments of Mind* (Cambridge, Mass.: The M.I.T. Press, 1965), pp. 46–66. More readable expositions of Formal Neuron Theory are available elsewhere, however.

instead. By convention, inputs are conceived as encountered by the system, in some sequence, serially in time, one after another. The order of writing the values of the next-state and output functions in the table is purely arbitrary; in tables in this book, descriptions of the elicited output sometimes will precede, and sometimes will follow, designations of the next state. Any given individual concrete system that would behave in the manner characterized by a given table is said, equivalently, to "satisfy," "realize," or "implement" that table, and the table is said to "characterize" or "describe" it.

No prejudices toward its subject matter are held by this mode of representation. Logically possible realizations of state tables include: an actual physical computer reading tokens of symbols from a magnetic tape or punched cards, a Cartesian "pure ego" reacting to sensory images or impressions arising in its *sensorium*, a central and peripheral efferent neural network responding to various ensembles of neural impulses as they arrive simultaneously on different afferent peripheral fibers, or a complete organism sensing and reacting to events and objects in its environment. Outputs respectively corresponding to these inputs might include: printing a new symbol in place of the old (erased) symbol and moving the tape, performing psychic acts of conation or "volitions," and moving bodily limbs. Some state table's concrete realization might also happen to be a universal Turing Machine, but this need not be the case.

Also it is assumed that realizations of a state table can "*distinguish*" each of the kinds of possible inputs listed separately in that state table; in other words, it is assumed that, at *some* juncture of operation, each distinctly listed kind of input can be the occasion of a differential or discriminating response by realizations of that state table. (So, in general, if i_j and i_k are separately listed inputs in a given state table, then that table contains a state, say S_m, such that some possible string of inputs containing i_j would elicit from a realization started in S_m a *sequence of outputs different from* the sequence of outputs that would be elicited from a realization started in the same state by a string of inputs exactly similar except with i_k in place of i_j.) Inputs of kinds not distinguished by a given state table will be regarded as inputs of the *same kind* (relative to that table).

Figure 1 abstractly portrays some system, M, characterized by this mode of representation. At any time, this system is assumed

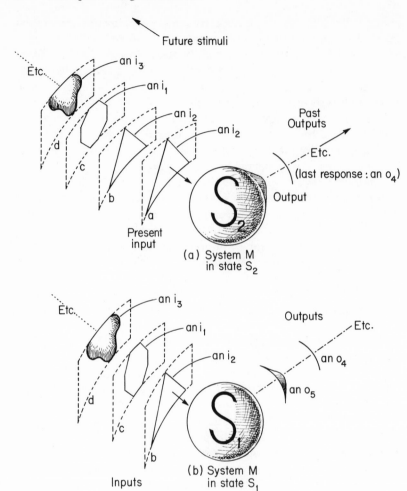

Figure 1

System M responds to an input.

to be in no more than one of the states $S_1, S_2, \ldots, S_n$ (or, possibly, in an indefinite state). At the moment shown in Figure 1(a), M is in state S_2 (after just outputting an o_4). This state (like any other listed in a state table) may be, perhaps, a state of the entire system, globally conceived. (*Nothing* [beyond what is implied by the general conventions associated with state tables] yet has been assumed or postulated about the definition or nature of these states.) In Figure 1(a), an i_2 confronts the system (after which, as portrayed in the illustration, it will encounter inputs in the sequence $i_2, i_1, i_3, \ldots$). The entry in Table 1–1 (assuming this table describes the system) for input i_2 in state S_2 shows that in this situation M will output behavior o_5 and pass into state S_1. Next, as Figure 1(b) shows, the system again finds itself confronted with (as it happens, another) instance of input i_2, in response to which, according to state Table 1–1, it will output an o_{12} and pass into state S_9. An instance of input i_1 next will be encountered, to which it will . . . , and so on, etc. However, one accidental feature of Figure 1 must not mislead readers; the picture must not be taken to imply that the nature and order of future inputs always is determined or fixed independently of M's previous output behavior, for M's output behavior at time t may influence subsequent inputs at time $t + k$. For example, if M is a human painter whitewashing a dingy wall, his successive outputs (brushing movements) eventually may cause a white (rather than gray) surface to face him, a new input resulting from his own past outputs, which may in turn cause him to stop painting. To avoid confusions, it is important to understand that application of this mode of representation does not preclude the existence, in the concrete situation, of external dependencies (additional to any implied by, or represented in, the state table itself) between outputs and subsequent inputs.

By itself, use of this mode of representation also implies nothing more about a concrete realization's internal nature and composition (its substance, constitution, structure, or inner configuration) than the conventions for applying state tables and the state designators themselves imply. The system appears from this standpoint as a "black box" whose internal nature, constitution, etc., is otherwise unspecified (and possibly unknown). Anything from a stochastic process, to an analogue computer, to a physical body controlled by an incorporeal interacting spirit, to a neural network, to an entire Turing Machine with an infinite internally located tape, could be inside the black box generating the actual and potential output behavior. For, any such system is characterizable (albeit, perhaps, incompletely) by *some* state table of the indicated sort, and since characterizability by such a state table is the only requirement a system must meet for this mode of representation to apply to it, therefore the assumption that a certain concrete system satisfies or realizes some state table of the indicated sort *itself* implies nothing more than what the particular state table entails about the system's internal structure. On this matter, the mode of representation is designedly neutral. The simple supposition that, e.g., system X realizes some state table or other itself entails almost nothing about system X; i.e., the assumption is "vacuous" or "trivially true." *Every* concrete entity realizes one or more state tables of the indicated sort, so the supposition that a system realizes some state table of the indicated sort presumes practically nothing about it.[42] To be sure, a given *particular* state table, as filled in, might characterize input-output properties that only certain sorts of systems could manifest, but in this event, it is the particular description constructed within the general framework of this mode of representation (i.e., the particular way the table is filled out) and not the general mode of representation itself, that engenders the restriction. Thus the supposition that a given concrete system realizes a state table of the indicated sort by itself entails practically nothing about the nature, constitution, configuration, etc., of the structure inside the system, although the supposition that a system is in one of certain states listed in some *given specific* state table may imply about its operation more detailed predictions than ever could be verified even by an infinitely long experiment (for proof, see Appendix II).

As previously explained, a system satisfying a state table is allowed to have states, behavioral dispositions, and input-output characteristics *in addition to* those shown in the table. It is understood by present conventions, in other words, that a state table need not show *all* the states or input-output characteristics of the system it describes. To realize a given state table, a concrete system need only be capable of acting as described by that table and of being in the states it lists; the table is *not* required to provide a "complete" or "exhaustive" description of the system, or to characterize how the system would act under all possible stimulations.[43] In particular, there may be possible environmental influences, capable of influencing a system's behavior, that are *not* listed as inputs in some state tables satisfied by the system. So, as understood here, a table genuinely satisfied by a concrete system nevertheless may describe that system only "partially" or "incompletely." For present purposes, a state table (and speci-

42. E.g., whether it is a universal Turing Machine, a probabilistic finite state automaton, a finite transducer, a stochastic generator, etc.

43. That such a requirement, if strictly adopted, would even make sense (for *concrete* systems) seems questionable.

fication of a state in that table) has essentially the logical status of a description (a monadic or one-place predicate conceived formally as a linguistic object true or false of particular concrete individuals) that need neither be "complete" nor the only such description truly ascribable to the system that satisfies it. One consequence of these conventions is that not only can the same state table be realized by many distinct individual concrete systems, but also each individual concrete system may satisfy, or be characterized by, many different state tables. (Illustrations appear in Appendix I.) These conventions also entail that a system possessing, in some sense, "infinite" behavioral capabilities nevertheless could satisfy and be characterized by (albeit, perhaps, incompletely) a finite state table. For, a concrete system with behavioral capabilities beyond anything that could be described or represented fully by a finite state table (supposing such a system to be possible in nature) nevertheless could satisfy a finite state table that (a) characterized only an initial finite subset of the system's possible behavior, and then (b) showed the system as passing out of the table into some unspecified state. So even infinite concrete systems (assuming the possibility of such entities) can satisfy finite state tables of the indicated sort.

Remarks: (1) Nothing yet has been said about how the "states," state names, or state predicates in the table themselves are defined. Intentionally, this now is left open and unspecified; as far as anything said so far is concerned, they might be further defined or specified in any of a variety of ways. (Their exact nature further develops in Chapter 3.) (2) When reified, *"states"* seem clearly to be the same kind of entity (viz., abstract objects or platonic universals) as the metaphysicians' traditional favorite, *"properties."* We commonly say that entities are *"in"* states (e.g., "rage," "third gear," "a discharged state") just as we say that they *"have" properties* or *qualities* ("hardness," "redness," "brittleness," "femininity," "consciousness"). Discussion of the question whether in some sense states could "exist" *apart from* the concrete systems which are "in" them (a special case, it seems, of the philosophic problem of universals) appears in the texts of metaphysics. (3) In the present context of the philosophy of mind, much is expressible most clearly in the *formal mode*, by speaking metalinguistically of individuals (such as persons) "satisfying" or "failing to satisfy" certain state descriptions (logical predicates such as 'is excited,' 'is solid,' 'is in third gear') or alternatively in terms of these linguistic expressions being "true of" or "false of" this or that entity. (To say in a metalanguage that the predicate 'is in state B' is true of entity *a*, of course, is equivalent to saying, in the object language or *material mode*, that entity *a* is in state *B*. So in particular, to characterize the conditions sufficient for some mentalistic state predicate or state description applying to, or being true of, an individual is the same as to characterize the conditions sufficient for an individual's being in that mental state.) (4) Just as an entity may have more than one property at once (e.g., be round, yellow, hot, and heavy simultaneously), there is no difficulty in conceiving it to be in several, or even countless, different states at the same time (e.g., be negatively charged, solid, and hot all at once). It suffices simply that various state descriptions (e.g., 'is negatively charged', 'is in a solid state', 'is hot') simultaneously be truly predicable of it at that time. Hence, in particular, although a realization of a state table of the sort described above is assumed, by convention, always to be, at any time, in no more than one of the states *listed* at the top of that table, this does not preclude a concrete realization of the table (while in a state listed in that table) from being simultaneously in any of a variety of other states not mentioned in it. At the beginning of Appendix I of this book, for example, a state table appears that characterizes a common typewriter; obviously, one can, without difficulty, suppose an actual typewriter to be in various other states (e.g., to be hot) at the same time it is in a state listed in the table. (5) Various considerations warrant presentation of the axioms of my theory serially in groups, and, naturally, only the implications of the axioms laid down (below) in this chapter will be discussed in this chapter. Thus, the initial talk of "states" in this chapter will be fully fleshed out later by axioms added in Chapter 3. (6) Whenever one feels that a theoretician is talking too loosely or without clear content about "states," one is entitled to demand specification or definition of the linguistic predicates that express the corresponding state descriptions.

Now comes the *model*. Consider the following two situations:

Situation I: There is an input on reception of which *M* goes into a certain state (which might be S_I). And for some inputs when in this state, *M* produces outputs having the following property: *They express in language* L *a description true of that input item.* For example, where *L* is English, part of the table for *M* might read as in 1–2.

	...	S_I	...
an apple	...	(*utter, 'Apple'*)S_J	...
an orange	...	(*utter, 'Orange'*)S_K	...
.	.	.	.
.	.	.	.
.	.	.	.

Table 1–2.

So in Situation I, M produces descriptions in L of the inputs it receives; more precisely, for some inputs it produces as outputs utterances that express in L descriptions true of those inputs. Thus, M here functions as a "description-renderer": put into state S_I and given an object within its repertoire, it produces a description true of that object. (This later will be taken as an analogue of the situation in transitional description.)

Situation II: Suppose that for some of its possible states, there is a special input item (which might be K^* or the query 'How-are-you?') such that if M receives an instance of this input when in one of these states, it produces an output with the following property: The output *expresses in language* L *a description which is true of* M *whenever* M *is in that state*, as, for example, in Table 1–3.

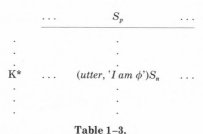

Table 1–3.

Here 'I *am* ϕ' expresses in L a description true of M when M is in S_p. So when M operates this way, it produces expressions which are, by the rules of L, descriptions of itself. In other words, here it functions as a self-describer: Give M an instance of the input K^* and (assuming it is in one of the states for which this works), it outputs an utterance telling its state. (This later will be used to model the situation in *nontransitional self-description.*)

Remark: The possibility of a state of affairs like Situation II first was suggested to me by Stephen Kleene's discussion of Turing Machines.[44] A Turing Machine with somewhat similar self-describing properties has been formulated and discussed by Hilary Putnam.[45] Putnam's model, however, develops very differently from mine. In his construction, the

44. S. C. Kleene, *Introduction to Metamathematics* (Princeton: D. Van Nostrand, 1952), chap. 13.

45. Hilary Putnam, "Minds and Machines," in *Dimensions of Mind: A Symposium*, ed. Sidney Hook (New York: New York University Press, 1960), pp. 138–164; reprinted in *Minds and Machines*, ed. Alan R. Anderson (Englewood Cliffs, N.J.: Prentice-Hall, 1964), pp. 72–97. Page references below are to the reprint in Anderson.

state mentioned in the output self-description is the state in the table itself and not, as in my model, simply a state it is in when in this state.[46] (The significance of this emerges in Chapter 3.) In Putnam's formulation, moreover, the self-description ('I am in state A') appears as an output in every row of the column under that state name in the table.[47] So on his model, the system could not do otherwise than output this self-description when in this state—that is, whenever in this state, for any input it will always report 'I am in state A'. Other features of Putnam's formulation rendering it unusable for our purposes are noted later.

The above two situations should be kept in mind. The first will be used to model, e.g., a person identifying a goldfinch. The second will be used to model someone reporting his mental state.

What system M does in both situations is similar in one respect. In both, he produces an output that expresses a description true or false of something. So in both cases, M can be said to have "described something." In another respect, however, M does a different thing in each case. In the first situation, M produces an output that expresses in L a description true of the input item.[48] Interpreting this as involving "observation" of that input item, in Situation I, M makes a transition in accordance with a rule of language from an object-of-description to a description true of that object. Also in Situation I, the truth value of the description uttered is independent of the state from which it has issued (depending instead only on the nature of the input item). In Situation II, on the other hand, M does not (in general) produce a description true of the prompting input item, and the truth value of the description expressed is not independent of the state from which it has issued; instead, whether it is true or false depends on M's state. But the description's truth value *is* independent of the nature of the input item received. In Situation II, M cannot be described as "making a transition in accordance with a rule of language from an object-of-description to a description true of that object" because the entity he describes (viz, himself) is, by assumption, not an entity he observed or perceived.

A general characterization detailing the respects in which Situation II resembles mental self-description appears below. The letter 'u' in it stands in place of a term designating the utterance

46. *Ibid.*, p. 79.
47. *Ibid.*
48. For all that has been said, this may even sometimes be M or some part of himself. Nothing has ruled out that some input-description, say 'k_i', be such that it would sometimes be satisfied by M itself (e.g., 'himself when bleeding').

token produced by *M*'s output action. (Later, where no confusion will arise, for brevity I sometimes will speak loosely as if this token itself, rather than the action of producing it, were the "output.")

THE MODEL OF NONTRANSITIONAL SELF-DESCRIPTION

General Characterization (Incomplete)[49]

1. If *M* produced *u* after receiving some input, it is not the case that the statement expressed in *L* by *u* is true in virtue of this input's presence.

2. Although *M* may have produced *u* as a result of receiving some input, *u* expresses in *L* a description of *M*—indeed, a description which, if true, is true of *M* solely in virtue of[50] *M* being in a state *M* was in when *M* was in the state as a result of (being in) which[51] he produced *u*.

3. The descriptive statement expressed in *L* by *u* is not, if true, true of *M* in virtue of the production by *M* of any output that *M* happens to produce.

The above is hypothesized to characterize (in part) nontransitional mental self-description. In applying this characterization, the "output" is understood to include the subject's physical behavior, and the "input" to be physical things or events that can affect his sense organs (i.e., in the terminology of psychology, the "inputs" are external stimulus objects and the "outputs" are behavioral responses, by stipulation). Thus a visible object, a ringing bell, a thorn in the foot all could be *inputs*; a swing of the arm, a wrinkling of the brow, or a vocalization might be *outputs*. (Regardless of how the "inputs" may be interpreted by other theoreticians in their applications of this cybernetic terminology,

49. Later these principles will be amended slightly.
50. As should be obvious, the phrase 'in virtue of' here expresses the relationship between a description and a state of affairs that satisfies it, a relation of truth conditions, not a causal relation.
51. *Re:* The awkward phrase "... being in a state [i.e., one of the states] *M* was in when *M* was in the state as a result of (being in) which he produced" the utterance: Principle 2 is couched this way so as to include cases where *the state of the speaker as a result of (being in) which he produced the utterance* is different from *the state of the speaker in virtue of (being in) which the description expressed by this utterance is true of him.*

in my theory *outward physical objects and events [or total environ-ments thereof]* are taken to be the "inputs.") To apply this charac-terization to a particular human case, e.g., that of Smith who (let's suppose) truly reported having a pain in his foot when asked this morning how he felt, we replace '*M*' with 'Smith', '*u*' with "I have a pain in my foot',' and '*L*' with 'English'. Thus applied, the characterization says:

> If Smith produced 'I have a pain in my foot' after receiving some input, it is not the case that the statement expressed in English by 'I have a pain in my foot' is true in virtue of this input's presence. Although Smith may have produced 'I have a pain in my foot' as a result of receiving some input, 'I have a pain in my foot' expresses in English a description of Smith—a description which, if true, is true of Smith solely in virtue of Smith being in a state [i.e., one of the states] he was in when he was in the state as a result of which he produced that utterance. The description expressed in English by 'I have a pain in my foot' is not, if true, true of Smith in virtue of the production by Smith of any output that Smith happens to produce.

If all these sentences are true, the characterization applies to Smith and his performance.

N.B. In my application of this characterization, the term "in-put" does *not* range over entities called "sensations." Only exter-nal physical situations or objects capable of affecting the subject's bodily sense organs (i.e., epistemologically public objects) are represented as possible inputs to him. In connection with this, several points deserve mention. (1) To posit "sensations" or other alleged mental objects, events or states of affairs as possible in-puts would be equivalent (when conjoined with the supposition that the subject identifies these as pictured in Situation I) to Application I of the Transition Model. It is thus fundamental that "sensations," "impressions," "subjective sense data," and the like not be included as inputs here. If necessary, such entities could be excluded as possible inputs by explicit fiat, but here this is unnecessary because the characterization's formulation itself precludes taking, e.g., sensations as inputs. (For anyone trying to do so will deduce from Principle 1, e.g., the absurdity that "If the speaker said 'I have a pain' after receiving some sen-sation, it is not the case that the statement expressed in English

by this utterance is true in virtue of this sensation's presence.")
(2) Notice, moreover and in particular, that treating, e.g., pain as a
state is not what precludes postulating, e.g., "pains" or "pain impressions" as inputs. For obviously one could affirm the statehood
of pain and yet hypothesize such entities as observational or
apprehensible input. For example, a classical theory of mind that
incorporated a transitional model of introspection might represent "pains" or "pain sensations" as introspectible inputs (to the
speaker's "mind," "self," "*sensorium*," or whatever), inputs perhaps that will cause the subject to be in or to pass into a state of
pain. (3) As the foregoing possibility illustrates, no issue at hand is
prejudged by my employment of a cybernetical mode of representation (with terminology like 'input', 'output', '*M*-system', 'state',
etc.). Every model of inner knowledge known to this writer is
representable or expressible in this terminology. (Appendix IV
contains additional explanation and illustration of this point.)

Remark: The cybernetical expressibility of different theories of mind
and introspection demonstrates that the problem is not *whether* to use a
cybernetical representation, but, if one is used, *how* to use it. My representation is distinguished, in part, by the specific concrete particulars
(namely, distal stimulus objects and outward physical behavior) chosen
as "inputs" and "outputs" in applying the characterization. Other theorists have employed similar cybernetical apparatus very differently. In
his use of it, for example, Patrick Suppes takes the *states* listed in the
state table to be realized by an organism's behavioral responses (that is,
by what I interpret as *outputs*).[52] And Putnam's "direct elicitation model"
is rendered unusable for nontransitionalists by its creator's postulating
"impressions" to "play the role of symbols on the machine's tapes"
(i.e., to be *inputs*) on the state table's psychological application.[53]
(Although somewhat difficult to comprehend, Putnam's model apparently
envisages these special entities as "imprinted" on a second [internally
located?] tape, an "*input tape*," by the action of the organism's physical
sense organs.[54] Putnam does not say whether these "impressions" are

52. Patrick Suppes, "Stimulus-Response Theory of Finite Automata," *Journal
of Mathematical Psychology*, 6 (1969), 329.
53. Putnam, "Minds and Machines," p. 84. In contrast I have taken the realization of the (external) "input tape" to be the sequence of events transpiring in the
organism's external stimulus neighborhood.
54. *Ibid.*, p. 77. See also Putnam, "Psychological Predicates," in *Art, Mind and
Religion*, Sixth Oberlin Colloquium in Philosophy, 1965, ed. W. H. Capitan and
D. D. Merrill (Pittsburgh: University of Pittsburgh Press, n.d.), p. 42, where the
"sensory inputs" are taken to be something for which the operation of the sense
organs is responsible. The same article is reprinted under the title "The Nature
of Mental States," in *Materialism and the Mind-Body Problem*, ed. David M.
Rosenthal (Englewood Cliffs, N.J.: Prentice-Hall, 1971); see p. 155.

conceived as *mental* entities produced in a Cartesian soul by the operation of the subject's sense organs, or as *physical* patterns of excitation produced in the afferent portions of the subject's nervous system [if he meant this, why would he use a mentalistic term like 'impressions'?], or even perhaps as something else.[55]) In any case, the same formal apparatus can be used in radically different ways to state extremely dissimilar claims or theories.

My account is most easily understood intuitively by viewing the diagram in Situation II as a picture or description of Smith. Suppose that the states in the state table (1–3) are states Smith may be in, and that 'K^*' is the input utterance 'How-do-you-feel?' Suppose also that when in S_p, the result of inputting this question is that Smith says 'I have a pain' which, as it happens, is true of Smith when Smith is in S_p. Then, according to this account, Smith produces the self-description 'I have a pain' neither by observing the fact(s) in virtue of which it is true nor by self-observation, but nontransitionally as shown in the diagram. (This diagram is the simplest expression I can formulate of the model's portrayal of the introspective situation. One must not, however, be misled by its simplicity. My hypothesis in particular does not entail that the speaker produces the self-description as a simple reflex response to some input. For one thing, the output might be "spontaneous" in the sense of being elicited by the null input [i.e., a person might pass into a state in which he produces this self-description with no outside input]. Also, even with external prompting, it is possible that the output issues only after the occurrence of computational processes involving many passages from state to state. Consequently, my model cannot be characterized correctly as a "direct elicitation model.")

This, I hypothesize, is how a person is able to say, and says, what mental state he is in when he is in that state; not by observation, but nontransitionally. Like the system pictured in Situation II, the subject is so constituted or arranged that, when in a certain state, receipt of an appropriate input[56] elicits output of an utter-

---

55. In another paper, Putnam classifies "certain configurations" of the physical body as "visual impressions," "tactile impressions," etc. But on the same page, he attacks the mind-body identity thesis, so this may be a slip of the pen ("The Mental Life of Some Machines," in *Intentionality, Minds, and Perception*, ed. Hector Neri Castañeda [Detroit: Wayne State University Press, 1966]; reprinted in *Modern Materialism: Readings on Mind-Body Identity*, ed. John O'Connor [New York: Harcourt, Brace & World, 1969], p. 275.

56. Or the null input.

ance expressing in the language a mental description true of him when in that state. Thus to possess the information contained in this description, the speaker need not receive observational input from anywhere. In cybernetic terms, no flow of information into the system is required because the relevant information is already inside it, stored in the form of its state. To convey this information outside the system, it suffices that the system do something distinctive, produce some special output, only when in this state.[57] Then, from the production of this special output, others can tell that it is (or was) in this state. (The possibility of physical systems capable of such operations is obvious; they need only realize a state table of the sort described.) Since this "special output" could be anything, in particular it can be a *token of some standard sign or symbol universally and conventionally used* to describe systems' states. Thus, Smith's case features the nicety that this special output is an utterance (viz., 'I have a pain in my foot') that expresses in English *a description true of him when he is in a state as a result of being in which he produces that description.* (The possible existence of physical mechanical systems having outputs possessing the additional property of expressing such a description is obvious. Skeptics, however, may turn ahead to Chapter 3 where an ordinary typewriter is converted to a simple system of this sort.) The hypothesis is that humans are such systems and that mental descriptions are among the state descriptions we so produce.

One qualification is required. Principle 2 is not satisfied by any statement whose truth value depends, in whole or in part, on something other than the speaker's own state. Thus the birdwatcher who reports, "That's a goldfinch," the chemist who observes, "This solution has turned green," and countless other cases do not satisfy the model. For the same reason, even some descriptions that *do* possess mentalistic implications also fail it. If, for example, the truth of 'X sees an apple' or 'X intends to beat his wife' requires that an apple seen by X exist or that X be married, then first-person utterances of these descriptions will not fit the characterization because their truth value depends on something other than the speaker's state. This is as it should be: these descriptions' possession of nonmentalistic implications (about apples and wives), as well as mentalistic implications, makes them "mixed"

---

57. The human case, of course, is complicated by the fact that the subject may lie.

rather than "pure" mental descriptions.[58] Strictly, the hypothesis is that for the class of *pure* (i.e., nonrelational) mental descriptions, the characterization always applies.

The relationship to this model of familiar epistemological concepts is obvious. Situation I, the transitional case, corresponds to a simple case wherein someone describes something perceived. The input is the *object-for-description*, and the subject's output utterance expresses a *description* true of it. (On this model, since only physical objects or events are inputs, these are the only entities a subject perceives; i.e., the present hypothesis strictly entails direct realism.) In Situation I the information conveyed in the subject's output is gained by observation. In Situation II, in contrast, the information conveyed in the output is *not* gained by observation. Instead, *when in a certain state*, the system outputs an instance of a description *true of itself whenever in this state*, and even if some external input has elicited this response, this input is not what the output describes. So no transition is made from an object-for-description to a description of it. Situation II is a case of "knowledge without observation," or, as I prefer to term it, "nontransitional self-description."[59] So Situation I corresponds to knowledge by observation and Situation II to nontransitional self-description.

Principle 1 of the general characterization implies of the nontransitional situation that the entity to which the subject responds as input is not also what his output describes; Principle 2 says that the self-description is produced as explained above. Principle 3, yet undiscussed, excludes action self-descriptions. That is, suppose someone utters the following words: 'I am now speaking.' This does not express a mental self-description, yet it satisfies Principles 1 and 2. Its truth does not depend on the nature of anything he observes, so it satisfies Principle 1. And on a lenient interpretation of "state," this utterance expresses a description true of the speaker in virtue of his being in a state he is in when he produces it (viz., the state of speaking), so it satisfies Principle 2.

58. The existence of "context-dependent" mentalistic descriptions (that is, descriptions that depend not only on the state of the subject but also on certain features of his external situation) has been widely noted and studied by philosophers. See, e.g., Errol Bedford, "Emotions," *Aristotelian Society Proceedings*, 57 (1956–57), 281–304.

59. To extend the concept "observation" to type II situations would be unadvisable because it would obscure the distinction just drawn between different ways of having knowledge and misleadingly would suggest that the Transition Model applies.

But it fails Principle 3 because it is true of the subject in virtue of his production of some output (viz., uttering the sentence itself). Action self-descriptions are discussed further in Section 1 of Chapter 4.

The neural mechanism underlying mental self-knowledge, on this model, can be highly unlike that postulated by David Armstrong and others. Armstrong hypothesizes that knowledge of one's own mental state is made possible by one portion of one's central nervous system "scanning" another part. On this theory,

> Consciousness of our own mental state becomes simply the scanning of one part of our central nervous system by another. Consciousness is a self-scanning mechanism in the central nervous system.[60]

Armstrong's underlying conception here obviously is again the Transition Model. His account differs from Application I only in explicitly locating the observational relationship between two parts of the speaker's nervous system. Armstrong's identification of the subject of self-awareness with "one part" of his nervous system (and his mental state with something in *another* part!) is somewhat difficult to comprehend, but in any event, as our model shows, for a system to be capable of reporting its own state, no such internal flows of information are required. In particular, no scanning operations need take place. Instead, it suffices if the system be so constituted that when in a given state, it can produce outputs that conventionally express this fact.[61]

Another physicalist, the psychological behaviorist B. F. Skinner, likewise unconsciously attempts to retain the Transition Model in his conception of mental self-knowledge and psychological self-description. On Skinner's application, the role of

60. David M. Armstrong, "The Nature of Mind," in *The Mind-Brain Identity Theory*, ed. C. V. Borst (London: Macmillan, 1970), p. 79. In *A Materialist Theory of the Mind* (London: Routledge & Kegan Paul, 1968), he presents the same view, claiming that "introspection is a self-scanning process in the brain," and stating, moreover, that it is impossible that the introspecting state and the state introspected should be identical (p. 324).

61. Of course, this is not to deny that more is involved in *self-awareness* than mere ability to produce true self-descriptions. This is discussed somewhat in Chapter 2 where it is shown that the only sort of awareness that need be assumed in order to understand the phenomena of "self-awareness" in one family of cases is awareness of external physical states of affairs and that phenomena of "subjective awareness" are merely altered or truncated states of objective awareness (that is, the awareness of objective situations).

object-for-description is played by "private stimuli" from inner
physiological events (a full or inflamed stomach, a stomach con-
tracting in hunger, a gallstone distending the bile duct, the
contractions or relaxations of small blood vessels in blushing and
blanching, a pounding heart, stimuli from muscles, tendons, and
joints generated by the position and movement of parts of the
body, etc.). On his account, a speaker's statements about, for
example, his own wishes or intentions (e.g., 'I'm strongly inclined
to go home', 'I intend to go home in half an hour') "describe states
of affairs which appear to be accessible only to the speaker."[62]
For instance, the statement, 'I was on the point of going home', he
says, "may be regarded as the equivalent of 'I observed events in
myself which [are of the sort that] characteristically precede or
accompany my going home'."[63] In contrast, without precluding
or excluding the involvement of peripheral afferent neural signals
from viscera, muscles, and other subparts of the body in mental
self-description, my model nevertheless shows that they are *not* in
general necessary, and it suggests a different conception of their
role when they are present. For example, being "strongly inclined
to go home" is a state into which as a consequence of various
possible stimulations (or their lack) a person may pass. When in
such a state, a given individual will have characteristic probable
responses to various different possible environmental circumstances (e.g., if someone suggests ending the party and all going
home, he will not disagree; if an opportunity to depart early grace-
fully arises, he will take it; etc.). When in this state, then, a given
subject will produce characteristic behavior in response to various kinds of environmental situations if they arise. Accordingly,
in particular, to produce a correct mental description of himself
as being in this state, no inward observation of "private stimuli"
or stimulus objects (muscles in tension, blood pressure, etc.) is
necessary. It suffices simply that among his characteristic behavioral responses (outputs) when in this state be uttering, for example, the words 'I'm strongly inclined to go home' when stimulated
with a query like 'What do you feel like doing?' or 'How do you
feel?'; responding 'Yes' to the question 'Do you feel like going
home?'; etc. No inner observation is required. It suffices for the

62. B. F. Skinner, *Science and Human Behavior* (New York: Macmillan, 1953),
p. 262. Cited by Norman Malcolm in *Problems of Mind* (New York: Harper & Row,
1971), p. 84.
63. *Ibid.*

subject to be so constituted that when in this state, certain kinds of external stimuli [or the null input] elicit characteristic responses of the kind described (a supposition that ought to present no difficulty to behaviorists or SR learning theorists). And in cases like pain or hunger where afferent signals transmitted from some bodily subpart *are* commonly involved in the organism's report of its psychological state, a different view of their role is offered by my model. The event in, or state of, the bodily subpart (stretched tendon, distended stomach, etc.) is not itself identical with the mental event or state, nor is it by itself an occurrence in virtue of which the mentalistic predications are true of the subject. For these events or states could occur in these bodily subparts without the subject being in a state of pain or hunger—e.g., if the incoming afferent pathways to the central nervous system from these subparts were interrupted, or if the overall state of the rest of the nervous system were modified or controlled (by drugs, general anesthesia, hypnosis, implanted electrodes, etc.) in certain ways. Having a pain or feeling hungry are states of the *whole* system, not just states of these bodily subparts considered in isolation. Although the occurrence of such *events in certain bodily subparts* and the transmission of neural impulses from them inward to the central nervous system on many occasions may be among the physical events that go to make up "having a pain" or "feeling hungry," or part of what causes the system to pass into these states, these events are not themselves the mental event, nor are they what the subject's report describes, or what his description (if true) is true in virtue of. Indeed, not only is the occurrence of such physical events in bodily subparts not itself sufficient for the occurrence of the psychological state (that is, for the truth of the mentalistic ascription); it is not necessary either. The same state that the psychological description attributes to the speaker (pain or hunger, for example) can occur without these usual preceding or accompanying events in bodily subparts (as in so-called "central pain"[64] or hunger produced by direct brain stimulation

<hr/>

64. Peripheral pain arises in the nerves of the extremities or body organs. Central pain begins in the spinal cord or in the brain itself and can be caused by spinal injuries, strokes or tumors. Central pain usually is very difficult to treat. See Valentino Cassinari & Carlo A. Pagni, *Central Pain* (Cambridge, Mass.: Harvard University Press, 1969). See also James C. White and William H. Sweet, *Pain: Its Mechanisms and Neurosurgical Control* (Springfield, Ill.: Charles C. Thomas, 1955). "Central pain" frequently is experienced as located in bodily extremities.

through implanted electrodes[65]). The truth value of the psychological ascription depends on the entire system as a whole passing into a certain state or configuration; the mistaken identification of the mental event with an occurrence in the leg or stomach, for example (the mistaken conclusion to which many psychologists are led by an application of the Transition Model like Skinner's), is avoided by completely repudiating that model. Nor does this mean that the organism's nervous system must receive stimuli, inflow, or neural signals from every part of itself to make such reports. For contrary to Skinner's initial mistaken assumption, psychological descriptions do *not* (as Skinner believes) "describe states of affairs . . . accessible only to the speaker"—they describe the speaker himself, and to produce such descriptions when true, these utterances need only be among the outputs characteristically produced as responses ("operants") to certain inputs when in the given state.

Remarks: The facts mentioned above apparently also disconfirm Putnam's functionalistic hypothesis. His formulation, like mine, employs a state table of a special kind (which he calls a "Functional Organization" or, for short, just a "Description") and interprets the "outputs" to be motor behavior. However, it slightly differs from mine in interpreting the "inputs" (called "sensory inputs") to be, as he says, something for which "the sense organs [are] responsible,"[66] rather than external physical events capable of affecting the organism's sense organs (as in my account). Putnam gives no further explicit specification of exactly what the "inputs" are. Thus, apparently, if dualistic interactionism were true and the sense organs functioned to cause psychic phenomena (Humist "impressions"?) to arise or exist in the mind or *sensorium* of the subject, then so specified, Putnam's "inputs" might be inner mental objects of the sort I am trying to avoid positing. If, on the other hand, one rejects (as presumably one should) a dualistic interpretation of Putnam's formulation and instead understands it as a purely physicalistic theory, then presumably the events for which the sense organs are "responsible" would be the physiological effects of their stimulation. For example, in vision, stimulation of the eyes activates

65. For a review of the literature on this topic see James A. F. Stevenson, "Neural Control of Food and Water Intake," in *The Hypothalamus*, ed. Webb Haymaker, Evelyn Anderson, and Walle J. H. Nauta (Springfield, Ill.: Charles C. Thomas, 1969), pp. 533–557. See also Konrad Akert, "Diencephalon," in *Electrical Stimulation of the Brain*, ed. Daniel E. Sheer (Austin: University of Texas Press, 1961), pp. 288–310.

66. Hilary Putnam, "Psychological Predicates," p. 42 ("The Nature of Mental States," p. 155).

retinal ganglion cells that in turn cause fibers in the optic nerve to fire, which, among other effects, excite brain cells in the so-called "primary visual projection area," which in turn activate neurons in the so-called "secondary visual projection area," and so on. Consequently, although Putnam does not precisely stipulate which link(s) in the chain of events for which the sense organs are responsible he takes as the "inputs," presumably something like either the activation of retinal ganglion cells, events in the optic nerve, or stimulations of the primary or secondary visual projection areas would be the "(sensory) input" to which his theory refers in the case of vision. In the case of pain, the "physical realization of the sense organs"[67] presumably would be the so-called "pain fibers" or "pain receptors" (i.e., apparently, peripheral A delta and C fibers whose distal endings normally are activated by damage to bodily tissue or the existence of conditions threatening such damage). So interpreted, the relevant "inputs" in the case of pain might be, for example, stimulated A delta and C fibers. [Although in our respective formulations the "inputs" are interpreted differently, in itself, this fact need not entail the incompatibility of the two accounts. The initial choice of what is to count as the "inputs" is to a great extent a matter of convention involving a more or less arbitrary delineation of the boundaries of what is to count as "the system" under consideration. If one model characterizes only a subpart of the entire system characterized by another, this need not imply any incompatibility between the two. Thus Putnam's choice of events for which the sense organs are responsible to be the "inputs" itself does not imply an incompatibility between the two models. A fundamental divergence does arise, however, between my nontransitional account and the axioms or principles that Putnam states using his interpretation.] With reference to pain, Putnam advances the following postulates. (For convenient reference, Putnam's original axiom numbers are retained while omitting statements not relevant to the present discussion.)

(1) *All organisms capable of feeling pain are Probabilistic Automata.*

(2) *Every organism capable of feeling pain possesses at least one Description ["Functional Organization"] of a certain kind (i.e., being capable of feeling pain is possessing an appropriate kind of Functional Organization).*

(4) *For every Description of the kind referred to in (2), there exists a subset of the sensory inputs such that an [any?] organism with that Description is in pain when and only when some of its sensory inputs are in that subset.*[68]

67. *Ibid.*
68. *Ibid.*

Interpreted physicalistically, Putnam's crucial principle (4) appears to entail, for an organism that realizes the indicated state table(s), that there exists a certain subset of sensory inputs (e.g., stimulations of the A delta and C fibers) such that the organism is in pain when and only when some of its sensory inputs are of this sort (i.e., when and only when stimulated peripheral "pain fibers" exist or are present in it). Briefly stated, then, this postulate seems to imply that an organism is in pain if and only if stimulated peripheral neural fibers of this sort exist or are present to it. But although this biconditional happens to be true (as an "accidental generalization") of many individuals at various times, it fails to express a fundamental invariance or true law of nature. For, as noted above, an organism can be in pain even when no sensory inputs of this indicated kind exist in, or are present to, it (as in "central pain" which exists without stimulation of any peripheral pain fibers), so the presence of such inputs is not a physically necessary condition for pain. Likewise, as noted above, an organism can have stimulated peripheral "pain fibers" without being in pain (for example, due to a spinal block, hypnosis, general anesthesia, etc.), so the presence of such inputs is not sufficient for pain either. Since no inputs are by themselves necessary or sufficient for pain, the empirical facts apparently disconfirm Putnam's formulation.

However, these same facts do not refute my nontransitional model because its postulates are different. Instantiated for the particular case of pain and formulated so as to facilitate a comparison with Putnam's, my Principles 1 and 2, in contrast, entail:

    1. *Whether an organism is in pain (or has pain) is logically independent of whether or not it receives or has received an input of any sort.*

    2. *Whether an organism is in pain at a time depends entirely on its state at that time.*

Obviously, neither of these statements conflicts with the empirical observations just cited. Sophisticated readers will note the great difference in ontological foundations laid in the different formulations. Putnam's model postulates that being in pain is a matter of having inputs (concrete particulars) of a certain sort present, while my formulation denies this and claims instead that it depends somehow only on the overall *state* of the system. (From these initial basic differences, great divergences develop. Indeed, in Section 3 of Chapter 4, it is proved that my model [with additional principles] is strictly and logically incompatible with Putnam's, and hence that the two theories are incompatible with each other.) So when the inevitable sleepy commentator pronounces the two theories identical simply on the grounds that both are "functionalistic," astute readers will recognize that the fundamental differences between them have not been comprehended.

The model so far constructed shows how a subject could give a mental description of himself without obtaining the description by observation of anything, and so shows how to avoid the problems generated by transitional accounts. It also explains the earlier feeling that knowledge of one's own mental state *"comes with* the state of which it is knowledge." For the state from which the information-conveying description issues (which is, in that respect, a state of knowledge) is also a state of the subject in which that description is true. So naturally the one "comes with" the other.[69]

Notice, furthermore, that from the standpoint of what goes on *inside M*, Situation I and Situation II are indistinguishable: *M* goes through a similar internal mechanical process in both cases. Even God, if he looked only inside *M*, could not tell which operation *M* was engaged in. Something *external* to *M* determines which (if either) of the two types of situation a given case is: namely, the output's meaning or interpretation in language *L*. Nothing unique going on inside *M* makes the output into a description of himself. It would not be surprising, therefore, if the subject should tell us that *he* can discern no difference in kind between what he does in Situation I and what he does in Situation II and that *to him* it seems that he does the same kind of thing in both cases. (For in a certain respect he does; the mistake would lie in thinking that the "same kind of thing" he does in both cases is to derive the description from that of which it is true.) Of course, if *M* had sufficient mastery of language *L*, he could categorize the cases as well as anyone. (All this becomes clearer in Chapter 3.)

In the next chapter, the decisive role of the utterances's linguistic meaning becomes especially important. If my model is correct, it should be possible, by holding every other parameter of the situation constant and varying only the interpretation of the output in *L*, to make a subject's performance fluctuate between being (a) an instance of making a transition from an object to a description true of it and (b) an instance of nontransitional self-description. For, as the model implies, nothing unique going on inside subjects makes what they do be a case of the one rather

69. Contrast this with Armstrong's view that in introspection "the mental state of affairs that we are aware of *brings about* the awareness of it" where this relation of *"bringing about"* is a *causal* one obtaining between two distinct mental states (*Materialist Theory*, p. 329). On the view I present, the relationship of the state reported ("introspected") to the state that is "knowledge" of it is not causal, nor need they be distinct states.

than the other. (In Chapter 2, this fact is exploited in an account of mental self-knowledge in cases such as pain description, after-image description, and dream description.)

My model also distinguishes what is right from what is wrong with Wittgensteinian assertions to the effect that "A person's mental self-description is a *manifestation* of his state and not a *description* of it."[70] If a person's characteristic actions when in a given state constitute "manifesting" that state, then producing a mental self-description as characterized by the model manifests one's state. So the first conjunct of the slogan is correct. But the output utterance also happens to express a description true of the subject, so it *also* can be said that the subject *is* "describing himself." Thus the second conjunct is literally false. (If it was intended only to mean that the subject does not derive his description from observation of the facts in virtue of which the description is true, then the point is correct but misleadingly put.) A more accurate statement would be: "A person's mental self-description is both a manifestation of his state and a description of it, although not a description derived from the facts it describes." For the same utterance both expresses a description and manifests the existence of the situation it says exists. It is produced by the subject as a consequence of being in the state he is in when the description is true of him, so in this respect, it is *evidence* that he is in this state; but since the subject's state also can be learned simply by interpreting his utterance in language L, his utterance also can be treated as a *description*. Truth conditions and utterance conditions here coincide; the utterance is both an assertion and evidence for what it asserts.[71] And as long as the state of the subject as a result of which he produces this sentence and the state of him in virtue of which the sentence is true continue to coincide, one is safe in treating it either way.[72]

Also explained are some of the facts behind the puzzling claim

70. This suggestion is found in Wittgenstein, *Philosophical Investigations*, sec. 244, and in the writings of many subsequent philosophers.

71. Thus psychologists who only regard subjects' utterances as behavioral data are justified, but so are those who regard them as statements of what the facts are.

72. Of course, if they failed to coincide, then the two approaches could lead to divergent results. If the subject produced a self-description false of himself (e.g., if he lied), then one could be led into error through going only by the meaning in the language of what the subject said. Whether in that event one could learn the subject's state by treating his utterance simply as evidence would depend, obviously, on how good that evidence was and the other evidence available.

that "a subject cannot misrecognize his own sensations." For the model shows why the (nontransitional) production of a mental self-description when false never could be attributed to the speaker's having misobserved something. This is not because there is some entity which the speaker could not misrecognize (i.e., respond to in a way that might be correct for some other entity but is wrong for this one), but rather because, in the nature of the situation, whether or not this has happened is irrelevant to the truth or falsity of what he says. For in nontransitional self-description, the truth value of the statement expressed by the output is independent of the nature of any input received. To illustrate: in Situation II, suppose that the input that activated M was actually an instance of k_1 but that M responded to it as he ordinarily would to K^* (i.e., by outputting the indicated self-description). This mistake would not affect the truth value of the self-description. For if true, what he says is true of M in virtue of his being in the state he was in when he produced the output and not in virtue of the nature of the input received. So even if M "misrecognized" some item, this would have no bearing on the truth or falsity of the output description. Thus the model explains why the nontransitional production of a mental self-description when false never can be attributed to the speaker's having misobserved something.

Does this model *uniquely* characterize mental self-description? That is, suppose the variable 'M' in the general characterization were restricted to the class of humans and 'L' were restricted to some language such as English. Would the resulting open sentences (with variable 'u') be satisfiable by utterances of all and only intuitively recognizable "mental" self-descriptions in that language? No. The characterization is satisfiable, for example, by someone who makes a policy of saying 'I have stimulated C fibers in my nervous system' every time he has a pain.[73] For the truth value of the statement he produces is independent of the nature of anything he observes (he does not examine or inspect his nervous system) and if true, is not true of him in virtue of any behavior he produces, so Principles 1 and 3 both are satisfied. And his utterance expresses a description that "if true, is true of the subject in virtue of his being in a state he was in when he was in the state as a result of which he produced it," so his performance

73. Putnam cites this example in "Minds and Machines," pp. 74f.

also satisfies Principle 2 (which nowhere was restricted to "mental" states). In fact, absence of any limitation on the kind of state involved in Principle 2 permits countless other nonmental self-descriptions also to fit the model. Someone, describing his own appearance, who says truly (not after observing himself but simply from memory), 'I'm tall and blond' produces an utterance that expresses in English a description true of himself in virtue of his being in a state (viz., the state of tallness and blondness) he was in when he produced that utterance, so this case also satisfies Principle 2 (as well as 1 and 3). Indefinitely many other "physical" self-descriptions ('I am short'; 'I am handsome'; 'I weigh 180 lbs'; 'I have dark eyes') similarly can satisfy the general characterization. So it does not characterize mental self-description uniquely.

Intuitively, 'I have a pain' is a *"mental"* description while 'I have stimulated C fibers in my nervous system' is not. But what is the real difference between these two descriptions? Since almost everyone seems sensitive to some distinction here (whether of kind or degree) and can apply it similarly to novel cases, the conjecture seems reasonable that a difference is based on some underlying principle—perhaps a principle that, if it could be uncovered, would greatly illuminate the relationship between "the mental" and "the physical" or between "mind" and "body". This conjecture is confirmed in Chapter 3 when the foregoing characterization is supplemented by a further principle nontrivially satisfiable by all and only the "mental" self-descriptions, a principle revealing the surprising fact that the so-called "mental" descriptions are actually set apart from others not by their reference to special mentalistic particulars (as was the Cartesian view, for example), but rather by a peculiar logical and epistemological property they all share.

Prior to this, however, a family of mental phenomena including hallucinations, afterimages, dreams, and bodily sensations receives special scrutiny in the next chapter because its members have appeared traditionally to classical theoreticians to substantiate, more than the members of any other group, the model of inner knowledge just rejected. Consequently, although not strictly essential to my model's further development, an analysis of these phenomena showing in detail that they fit the part of it already constructed is desirable. Since it is obviously logically impossible for a general characterization satisfiable by *all* mental self-descriptions to distinguish one subclass of them from another, the characterization of a specific subclass requires the general model's supplementation by an additional more specific model. Hence this family of mental phenomena (like any other subset) is characterizable in contrast to others only by *conjoining* to the general characterization a *further* model satisfiable only by its members. In the next chapter, hallucinations, afterimages, dreams, and bodily sensations are shown to satisfy both the portion of the general model given above and the specific model introduced there.

CHAPTER 2

The Apparent Existence of Private Mental Objects in One Family of Psychological Phenomena

1. Preliminary Remarks

Chapter 1 explained that what a subject does to arrive at a correct mental description of himself should not be represented or conceived as making a transition from something to its description. Nevertheless, with such experiences as hallucinations, afterimages, dreams, and bodily sensations, this is exactly how it seems to the subject himself that he arrives at a true mental self-description. That is, in the case of these phenomena, when a subject is constructing a mental self-description, it seems to him as if he were deriving a description from something which only he observed. (In this respect, these phenomena differ from all other mental phenomena; when someone announces his hopes or intentions, for example, it usually does not seem to him as though he were describing something privately perceived.) For this reason (and because, as Thomas Nagel emphasizes, "a physical theory of mind must account for the subjective character of experience"[1]), it is imperative to show clearly by detailed analysis that subjects in such cases do *not* (as it appears) make a transition from a directly apprehended mental particular to its description, but instead (as I have posited) produce self-descriptions nontransitionally.

What the preceding chapter characterized from an objective external viewpoint will be described in this chapter from the

1. Thomas Nagel, "What Is It Like to Be a Bat?" *Philosophical Review*, 83 (1974), 437.

subject's viewpoint. Such a description is needed because very little about the speaker's performance as undergone subjectively (i.e., how the subject actually forms the mental description of himself, the rational procedure he uses, the acts of judgment he must perform, etc.) is shown by the general characterization of Chapter 1. Indeed, for all it says, mental self-descriptions might simply pop out of one's mouth like hiccups with no steps of ratiocination or judgment behind them whatsoever.[2] This chapter, then, characterizes in detail what, in cases of the phenomena listed, a system does, qua rational agent, to arrive at a mental description true of itself, a characterization showing how, in doing so, a subject may engage in processes of reasoning and reflection fully as much as in any case where he really derives a description from something.

This chapter investigates two important features of these mental phenomena: (1) the respect in which the experience (e.g., of having a pain) resembles the experience of perceiving or observing something; (2) the respect in which what the subject does to form or to construct a true mental self-description in these cases is like what he does when he derives a description from something. This chapter also can be viewed as giving an answer to the traditional "argument from hallucination" (as J. L. Austin showed we should call it) and an account of the apparent "perception" of pains, afterimages, etc., consistent both with direct realism and with the view that the only objects or events we ever perceive are physical.

2. The Model of Truncated Awareness and Description

In investigating hallucinations and their subjective description, we shall begin with a "full-blown" case of normal perception (i.e., a case where a subject sees and describes an external public object) and then imagine features or components of the case cut

---

2. Some contemporary philosophers convey precisely this impression by making assertions like "A man's utterance is not a description of his pain but an expression of it" and comparing the subject's output to a wince or a moan. For example Norman Malcolm, "Knowledge of Other Minds," *Journal of Philosophy*, 55 (1958), 978. But no account ignoring the activities of judgment and rational agency underlying these performances can be considered adequate.

away until it degenerates into pure hallucination.[3] Thus by a process of subtraction, so to speak, a paradigm will be created for use in the analysis of hallucinatory experience.

Suppose that you are walking the grounds of your country house with a friend when suddenly he spies a rabbit: "A brown and white rabbit with one ear longer than the other," he says, pointing to a furry creature by the gorse answering this description. Take this as the full-blown case. In it, we assume, the object of perception (i.e., the rabbit) is involved in a chain of events by which the subject is affected through his sense organs: sunlight reflected off the rabbit strikes his eyes where it is focused on his retinas stimulating receptors that initiate a series of events ultimately terminating in his passage into a certain sensory state and production of the rabbit description. It also is assumed that if, at any point, this causal chain were broken and an event of the same kind produced as an effect of some other cause, the same subsequent effects still would ensue.

Now imagine the full-blown situation slightly altered. Assume light reflected in *exactly the same pattern* as before, but now, say, from a clump of leaves rather than from a rabbit. In such a case,

---

3. In *A Materialist Theory of the Mind* (London: Routledge & Kegan Paul, 1968), and also *Bodily Sensations* (London: Routledge & Kegan Paul, 1962), D. M. Armstrong employs a similar strategy in analyzing hallucinations and bodily sensations, but uses a different model and so ends up with a different account. Armstrong conceives of introspective awareness as an "inner sense" comparable to sense perception (*Materialist Theory*, p. 323) having for its object certain brain or neural events (which he identifies with mental states). In contrast, I represent introspection, in cases such as those here under consideration, as the truncated awareness of apparent objective situations, not of brain or neural states. So complete is Armstrong's assimilation of introspection to perception (Application I of the Transition Model) that he even defends the possibility of nonveridical introspective images, analogous to nonveridical sensings (*ibid.*, p. 330).

The account developed in this chapter can be regarded, however, as an extension and detailed development of the idea, suggested in scattered remarks by Ryle and J. J. C. Smart and endorsed by James Cornman, that sensations may be understood in terms of nonrelational, objectless states of sensing (states of sensing "F"-ly, sensing "G"-ly, etc.). For a thoroughgoing criticism of the traditional conception that sensations are sensory objects or sensa (that is, entities one senses) and of other approaches materialists have taken in trying to deal with sensations, see James W. Cornman, *Materialism and Sensations* (New Haven: Yale University Press, 1971).

Also, this chapter's apparent-object analysis of sensations could be viewed as providing a possible content for Wittgenstein's mysterious aphorism that "the sensation itself" is "not a *something*, but not a *nothing* either!" Ludwig Wittgenstein, *Philosophical Investigations*, trans. G. E. M. Anscombe (New York: Macmillan, 1953), sec. 304.

although no rabbit is involved (there being, let us suppose, no rabbit even in the neighborhood), in an obvious respect, for the subject the situation still will be the same as before: standing there and looking in that direction, for him it is just as though he saw a rabbit before him. Of course, if he walks closer and investigates, he will find only a ball of leaves; but standing where he is, he is in exactly the same sensory state (and so has the same sensory experience) as in the full-blown case. As the word is ordinarily used, he does not actually *see* a rabbit since there is no rabbit to be seen, but for him it is as though he did. He may or may not be led into error by this illusion, for he may know independently that there is no rabbit before him, but even if he knows this, the respect in which it is for him just as though he saw a rabbit is clear.

Convert this now to a case of hallucination by deleting in your imagination not only the rabbit but also the rabbitlike pattern of light. Imagine, for example, that the subject's retinal receptors simply spontaneously fire in the same pattern as earlier when irradiated by light from the leaves.[4] (Thus another person standing in the same location will not also seem to see a rabbit.) In other words, imagine now something amiss in the subject rather than in his environment. But *subjectively*, of course, his state remains the same; for him it is still as though he saw a rabbit.

Be careful, at this point, to avoid supposing that the subject could not be in this state (and have this experience) unless he now perceived some other entity rather than the rabbit and so introducing some further object ("sense data," "sense impressions," etc.) to be what he perceives. To understand this situation, no object of perception need be imagined or postulated. The present case is merely a degenerate version of the full-blown one.[5] In the latter, an object (the rabbit) affected the subject, putting him into a certain sensory state, and his "perceiving" the entity involved or consisted in his being in that state in those circumstances. In

---

4. I am well aware that this is not the usual cause of hallucinations. The cause usually lies deeper in the nervous system. The subjective experience of a hallucinator, moreover, is rarely identical with any veridical experience he might have. But the present analysis is most clearly elaborated by first applying it to the simplest possible paradigm, even if it idealizes. Less unusual cases will be discussed later.

5. The term 'degenerate' is used here in a nonethical sense (as when one speaks of a "degenerate hyperbola") and is not meant to suggest that having these experiences is in any way morally reprehensible. Armstrong uses the same word in *Materialist Theory*, p. 329.

the present case, the external object and circumstances have been cut away, leaving only the subject in the same state as in the full-blown case. Here there is nothing he perceives; he is merely in the same internal state as normally when he does perceive something. And because he is in this state, naturally it seems to him as if he sees something (viz., a rabbit), when actually he does not. (That it should seem to some epistemologists that in this case something exists that only the subject perceives is not altogether surprising since it seems that way to the subject too.)

Since the subject is in the same internal state as in the full-blown case, naturally he also can go through rational computations similar to those he could go through in the full-blown case. In particular, if in the full-blown case, he could describe what he saw, then he still can go through the same sequence of internal operations now, even though there actually exists no object of perception to which the description he constructs will apply. He can pass through all the same steps of reasoning, reflection, cogitation, and judgment as in a full-blown case and even end up with the same verbal (rabbit) description. (In fact, his activity here may be indistinguishable subjectively from what he does in the full-blown case; the hallucinating subject may be unable to tell whether or not he really is deriving a description from something.) Such a performance will be called "truncated description." In truncated description, then, the subject engages in the same ratiocinative activities as he would in a full-blown case (where there was an object that he perceived and was describing) except that no such object exists. It is like "treading water" in a vacuum: the same activity and events in the subject still take place, but without the appropriate surroundings. (And, of course, if one looked into his brain, one would expect to observe occurring a series of neural processes similar to those that normally occur when the subject is cogitating over the correct description of something he sees.) This same activity, in different circumstances, would constitute deriving a description from something, but not here, for there is no object from which he is deriving the description. The concept of truncated description and its relationship to the epistemological, subjective, and mechanical descriptions of the situation is fundamental to all that follows.

Should it be said that this person is "describing a rabbit"? On the one hand, he goes through the same steps he would in deriving a description from an object and he does end up with a rabbit description (e.g., "It has long ears, is brown and white, . . ."). So if one thinks only of the activity in which he is engaged, it might seem natural to characterize him as "describing a rabbit." On the other hand, to say this suggests that there is a rabbit he is describing, which is false. To avoid possible confusion, I will say that the subject "describes a rabbit" only when there exists a rabbit from which he is deriving the description.[6] And I will use the term 'truncated description' to refer to the subject's activity as of deriving a description from an object when there is no such object.[7]

Consider next the *uses* to which the end product of the subject's truncated description may be put. Rabbit hunters should pay no attention to what this hallucinating subject says, obviously, but a physician treating him should. The doctor will regard the description produced by the subject not as a statement about something answering it (viz., a nearby rabbit), but as an output indicating the speaker's state. If the subject is unaware that he is hallucinating, he may simply continue the truncated description while others study him to try to ascertain what is wrong with him. But even if aware of the problem, he can, so to speak, set aside the realization that he is only hallucinating and cooperatively engage in truncated description anyway: "Tell me what you see" or "Describe your hallucination," the doctor says, and, after concentrating for a moment, the subject replies, "It's a rabbit, brown and white, with one ear longer than the other. . . . " (*"Deliberate truncated description"* I will call it when, as here, a subject accommodatingly "derives" a description [of what it seems to him he sees] while realizing at the same time that actually he perceives no such object.) The outcome of a subject's truncated description not only indicates his state, but can be incorporated in third-person descriptions of him. Thus the doctor may say of our friend, "He is hallucinating a brown and white rabbit with one ear longer

6. Normally no terminological problem arises, since usually when one is engaged in the activity of describing something, there is something which one is describing. But in the *un*usual case where object and activity go separate ways, the problem arises which way to go with the terminology.

The same problem does not arise with the technical term 'derives a description' since it is referentially transparent. Someone "derives a description from a rabbit" only if there is a rabbit from which he derives the description. In contexts where the meaning is clear, however, I sometimes use the word 'derives' in "raised-eyebrow" double quotes when discussing the activity of truncated description.

7. The phrase 'activity *as of* deriving a description' is shorthand for "internal activity on the part of the subject identical to, or resembling, what takes place in him when he really describes something." In other words, truncated description.

than the other," using the patient's own words to form a description of him. Here the description the subject constructs by truncated description is used to form a new description which, if true, is true of him in virtue of the fact that he is in the state as a result of which he produced it.

A further twist completes the case. Suppose now that the *subject himself* presents his "derived" description (i.e., the expression constructed by truncated description) in a way that, by the rules of the language, transforms it into a description of himself. For example, he might say, 'I have the hallucination of: . . .' and then give the description he obtains by truncated description ('. . . a brown and white rabbit with one ear longer than the other').[8] If he does so, the subject will produce a description that is true of himself, but arrive at it by a process like that of deriving it from something he perceives. This I will call the "total case."

In Chapter 1, the possible existence was noted of situations in which someone produces a description true of himself without deriving it from observation of the thing (viz., himself) of which it is true [nontransitional self-description]. More recently, it has been noted that a person may go through a process as of deriving a description without there being anything from which he derives that description [truncated description]. Both occur in the total case. The subject goes through a process as of deriving a description from an object that he perceives, but outputs the verbal end product of this operation in a form converting it into a description of himself—indeed, a description that if true, is true of him in virtue of his being in a state he was in when he was in the state as a result of which he produced that description.[9] In this way, then, a subject can arrive at a true mental self-description without deriving it from observation of himself. He arrives at it by a process as of deriving a description from something he perceives,[10]

8. A language could have a single operator 'ϕ____' which prefixed to a description 'D' obtained by truncated description, produces a new description ('ϕ:D') that is, by definition, true of the speaker when the speaker is in such a state that he produces 'D' when he tries to describe what he perceives. Then a speaker could generate true mental self-descriptions by going through the same computational procedure he would go through to construct a description of what he perceives and then prefixing the result of his efforts with 'ϕ____.' English has many such operators.

9. Notice that the total case hereby satisfies Principle 2 of the Model of Nontransitional Self-description.

10. This fact undoubtedly has contributed greatly to the mistaken view that the subject obtains his mental description by introspective examination of a private object.

true, but the "facts" from which he "derives" it are not the facts in virtue of which the self-description is true.

Remark: Confusion is again possible over the verb 'to describe'. In the total case, should we say that the subject "describes himself"? His production of a true description of himself supports saying this. On the other hand, however, saying that someone "has described something" suggests that he has derived the description from the facts it describes, and this is not so in the total case. As before, here too, then, the term 'describes' should be used only with qualification.

The foregoing lengthy account of what the rabbit hallucinator does can be condensed into a general characterization applicable to other cases as well:

MODEL OF TRUNCATED AWARENESS AND DESCRIPTION

1. *(The subject)* produces *(the description)*.

2. *(The subject)* does not derive *(the description)* from anything.

3. What *(the subject)* does in obtaining *(the description)* involves the same cognitive processes of reasoning, reflection, and ratiocination that would be involved in a case where he really did derive a description from something. It is (or was) for the subject in some ways as if he perceived something from which he might derive its description and were now describing it.

4. The production of *(the description)* by *(the subject)* indicates his state, and others may incorporate *(it)* into a further description which, if true, is true of *(the subject)* precisely in virtue of his being in a state he is in when he produces that description.

Truncated description in general fits Principles 1 through 4. The characterization can be restricted to cases where the subject expresses the result of his descriptive efforts in the form of a self-description by adding:

5. *(The description)* produced by *(the subject)* is true of himself.

The relationship between this model and the earlier characterization of nontransitional self-description is that this model provides an additional, more specific characterization of one *subclass* of the phenomena that satisfy the earlier, more general model.

This model of truncated awareness and description has a number of important features. (1) It does not represent the subject as deriving the description from something to which only he has access. (2) It does not represent him as obtaining his description from observation of himself. (3) It explains the fact that what the subject does in obtaining this description is like what he does when he derives a description from something. (4) It explains in more detail how a subject's epistemic position with regard to his own mental description is unique in at least two ways. First, the subject is the only one whose truncated describing's outcome is relevant to the truth of the mentalistic predication, for he is the only one for whom the production of this description by this process is a consequence of the state of affairs that it asserts to exist. If others also engaged in truncated description, their results would be unrelated to this mentalistic description of him. Second, the subject arrives at the description of himself by a procedure different from that used by anyone else. Others derive it from that of which it is true (viz., him). He does not, and only he can arrive at it by the procedure he uses.

The above also shows in more detail what is right and what is wrong with the claim that "What the subject does is not to describe his mental state but to manifest it."[11] For to say that what the subject does to produce the mental self-description may include truncated description means that it may involve going through the same series of steps as when he derives a description from something observed. It is thus a mistake to assimilate the subject's production of the self-description to nonrational, noncognitive, or nondeliberate behavior like wheezing or moaning, as philosophers endorsing this dictum sometimes suggest. Putnam, for example, in discussing his model, says we must suppose that

---

11. Chapter 1 showed that this claim is correct in several respects. First, the subject's utterance *is* evidence that he is in this state. Second, if one takes "describing something" to entail deriving a description from it, then the claim is right in denying that the subject describes his mental state. But Chapter 1 also pointed out that in another sense, the subject *can* be said to have "described his mental state," for he does produce a mental state description true of himself.

the subject

> simply says 'I am in pain' "without thinking," i.e., without
> passing through any introspectible mental states other than the
> pain itself. In Wittgenstein's terminology, Jones simply *evinces*
> his pain by saying 'I am in pain'—he does not first reflect on it (or
> heed it, or note it, etc.) and then consciously describe it. (Note
> that this possibility of uttering the "proposition," 'I am in pain'
> without first performing any mental "act of judgment" was
> overlooked by epistemologists from Hume to Russell!)[12]

Such a supposition is as objectionable in the case of pain as it is
in instances of hallucination. In cases of both kinds, it is an empirical fact that people generally reflect and cogitate in order to
construct the description they give. (In fact, it is doubtful that
subjects *ever* produce mental self-descriptions in the way Putnam
describes.) So the supposition is generally false. It is also theoretically superfluous. My model shows how to understand the subject's rational activity without positing any private sense data,
inwardly apprehended mental objects, or other "objective constituents"[13] of the situation. The subject merely passes through
a series of internal states[14] similar to those he would pass through
in really attending to, inspecting, and describing something
perceived, a succession of internal operations involving changes
of state similar to those occurring when he performs other deliberate, rational acts of judgment. Through such operations the
subject can construct a hallucinational description true of himself, just as the rabbit hallucinator arrived at his self-description.
(Notice, incidentally, that being in one state [whether of pain,
hallucination, or whatever] does not preclude simultaneously
being in many other mental states, including those passed
through in constructing the mental self-description. Some of these
other states may also be states he could report [i.e., "introspectible" states].)

Special additional terminology will condense subsequent discussion. The modifier 'truncated', already used in the phrase
'truncated description' to cancel certain implications of the term

12. Hilary Putnam, "Minds and Machines," in *Minds and Machines*, ed. Alan R.
Anderson (Englewood Cliffs, N.J.: Prentice-Hall, 1964), p. 79.
13. C. D. Broad, *The Mind and Its Place in Nature* (1925; London: Routledge &
Kegan Paul, 1968), chap. IV.
14. Chapter 3 analyzes the nature of these states.

it modifies (in particular, the suggestion that there exists something from which the speaker is deriving its description), will be used similarly to modify other nouns. A case in which it seems to the subject as if he were observing an X but no X exists which he observes will be called "truncated observation." Likewise, an instance where it is for the subject as if he were aware of an X, but there is no X of which he is aware, will be described as an occurrence of "truncated awareness." A case where it seems to the subject as if he recollects some event, but no such event existed, will be called "truncated recollection." And so on. The noun phrase 'apparent object' also will be used to perform the same function, serving as a dummy term filling a sentential position ordinarily occupied by a referring term and indicating the same situation as the adjective 'truncated' indicates. Thus I shall speak of "describing an apparent object," "observing an apparent object," "being aware of an apparent object," "recollecting an apparent event," and so forth. "To describe an apparent object" is just to engage in truncated description; likewise, "observing an apparent object" is simply truncated observation. Thus, for example, it may be said of the rabbit hallucinator that he "sees and is describing an apparent rabbit," meaning not that there exists some entity called "an apparent rabbit" which he sees and is describing, but only that he is in a state similar to that of someone who really sees and is describing a rabbit. Whether the subject himself *knows* that there really is nothing that he is describing, observing, etc., will be irrelevant to the application of these terms.

Some hallucinationlike phenomena cannot be treated simply as truncated versions of full-blown perceptual situations because the experience they involve is unlike any possible veridical perceptual experience. For example, a patient whose hand has been amputated may suffer a peculiar phantom-limb syndrome in which he seems to be aware of the missing hand continually opening but never closing. Obviously, there could be no full-blown analogue for this experience since, in a full-blown case, the subject's hand would cease opening after a short time and would have to close before opening again. Likewise, people who are struck on the head sometimes "see stars." Although the experience is similar to that of really seeing star shells, the two are not identical. Hallucinatory drugs also can produce experiences unlike any possible veridical experience. Sometimes a subject may experience an apparent train of events which, as in a dream, is unrealistically indefinite or incomplete, filled with lacunae and impossibilities. Similar phenomena also occur in more complicated mixed situations where a subject actually perceives something, but in a nonveridical way. In experiments in autokinesthesia, for example, subjects looking at an isolated point-source of light in a dark environment seem to see it as "moving but not getting anywhere." The subject perceives the light, and it seems to him to move but never to be in a new location. Not only does nothing in reality correspond to this apparent movement, but nothing could, since to say that something is "moving but not getting anywhere" is self-contradictory.

In such cases, although a perceptionlike experience occurs, there is no possible object or event such that in perceiving it the subject would be in this state. In these cases, consequently, one cannot combat the temptation to say that the subject is privately perceiving something by pointing out that he is merely in the same state he would be in if he were perceiving such-and-such real state of affairs (so that naturally it seems to him as if he were perceiving something, although he really is not). However, these experiences still can be understood without postulating private objects. The struck man who "sees stars" has gone into an internal state similar to, but not identical with, the state he would be in when viewing star shells. Hence, it seems to him somewhat, but not exactly, as if he saw stars. Likewise, inside the patient with the peculiar phantom-limb syndrome are taking place some of the same processes that before the amputation occurred when he was aware of the opening of his hand; but these processes are different also in some ways from those that occurred before the amputation (e.g., they do not terminate after a short period of time).[15] As a result, it continuously seems to him as if his hand is opening and never as if it is closing. In other words, as the examples illustrate, these phenomena are treated as degenerate versions of pure truncated cases. To apply the model, one need only explain the respect in which "it is for the subject as if he perceived something from which he might derive its description" (Principle 3). Talk of truncated perception or apparent objects is

15. The precise nature of these processes is not yet known, but this does not vitiate the present analysis.

one easy way of doing this, but other ways also exist, and application of the model is not restricted to cases where the subject's state is *identical* with his state in some possible full-blown perceptual situation.

No theoretical difficulty arises, then, over the occurrence of such bizarre or incomplete experiences. Given a sensory system so constituted as to be capable of veridically perceiving its environment, it is not surprising that tampering with it may result in strange experiences. Such experiences might indeed seem perplexing if one assumed that they involved the (veridical) perception of something correspondingly bizarre, but, as has been seen, the positing of such objects is unnecessary. Even apparent objects whose description involves a logical contradiction (or even apparent states of affairs that the subject is unable to describe) present no difficulty. If descriptions of sensory states are constructed by truncated description of apparently perceived objects and events, then if the subject's state is sufficiently unlike any veridical sensory state he might be in, it is possible that none of the normal operations that lead to the production of descriptions of perceived entities will come into play, or if they do, that they will lead to strange results. For example, suppose that it is logically impossible for a thing to be red and green at the same time. Still it might be possible for a perceiving system capable of recognizing colors to break down and simultaneously be *both* (a) in the state it normally is in when confronted with something red and (b) in the state it normally is in when confronted with something green, and so "seem to see something that is red and green all over" and even to report this. Indeed, if a subject were sufficiently disorganized or dysfunctional, he might even go into a perceptionlike state that could not be connected with any external physical situation he has been taught how to describe. This would manifest itself as an "ineffable experience": a state resembling perception, but for which the subject is totally unable to produce a state description.[16] An indescribable experience would seem mysterious if it were assumed that the subject actually was perceiving something so extraordinary that no words could describe it, but as has been demonstrated, no such assumption is necessary.

---

16. The state may have other features or components too; for example, emotions like horror or wonder.

3. Afterimages

Afterimages are unlike hallucinations. The cause of after-images *does* lie in the retina,[17] while the cause of hallucinations probably does not. Hallucinations, moreover, often involve a general derangement of judgment not associated with after-images. For this reason and because normally they are preceded by distinctive stimulus conditions, afterimages seldom lead any-one into error. Also, the surface grammar of the terms 'afterimage' and 'hallucination' is different. It is permissible not only to say that someone "has" an afterimage, but also that he "sees" one, whereas we ordinarily say only that someone "has" a hallucina-tion. However, this linguistic fact counts for little and, needless to say, does not mean that all the inferences permissible in other cases where we speak of "seeing something" are also permissible here.

In other respects, afterimages may be treated like hallucina-tions and the preceding model applied to the phenomenon. As with hallucinations, so too with afterimages it seems to the sub-ject as if he saw some entity although really he sees no such thing (for example, it may seem to him as if he sees a green lumi-nous disk floating before him). And just as he could describe it if he really saw such an object, so here too he can go through the same ensuing series of changes of state, the same series of cogni-tive steps or operations, even though no such object is present before him. The activity of "describing an afterimage" is trun-cated description, and the linguistic result of this process (e.g., 'It's round and green') is an afterimage description. It can be com-bined with other sentential forms to yield mental self-descriptions like "I have a round green afterimage" or "I see a round green afterimage." Other general points made earlier about hallucina-tions also apply to afterimages and will not be repeated here.

To appreciate the relationship between the situation as it appears from the first-person standpoint and the situation as viewed from the objective standpoint, perform the experiment of putting or imagining yourself in the position of the subject (Wittgenstein to the contrary not withstanding). Generate an afterimage (say, by looking at a bright light). With eyes closed, try to "look at" it. From your subjective standpoint, it will seem

17. See, e.g., G. S. Brindley, "Afterimages," *Scientific American*, 209 (October 1963), 84–93.

to you as if you perceived something and could perform various cognitive operations in relation to it—attend to it, noting its color, shape, apparent location and movement, and describing these. Although actually nothing exists that you are looking at and making judgments about, you can engage in certain activities or perform certain operations in compliance with these directions. Moreover, you will be "consciously aware" of these (mental) operations in the strict sense that if asked, you can report their occurrence (e.g., "First I noted its color and then I tried to ascertain its shape"). These are what the model represents as truncated versions of looking, noting, and describing. You have passed through a series of states similar to those that normally occur when you really are looking at, attending to, or describing something. Because of this (i.e., because you go through similar internal states and changes of state) it *seems* to you as if you were looking at something and making judgments about it, when actually you are not.

Remark: The foregoing underscores an important methodological point. Theoreticians who approach the problem of characterizing mental phenomena by imagining *themselves as the subject* may, if they are not careful, be led mistakenly to conclude that there *is* something private from which the subject derives its description (because this is exactly how it seems to the subject). Empathy here can be a dangerous heuristic, especially when the state in question is delusory. Not that anything is wrong in asking, "How would it seem to me if I were in that state?" and trying to relate how it would seem from the subject's standpoint to what really is going on. But then, while doing this, it must not be assumed that what seems to be the case really is the case.

Another basic error is to think that the subject with an afterimage actually is looking at or perceiving a portion of his own retina or an event taking place in his brain, or that the afterimage itself is identical with some event in his nervous system.[18] To be sure, afterimages occur only after a bleaching of visual pigments in retinal receptors and the integrity of certain structures in the brain also is necessary. But these neural events are not what the subject sees when he "sees" an afterimage. In the first place, they are not even what he *seems* to see. Afterimages generally do not even appear to have the same visible qualities as parts of the retina or brain. The afterimage in the above illustration, for exam-

---

18. Some early versions of the mind-body identity thesis were so formulated. See, for example, J. J. C. Smart, "Sensations and Brain Processes" in *The Philosophy of Mind*, ed. V. C. Chappell (Englewood Cliffs, N.J.: Prentice-Hall, 1962), pp. 160–172.

ple, was green, but the retina is black and the brain gray or white. Second, these physiological objects or events are not in the right relation to the subject to be seen. Most people, in fact, *never* have seen their retinas or any other part of their nervous system. In "seeing" an after-image, the subject is not really seeing anything; it only seems to him as if he is.

The fact that certain events in the body cause neural occurrences that underlie a sensory experience is not a good reason for thinking that these events are themselves the objects of perception.[19] Such reasoning confuses the *causes* of a sensory experience with its *object*. The two are not always the same. For some sensory states, none of their causes is an object of perception. This is the case with afterimages. The subject goes into a certain sensory state, the state of seeming to see, for example, a luminous disk floating before him. The *causes* of this lie in the retina and nervous system, but they are not *objects* of the experience. Of course, in *veridical* perception, one of the causes of the subject's being in the proper sensory state is normally (always?) the external object of percep-tion, but its being among the causes of this state does not alone suffice to make it be a perceived object. The experience also has many other causes, most of which are unperceived, including the underlying neural processes. How all the underlying processes in the subject unite around *only one* of their causes to make *it* the object of perception is unknown, but clearly they do.[20] Some feature of the *overall* operation or mass action of these processes determines what the object of perception (or, in the case of afterimages, the apparent object of perception) will be; it is not simply the most peripheral stimulus. Thus the fact that something stands at a distal starting point of the causal chain of neural signals does not mean that it is the thing perceived.[21]

4. Dreams

The same model also characterizes dreaming and dream re-porting. The result contrasts interestingly with the account of

19. George Pitcher, for example, mistakenly takes the fact that tissue damage is a causal factor in most cases of pain to support his claim that to be aware of a pain is to perceive (via neural pain tracts) a part of one's body that is, or is in dan-ger of being, injured or damaged ("Pain Perception," *Philosophical Review*, 79 [July 1970], 371).

20. In general, a sensory state neither has nor seems to have *any* of its under-lying constituent neural processes as its object. In vision, for example, what we see (or sometimes only seem to see) are objects, like tables and chairs, located outside our bodies. The events on our retinas and in our nervous system are among the causes of this experience, but generally not its object.

21. In fact, the thing perceived is usually not at the starting point of the causal signal at all. In vision, for example, the point of origin of the causal signal is the source from which the light reflected from the object originally came (e.g., the sun).

dreaming given by Norman Malcolm as *his* alternative to the introspectionist account.[22] Malcolm wishes to oppose the view that dreaming is an "inward state or process of the soul" which the dreamer notes and recounts in a dream report, pointing out that this view gives rise to "insoluble problems."[23] In opposition to it he suggests we allow "that the *descriptions* that people give of their private states provides a determination of what those states are and whether they are the same [as earlier or later states]".[24] Malcolm continues:

> But if one takes this line (which is correct) one cannot then permit a question to be raised as to whether those descriptions are in error or not—for this would be to fall back into the original difficulty. One must treat the descriptions as the *criterion* of what the inner occurrences are.[25]

Much has been written about the Wittgensteinian notion of a "criterion,"[26] but whatever else it may involve, this postulated criterial relationship between dreams and sincere dream reports entails, says Malcolm, the incorrigibility of the latter.[27] Malcolm's critics have focused on this consequence of his account, arguing that it must be wrong since clearly a person can dream one thing and later think that he had dreamt something else or even forget the dream entirely.[28] Also it is an empirical fact that it sometimes takes a dreamer some time and several attempts before he can achieve a satisfactory dream recountal, and if he corrects himself, he does not explain the retracted version by saying that it was the result of insincerity.[29] Other

22. Norman Malcolm, *Dreaming* (New York: Humanities Press, 1959). Reprinted in part in Donald Gustafson, *Essays in Philosophical Psychology* (New York: Doubleday, 1964). Page references below are to the reprint in Gustafson.
23. *Ibid.*, p. 265.
24. *Ibid.*
25. *Ibid.*, p. 265–266.
26. See Rogers Albritton, "On Wittgenstein's Use of the Term 'Criterion'," *Journal of Philosophy*, 55 (1959), 845–857; also Charles S. Chihara and Jerry A. Fodor, "Operationalism and Ordinary Language: A Critique of Wittgenstein," *American Philosophical Quarterly*, 2 (1965), 281–295.
27. Malcolm agrees with Wittgenstein: "The question whether the dreamer's memory deceives him when he reports the dream after waking cannot arise, unless we introduce a completely new criterion for the report's 'agreeing' with the dream" *Philosophical Investigations*, trans. G.E.M. Anscombe [New York: Macmillan, 1953], pp. 222–223.
28. See, e.g., V. C. Chappell, "The Concept of Dreaming," *Philosophical Quarterly*, 13 (1963), 211–212.
29. D. F. Pears, "Dreaming," *Mind*, 70 (1961), 146.

accepted ideas about dreaming—e.g., that it occurs at a time earlier than the dream report—also appear to support the possibility of a person's dreaming one thing and later believing that he or she dreamt something else.

Malcolm encounters related difficulties in dealing with the phenomenon of "remembering a dream." He would allow us to continue so speaking, but he denies that what happens when we "remember a dream" is like what usually happens when we remember something:

> We speak of "remembering" dreams, and if we consider this expression it can appear to us to be a misuse of language. . . . When I speak of "remembering" a dream, there is nothing outside of my account of the dream (provided that I understand the words that compose it) to determine that my account is right or wrong. . . . Since nothing counts as determining that my memory of my dream is right or wrong, what sense can the word 'memory' have here?[30]

Malcolm opposes the idea that "memory" is involved because he wishes to deny that there is something (viz., "a dream") from which the dream description is derived and because he thinks that, if it genuinely occurred, "remembering a dream" or "recalling a dream" would have to involve making a transition (one utilizing memory) from such an object or event to a description true of it.

The question thus arises whether it is possible to acknowledge that a dream report might in some way fail to agree with earlier dreaming without postulating a realm to which only the subject has access: In other words, is there any way to understand the phenomenon of recalling a dream other than by employing the model of inner recognition? For, "Surely," one might think, "if a person remembers (or misremembers) at all, then there must be something which he remembers (or misremembers). And if what he remembers is a dream, then this must be something to which only he has access since he alone has his dream." Malcolm sees clearly that if remembering a dream is represented as recalling a psychic occurrence that one earlier had apprehended in some way, this would constitute an application of the Transition Model (analogous to Application I) generating the problems cited in Chapter 1. But in his concern to deny that "remembering a dream"

30. Malcolm, *Dreaming*, pp. 267–268.

involves making a transition from a psychic object to a description of it, Malcolm overlooks the respect in which something very much like real remembering occurs when one "remembers a dream." This mistake connects with another. Wishing to apply to dreaming an analogue of the Wittgensteinian point about the impossibility of misrecognizing sensations, Malcolm locates the corresponding impossible mistake, so to speak, between the dreaming and the subsequent awakened report. But the impossibility of making a mistake in subsequently recounting a dream description would not be analogous to the impossibility of misrecognizing a sensation. In dreaming, what corresponds to *having a pain*, e.g., is not *remembering* the dream but *having* it. And what corresponds to the impossibility of misperceiving a pain is the impossibility of misperceiving one's dream. That is, if as he dreams, it seems to someone that he is riding on a train, say, then it is not possible that his dream is really about his first-grade teacher, but that he has misrecognized it. One cannot misview a dream (because one does not view dreams). But this does not entail that one cannot make a mistake in subsequently recounting the experience, anymore than the impossibility of misperceiving a pain entails that one cannot err in a pain description.

My models enable dreaming and dream recounting to be understood in a way that avoids both the paradoxes of Malcolm's treatment and the problems of inner access, and its resulting account of the relationship between dreaming and dream describing permits a question to be raised as to whether those descriptions are in error without falling "back into the original difficulty" as Malcolm feared.[31] First, by an application of the Transition Model analogous to Application II, dream self-descriptions (e.g., "I dreamt that first A happened, then B happened . . .") are represented as descriptions true or false of the subject (as opposed to being descriptions of an entity called "a dream"). In the present case, these will be descriptions in the past tense, referring to an earlier occurrence. To characterize the first-person situation, the Model of Truncated Awareness and Description is used, representing dreaming as a kind of somnolent hallucination that occurs when the sleeper is caused to pass through a series of internal states similar to those he would pass through if he actually were experiencing events of the sort dreamed.[32] Conse-

31. *Ibid.*, pp. 265–266.
32. This undoubtedly is related to rapid eye movements (REM) during dreaming.

quently, for the dreamer it is as though he were actually witnessing or undergoing those events. Dreaming is a state of truncated awareness, and dream events are apparent events experienced by the dreamer. A dream description (e.g., "first A happened, then B happened . . .") is a description of these apparent events.[33] The phenomenon of "recalling a dream" now may be understood as follows. Assume that if the subject had passed through this sequence of states in really witnessing or undergoing such events, he could have recalled and described them later from memory. Then there is no difficulty in supposing him to go through the same (or similar) processes now even though he never actually experienced such events; upon awakening, it seems to him as though he recently experienced the dreamed events and he can recall and recount them in detail in just the same way he would if he really had experienced them. Everything he can do in a full-blown case he can do here too, except that he will not be recalling events that actually occurred. Let us call what the subject does "truncated recalling" or "truncated remembering." "Remembering one's dream," then, is the truncated recalling and recounting of these apparent events just as if one actually had witnessed their occurrence and were called upon to describe them from memory. In rare instances, someone (especially a child) may believe that he really did witness some such events and consequently will affirm as true the description he gives, but ordinarily the awakened sleeper recognizes the nonveridical nature of his experience. He nevertheless goes through a process of telling what he "saw," "heard," "felt," etc. (deliberate truncated recounting), not to inform others about the occurrence of events fitting the description he gives but to let them know the nature of what he just underwent.

Others then can construct a dream description of the subject from his narrative by prefacing it with words like, 'He dreamt that . . . ' (and possibly changing pronouns, verb tenses, etc.). Or the subject himself can deliver his tale prefaced with the first-person form of this phrase ('I dreamt that . . .'), producing thereby

33. In the simple case, this will be a description such that events satisfying it would, if the subject witnessed or underwent them, put him through the same sequence of states he has just gone through. In a more extraordinary case, the dreamer might go through a sequence of states that no possible observed external situation could stimulate, and he might produce a description that nothing could satisfy (e.g., he might dream that he witnessed events that are physically impossible).

a dream description true or false of himself. (We may say that in doing so he has "described himself" or even "described his dream" as long as this does not suggest that he arrives at his description by observing something and describing it.) In this way a subject can use the results of his truncated remembering to construct a dream description true of himself.

Viewed thus, it is not surprising that in trying to recount his dream, the awakened sleeper may experience the same difficulties and uncertainties as he might in a full-blown case where there really were observed events which he was trying to recall. He could be uncertain, falter, halt, stop and restart, and, in general, experience all the same difficulties as in a full-blown case in which he tried to recall something observed. Likewise, if his memory could fail him in the full-blown case, the same could happen in the truncated case: he could make what would constitute a mistake in a full-blown case (a truncated mistake). Of course, in dream recounting, a truncated mistake will not have the consequence that his narrative fails to describe events that actually occurred (since if he only was dreaming, this failure would have occurred in any case). But it could have the consequence that his subsequent dream report fails to reflect accurately his sequence of states during the preceding period of sleep; his recollection could fail to recapitulate his earlier dreaming accurately or he might even be left with no recollection whatsoever and his dream consequently go undetected. Thus the model enables one to understand how a breakdown can occur between the dreaming and the reporting without positing something privately apprehended.

5. Pains

The pain experience characteristically involves two components: a locatable sensation and the associated suffering. In the following, I shall call the former "the perceptual aspect" and the latter "the passional (or affective) aspect." In its perceptual aspect, pain may involve, for example, a stabbing or burning sensation felt in some part of the body. In its passional aspect, pain involves the subject's agony or distress. Both appear in the normal case: the victim has the sensation and, in some way not yet understood, suffers over this. The perceptual aspect has dominated recent philosophic discussions of pain. In fact, pain has almost become the standard example of a "sensation" cited in

discussions of behaviorism, avowals, private objects, etc.[34] Pain
as a source of suffering has received little recent philosophic
attention, and some philosophers even have difficulty recognizing
that pains have a feature (viz., apparently causing suffering) that
sets them apart from other sensations and generates special philosophic problems.[35]

The distinction between these two aspects of the psychological
phenomenon is obscured in English by the use of the one word
'pain' for both. As a count-noun, 'pain' is used to refer to the
sensation ("He has one pain in his leg and another in his hand,"
"He has two pains in his foot").[36] Used to refer to the state of
suffering (e.g., "He is in pain," "Pain degrades its victim"), it
does not function as a count-noun. In this use (where its role in
the language as a state description is immediately obvious) it
admits of modification by terms like 'more', 'less', 'some', 'no'
without forming the plural. Other terms for bodily sensations like
'itch', 'tickle', and 'ache' do not have this dual use. We can say,
"He has a tickle in his throat and an ache in his back," but not
"He is in tickle" or "He is in ache." The word 'pain' has other
subtleties. For example, to say of a person, "He is in pain," suggests significant suffering; not any little ache or pain will do.
Also situations exist in which we would say of someone, "He is
in pain," but probably not "He has a pain." For example, if we
know that someone has a bullet in his leg, we would not ordinarily say, "He has a pain in his leg." But if it felt to him as if he had
been shot in the leg but no wound was apparent, then we might
say that he "had a pain" in his leg. We tend to speak of "pains"
when nothing further is known about the cause of the suffering.

The distinction between sensations of pain and the attendant
suffering is reinforced by their apparent clinical separability.
Prefrontal lobotomy in the neurosurgical treatment of intract-
able pain appears to relieve the patient of his distress without

34. It may surprise some to learn that the classification of pain as a sensation
is widely disputed. Aristotle, for example, classified pain among the "passions of
the soul," and disputes over whether pain is a sensation, continuing into this century, figure prominently in speculation on the neuropsychology of pain. For a history of this dispute, see Karl M. Dallenbach, "Pain; History and Present Status,"
American Journal of Psychology, 52 (1939), 331f.

35. This problem receives attention in an article by George Pitcher, "The Aw-
fulness of Pain," *Journal of Philosophy*, 67 (1970), 481–492.

36. A "count-noun" accepts numerical qualification and forms the plural under
modification by words like 'some', 'all', 'any', and 'no'. 'Shoe' is a count-noun;
'footwear' is not.

affecting the pain sensation.[37] After the operation, a lobotomized patient may say, "It still hurts; it just doesn't bother me anymore."[38] Morphine often has the same effect, merely diminishing the affective component of the experience and depriving the sensations of their unpleasantness. The sensation apparently remains present but no longer produces suffering.

Their power to produce suffering sets pains apart from other sensations. Most sensations are affectively neutral, neither pleasant nor unpleasant in themselves, and even other unpleasant sensory experiences are not unpleasant in the way pains are. A person may be irritated and annoyed by an afterimage or a ringing in his ears, for example, vehemently wish it would stop, and yet not find it painful. Thus there is more to being painful than just being unpleasant; painful sensations are unpleasant in some special way. This has led some theoreticians to posit "pain quality," a specific sensory quality that other sensations lack, but pains allegedly have. As Roger Trigg remarks, "The concept of a 'pain-quality' becomes necessary when it is realized that pains are not defined as merely unpleasant sensations."[39] On this analysis, the experience of pain associated, say, with having a thorn run into one's finger does not consist solely of the felt intrusion of this foreign object together with an aversion to that state of affairs. The experience involves the presence of the thorn *felt as having pain quality* and an aversion to that. "Pain quality" is very difficult to characterize verbally, but almost everyone has experienced what this term is intended to denote.[40] For example, when one's skin is pinched very gradually, first only sensations of pressure are felt, but as the pressure increases, what is perceived suddenly seems to have a new quality. The pinch *becomes*

37. James C. White and William H. Sweet, *Pain: Its Mechanisms and Neurosurgical Control* (Springfield, Ill.: Charles C. Thomas, 1955), pp. 327, 329. As sources, White and Sweet cite Y. D. Koskoff, W. Dennis, D. Lazovik, and E. T. Wheeler, "The Psychological Effects of Frontal Lobotomy Performed for the Alleviation of Pain," *Research Publ. Assoc. Nerv. & Ment. Dis.*, 27 (1948), 723–753, and J. W. Watts and W. Freeman, "Frontal Lobotomy in the Treatment of Unbearable Pain," *ibid.*, 715–722. In their writings on the topic, these authors distinguish between *suffering* and *pain*, and they emphasize that frontal lobotomy is surgery for the relief of suffering rather than for the relief of pain. (By 'pain', they mean the sensation of pain.)

38. See, e.g., Ronald Melzack, "The Perception of Pain," *Scientific American*, 204 (February 1961), 47.

39. Roger Trigg, *Pain and Emotion* (Oxford: Clarendon Press, 1970), p. 26.

40. A few people appear to be congenitally insensitive to pain. They evidently cannot experience this quality.

painful. This new quality arising in the experience is what these theoreticians call "pain quality." Its emergence does not consist simply in one's suddenly coming to dislike being pinched. Rather, "pain quality" somewhat resembles a visible color. Like a color, it simply seems to arise or be "given" in sense experience prior to and independent of any attitude or judgment on the part of the subject. To assimilate experiencing "pain quality" to seeing a color, of course, makes it no less mysterious, but at least suggests the kind of company in which it travels and that this company is respectable. As much as any quality is, this quality is a *perceptual* one, something new appearing in sense experience, and because of its appearance, one acquires the sudden strong dislike for being pinched.

The Model of Truncated Awareness and Description will now be applied to the phenomenon of pain. As will be seen, it provides no explanation of "pain quality" or of the relationship of pain sensations to suffering. This does not mean that its application is false; it is true if what it says about the experience is true. Nor does the fact that it provides only a partial and incomplete characterization of the pain phenomenon render it valueless. Earlier applications of the model to hallucinations, afterimages, and dreams also provided only partial accounts of these phenomena. To give a complete account of pain a further special pain model would be necessary. Later in this section are sketched some suggestions toward such a model.

To apply this model to the phenomenon of pain, begin by considering the case of someone who has run a thorn into his finger. Assume he feels the thorn in his finger and that it hurts (whatever "hurting" consists in). He may say, "My finger hurts" or "I have a thorn in my finger and it hurts" or the like. He can give other descriptions of it, too. He can say more exactly where in his finger it is located. He can describe the extent of the felt intrusion (e.g., at a small, specific point rather than over a large, diffuse area). If its effects are intermittent, he can say when he is aware of it and when not. And so on.

Taking this case as the "full-blown" one in applying the model may provoke the following *objection*:

Although the subject certainly can be said to "feel" this thorn, is unclear whether he can be said here to "perceive" it. This in part may be because none of the conventionally recognized five senses is involved. He certainly does not see, hear, taste, or smell the thorn, and it would sound odd to say that he "perceives it by touch," even though he is in physical contact with it. For the situation is not such that he can examine or investigate the thorn by the kind of tactile perceptual operations that normally enable a person to acquire some knowledge of an entity's tactile qualities. In tactile perception, moreover, one usually can learn (perhaps by a series of operations) some or all of a thing's size, shape, texture, weight, and possibly temperature. But in the case of this thorn, the subject's sensory position enables him to gain none of this information. He is aware of the presence of something in his finger hurting him, but has no awareness through sensation of any of its other qualities. The content of his experience is totally exhausted by the description "something tiny in a small region of his finger hurting him now," and although the thorn indeed has that size and location, these properties alone are insufficient to constitute anything that could be counted as a full-blown object of perception. Not enough perceptual qualities are manifested in the experience to make up a perceptual object or to justify saying that he *perceives* what is in his finger.[41] Thus, although it is correct to say that he "feels" the thorn, to say he "perceives" it sounds strange.

Reply: Even if his experience does not constitute perception, one may respond, it resembles perception in obvious respects. In the first place, *subjectively* his experience is similar to other experiences of perceiving things. It seems to him that he is aware of an entity situated in a certain place (his finger). Let us express this more succinctly by saying that his experience is "objectlike" in nature, meaning that it is like the experience of being aware of an object. Second, the *relationship between* the subject and the thorn is similar to the relationship existing between subject and object in standard cases of perception. The thorn manifests its presence to him through sensation, and some of its properties (e.g., size and location) are given in his sensory experience. His consciousness seems to be of something located at a certain point in his body affecting him painfully, and the physical thing in his fingertip answers this description. Moreover, he gains awareness of it through peripheral neural stimulation analogous to that

41. This formulation of the point is due to Barbara Klein.

involved in other kinds of perception. Thus, even if the situation is not fully "perceptual," it is clearly perceptionlike. Even if he does not sense enough of the thorn's properties to constitute full-blown perception, he is aware of it in some of its properties. As a response to the objection, one might introduce special qualificatory terminology: rather than describing the situation by saying, "The subject perceives the thorn in his fingertip," we might say something like, "The subject partially perceives the thorn in his fingertip." But since the following account of pain is completely independent of this terminological issue, I shall avoid it by using a disjunction that should please everyone, saying simply that the subject has (full-blown) *"perception or partial perception"* of the thorn in his fingertip. In this terminology, then, the situation is described by saying that the subject perceives, or partially perceives, the physical entity or state of affairs in his fingertip, and that this entity or state of affairs is the *object* of his perception or partial perception, or the "objective constituent" of his perceptual situation. (If I sometimes forget myself and speak only of the subject's "perceiving the thorn in his fingertip," I would be understood as meaning the longer disjunction.) Other cases will be modeled as truncated versions of this "full-blown" case.

Next let us imagine a case to which the Model of Truncated Awareness and Description applies. As in the other instances, we simply imagine the perceptual object removed while leaving the sensory state unchanged. One might begin, for example, by supposing that the the thorn is removed from the victim's finger, but that (as is common in such cases) everything still feels the same. His situation is now analogous to that of someone who has a visual afterimage after looking at a bright light (in fact, one could say that he has the "afterimage of a thorn" in his finger). No thorn is embedded in his finger, but it feels to him as if one were there. I will describe this situation by saying that he "feels an apparent thorn in his finger."

Now slightly change the imagined case. Suppose that the subject somehow passes into this same state without prior injury by a thorn. (Perhaps some of the same nerve fibers fire spontaneously in the same pattern as before.) When this happens, he may say, "I must have a thorn in my finger," and look to find it. However, when he discovers no thorn or other detectable injury he may modify his statement to, "It feels as if I had something sharp in my finger and it hurts." If so, we have a total case. His output no longer asserts the existence of a thorn in his finger, but expresses a description true of him in virtue of his being in a state he is in when he is in the state as a result of which he produces this description. (Notice, too, that the formulation and production of this self-description may involve the same series of operations and cognitive steps as were involved in the earlier judgment about a thorn in his finger.[42]) Equivalently, he may use the count-noun 'pain' and speak of there being "a pain" in his finger: "I have a sharp pain in my finger," he says, indicating the place where the apparent thorn is located.

The true nature and ontological status of "pains" now begins to emerge. The subject's experience in this case of pain involves an apparent object: it seems to him as if he were aware of the presence, in a certain part of his body, of something affecting him hurtfully. This apparent object he calls "a pain." (Calling it 'a pain' implies its hurtfulness; this feature of the apparent object will be discussed later.) The subject who is aware of an apparent hurtful thorn "has a pain"; nothing more is required. In fact, the apparent hurtful thorn is identical with his "pain."[43]

The analysis shows that there is nothing bizarre in the fact that pains seem to have various properties including bodily location. They "have" location and other properties (i.e., apparent location and other apparent properties) in the same unproblematical way that afterimages do. Just as an afterimage can seem to be located on a distant wall, so an apparent hurtful thorn can seem to be located within the finger.[44] The same is true for other properties such as size and temporal duration. The analysis also elucidates the fact that the subject uses the word 'pain' as if it referred to something only he perceives. He operates with this word as if it were a general term true of the apparent object. Told, "Point to the location of your pain," he will point to the location of the apparent object. Directed, "Close your eyes and focus your atten-

---

42. Cp. Principle 3 of the general characterization of truncated awareness and description, p. 91.

43. Compare this with, for example, Armstrong's account that identifies "the pain itself . . . not with a physical happening at the 'place of the pain', but with an event in the central nervous system" *(Materialist Theory)*, pp. 319–320. On the present account, in contrast, *"the pain itself"* is "identified" (so to speak) with no occurring physical event but with an apparent partially perceived hurtful something located at the place of the pain.

44. This part of the analysis *is* consistent with Armstrong, *ibid.*, p. 315.

tion on your pain," he will close his eyes and focus his attention on the apparent hurtful thorn (i.e., do the same thing he would in the full-blown case if asked to focus his attention on the thorn in his finger hurting him).[45] The analysis also explains the fact that in producing a pain self-description, it is for the subject as if he were describing an entity which he inwardly perceives or is aware of. For in arriving at the self-description, he goes through the same steps that in other circumstances would constitute deriving a description from something he partially perceives (viz., a thorn in his finger). But here, the end result of this process (viz., the utterance, 'I have a pain in my finger') expresses in the language a description which, if true, is true of him in virtue of his being in the state as a result of which he gives that description.[46]

Many properties of the pain experience are explained by this model. It explains how a pain, presumably not something physical, nonetheless could have location at a particular bodily place. It shows how having a pain is like perceiving something objectlike (even though this is not what is really going on). It explains why in describing his pain, it seems to the subject as if he is describing something that he, and only he, perceives. And it explains why, in responding to others' statements, questions, orders, requests, etc., mentioning his pain, it seems to the subject as if he is dealing with and referring to a private object. And, of course, in explaining all this, it accounts for major sources of the mistaken idea that pains are inwardly perceivable and describable private objects.

Pain experiences, of course, vary considerably in the degree to which they are objectlike. Some pain experiences manifest more objectlike qualities than others. At the one extreme, a subject sometimes can tell from feel that he has a thorn or a sliver in his finger, or that his pain is the effect of a certain sort of blow to the abdomen. At the other extreme, headaches or toothaches, e.g., simply may involve pain quality associated with some bodily

45. A reader comments, "On questions of location (of 'private objects') it might help to point out that the fact that a pain is in my gloved hand does not entail that a pain is in my glove. Physical location is usually transitive." This is not at all obvious. If one talks at all about spatial location in connection with apparent objects, one might say they are located where they appear to be. Rainbows and "virtual images" formed by lenses or curved mirrors are not actually existing substantial entities located in space, and yet we assign them spatial location (we say that they are where they appear to be located, e.g., in the sky or so many inches behind the mirror).

46. Cp. Principle 2 of the general characterization of nontransitional self-description.

region. In such cases it is very difficult to think of any objective state of affairs that one could say is partially perceived (or apparently partially perceived) in such cases. While an attempt might be made to describe a given headache as feeling, for example, "as if a band were being drawn tightly around my head," many headaches involve less specific feelings. As a result, the subjective experience is not, with naturalness, representable as the truncated version of the partial perception of anything. Too few objectifiable qualities are given in the experience. In most headaches, for example, probably the subject simply undergoes an experience of pain quality associated with a diffuse general region of his head; his experience has only the two components, pain quality and vague location.

But the difficulty in treating such experiences as truncated cases of partial perception does not mean that here at last the existence must be posited of something privately perceived (perhaps a similarly indefinite psychic object?). These cases can be regarded as degenerate versions of truncated cases. Some features present in the thorn case (e.g., sharp location) simply are absent from the headache case. Also, the phenomenon is not unlike others previously characterized. Earlier we noted that in having a visual afterimage, a subject's experience is of *color* diffusely located within a certain area at a certain place. With a headache, his experience is of pain quality diffusely located within a certain area at a certain place. The two situations obviously are analogous. Of courses, pain quality is different from color, but this does not affect the theoretical argument. If we do not need to posit something privately perceived in the afterimage case, neither do we in the headache case. We still can posit that the only existent is the subject in a certain state, and the fact that this state resembles a state-as-of-perceiving-something does not entail that an object of perception also exists. Of course, an explanation of what it is for a person to experience pain quality as located at a certain place still is needed, for the Model of Truncated Awareness and Description provides none. A special additional model is required to explain "pain quality" and how one *suffers* with pain. While I offer no complete pain model, I have a few suggestions about how these unique aspects of the pain phenomenon might be analyzed.

It seems impossible to analyze pain quality into atomic constituents or to explain it as somehow built up out of other perceptual qualities. Pain quality appears to be a simple, unanalyzable, perceptual quality, in no way reducible to other perceptual qualities. In this respect, it resembles sensations of color or feelings of heat and cold. If no reduction of pain quality to other phenomenal qualities is possible, the analysis must proceed in some other way. One way is to describe a set of properties such that a structure having them could experience this quality. That is, one might try to blueprint a system capable of experiencing pain quality. Thus the quality would be characterized by describing a system in which it emerges. A sufficient condition for convincing skeptics of the adequacy of such an account might be displaying a set of properties such that they would agree that if *they* were systems having those properties, they could experience pain quality.

Although intimately related to it, aversion to pain is not identical to pain quality. Pain quality is a perceptual quality, suffering and aversion are affective reactions. But the two are connected through the fact that one suffers over sensations having pain quality and, in some sense, suffers over them *because* they have this quality. The real relation behind the word 'because' here obviously bears scrutiny. Although one suffers over pains "because" they hurt, it may turn out that in another sense, one experiences them as "hurting" because one suffers over them—that is, that their "hurting" in some way consists in the aversion one feels toward them. If so, an analysis of pain quality and an analysis of the special kind of suffering involved in pain should go hand in hand.

Several possible approaches fail through omitting one or another aspect of the phenomenon. Pain cannot be analyzed purely as a perceptual phenomenon because there is no entity such that merely perceiving it would constitute pain. A person might perceive a thorn in his finger or drilling on his tooth without experiencing pain. Experiencing pain is not like the affectively neutral simple perception of something. Pain exists only when one is affected in such a way that he feels aversion or suffers. Nor can pain be interpreted simply as the perception of some physical situation together with an aversion to it, for the appearance of pain quality in the subject's *sensory* experience seems to be an essential component of the pain phenomenon. That pain does not consist simply in an attitude of aversion toward some perceived or perceivable state of affairs (e.g., being cut) is established by the common effectiveness of local anesthetics in relieving pain. It is possible (indeed, frequent) for a local anesthetic successfully to eliminate the pain and yet for the patient to continue to have an attitude of aversion toward the bodily injury or damage. Thus having a pain is not the same as having an attitude of dislike or aversion toward some perceived bodily state of affairs.

Normal cases of pain seem to involve a sensation with pain quality and an aversion attitude or reaction directed toward it. The Model of Truncated Awareness and Description shows how to deal with one potentially puzzling aspect of this situation. It permits understanding how aversion could be directed toward "a pain," something whose ontological status is that only of an apparent object. According to the model, one can carry the problem over to a full-blown case in which, e.g., there really is a thorn embedded in the subject's finger and try to explain what it is for *that* to hurt. For the suffering and aversion in a full-blown case is no different from the case where it only feels to the subject as if there were a thorn in his finger. Thus we need not puzzle over how someone could suffer over something that does not really exist. We can speak of the subject's aversion as being directed toward a pain, knowing that this can be unpacked in an apparent-object analysis without entailing the existence of something privately perceived that is the object of his aversion. Any successful explanation of the full-blown case then can be carried back to the truncated case.

This fact together with the general model permits another move. We may omit the thorn and take *states* as our ultimate objects of analysis. On this account, the normal experience of pain involves a sensory state and an affective state, and the problem is to characterize these two and the relationship between them. This reformulation of the problem helps by permitting kinds of relationships that might seem to be precluded by other ways of stating the problem. Describing the situation as one of aversion to an apparent intruding thorn, for example, suggests that it involves an attitude directed toward an independent entity and should be treated like fear of a wolf or love for a person. But in the case of a pain, the "object," and its relevant properties (especially pain quality), may not be completely separable from the attitudinal state. Taking states instead as the objects of analysis opens the way to other kinds of treatments. For example, the two states might be analyzed as parts or aspects of some further single

state encompassing both.[47] Then the problem would be to characterize some single state that has both these aspects.

The relationship between pain and aversion is puzzling in a
number of ways. For one, dislike of pain seems to have no further
rationale. If the question is raised, "Why do you dislike pains?"
one can give no reason. Someone might say, "I dislike them because they hurt," but this accomplishes nothing, because now the
same question reappears as, "But why do you dislike things that
hurt?"[48] Nor does it help to say that the thing is experienced as
"having pain quality." Imbue it with any quality you like, the
question still can be raised why one dislikes something with that
quality. Someone might suggest that we dislike pains because
they are a symptom of something amiss in our body, a "warning
signal." But this answer fails even to meet the question. Knowledge of this fact certainly may add to a sufferer's distress, but he
would dislike pains whether or not they were symptomatic of
organic disorder. Moreover, people (and presumably other organisms) who have no knowledge of the physiological significance
of pain nevertheless dislike it. Dislike of pains, then, seems not
to be based on any further reason the sufferer has for disliking
them.

But if I have no reason to dislike pains, why do I not look upon
them with detachment instead of responding to them as I do? How
does something that I have no reason to dislike bother me? Why
can I not respond to pains with equanimity, especially when I
believe this would be in my best interest (for example, if I were a
terminal cancer patient who at least could spend his last days
peacefully if he did not let the pain bother him)? But on further
reflection, of course, nothing is paradoxical in the fact that some
aversions and affinities have no further justification. As many
philosophers have pointed out, every chain of justifications must

47. There is nothing strange about this. Being hot and being gaseous, for example, are both states of something that is also in a certain molecular state. The
molecular state underlies the other two states, and the relationship between them
may be explained by reference to it.

48. To say that the meaning of the word 'pain' entails that pains are unpleasant
and disliked does not help either. Assume that as a matter of language, a sensation
cannot be said to "hurt" or to be "a pain" unless it is disagreeable in some special
way. The question still arises why some sensations are disagreeable in this way
while others are not. Why does one dislike these sensations while not minding
others? Why are they associated with suffering and what is their relationship to
it?

end somewhere. We must like or dislike some things for their own sake, and here perhaps is one place rock bottom is reached. Other things might be disliked because they lead to pain, but pain is disliked for its own sake. Other attitudes have justifications as well as causes; aversion to pain has only causes. Perhaps, then, aversion to pains is a pure dislike of something for its own properties and not for some further reason.

To establish that there is nothing paradoxical in this, let us begin by comparing aversion to pains to other dislikes that are not based on further reasons. For example, many people have an extreme aversion to slimy or crawling insectlike creatures (e.g., spiders, slugs, centipedes). Their reaction is primitive, spontaneous, almost violent, and often without further justification. In some ways, aversion to pains is like this, in other ways it is not. One obvious difference is that a subject can escape from crawling or slimy creatures by brushing them off or running away, but pains stay with him wherever he goes. He cannot run from them or brush them away. So to obtain a less dissimilar case, one might imagine a nightmarelike situation in which a spider or similar creature sticks to the arm of someone who has this extreme aversion so that he cannot get it off. In a frenzied panic, he first tries to rid himself of it, but when he realizes this is hopeless, he simply lies still in a cold sweat hoping it somehow will go away. This is more like pain. A second important difference between aversion to spiders and aversion to pain is that although one may be revolted at the idea of being touched by the creature, the aversion is toward the creature and not toward the feeling per se. This is demonstrated in the famous prank in which the hand of a blindfolded subject is put into a bowl of spaghetti. Told that it is a bowl of worms, he reacts with violence, whereas if told that it is a bowl of wet noodles, he is bothered little, even though, in fact, he cannot tell the difference by feel. In the case of an embedded thorn, by contrast, not simply the impinging object, but some quality it produces in the experience is the object of the reaction. Most of us scarcely would mind being pricked by a thorn if it were not for the feeling it produces. So aversion to pain is more like an aversion to some sensory quality than like an aversion to some objective physical thing or situation.

In this respect, aversion to pain is more like some people's aversion to parsnips. In the case of a pain, one dislikes the way it feels; in the case of a parsnip, they dislike the way it tastes. Otherwise, they are indifferent to parsnips (they have no desire, for example, to see the species eradicated). But there are differences here, too. Dislike of parsnips is, as we say, a matter of taste, whereas dislike of pains is not simply a matter of taste. In the end, however, this may mean nothing more than that there is not the divergence of attitudes toward pains that exists toward parsnips. Some people like the taste of parsnips, but nobody likes pains,[49] not even masochists.[50] Nor can one imagine coming to enjoy the feeling of pain as one might come to enjoy the taste of parsnips. So if aversion to pains is like a distaste, it appears to be a universal and inflexible one. Another difference between parsnips and pains lies in the strength of the aversion reaction. The aversion reaction to parsnips usually is mild. In polite company, one may have to suppress a facial contortion (probably related to a spitting-out reflex), or in the extreme, feel for a moment as if about to vomit. Reaction to an intense pain, in contrast, is stronger, less detached, and more global. In this respect, it is more like the response to slimy or crawling creatures discussed earlier. People with extreme reactions to such creatures shrink from contact with them, draw back, and shudder. If a spider crawls onto the back of their hand, they shake it off with a violent, jerking, almost involuntary movement, perhaps even trembling uncontrollably for a few seconds afterward. They often are completely unable to restrain these reactions. In such cases, although the reflexes are not simple, it does not seem strange to say that the stimulus simply causes the reaction without the mediation of justificatory deliberations.

Reactions to pain-producing stimuli are similar. Often these are avoidance reactions (usually automatic responses of withdrawal from the source of infliction). These reactions are so primitive and undiscerning that they tend to continue even after they no longer serve a function. Long after the bee has passed, the person stung

49. As an example of someone apparently liking pain, the case is sometimes cited of someone with a sore tooth who periodically touches it with his tongue setting off a twinge of pain. But his doing this does not show that he likes pain. He might just be experimenting to see if the tooth is still sore. That he dislikes this pain would be shown by his response if we offered to fix his tooth so that it produced this pain constantly.

50. The masochist of clinical fame likes not the pain itself but certain situations in which pain is inflicted on him. Masochists do not choose situations that will inflict the most severe pain, but rather, situations with other interesting properties in which mild pain is inflicted.

by it may continue to shake his hand rapidly, or to restrain himself only by a conscious effort, perhaps quieting the injured hand with his other hand. (Of course, swollen tissue, the local present effect of the sting and bodily cause of the reaction, continues to be present after the bee has left.) A violent blow to the abdomen sets off a persistent doubling-over reaction that is overcome only with difficulty. In a sinus headache, pressure from swollen nasal membranes causes facial muscles to contort. These I will call "positive bodily reactions," because they involve positive bodily movements that must be restrained if they are not to take place. They are continuing, automatic reactions, not initiated through deliberation, that can be overcome only by a conscious, deliberate effort. These automatic positive bodily reactions comprise one component of the "suffering" associated with pain and part of what it is to experience "pain" at a bodily place.

A second component of the phenomenon of pain, more difficult to characterize, involves the *blocking* of certain bodily movements. To illustrate, suppose that as an arthritic person is sitting quietly in his armchair, certain chemicals are collecting in his elbow joint such that, when he bends his arm, an intense pain will be produced, but that he does not know this because his arm is outstretched and he has not yet tried to move it. He starts to get up, a movement that involves bending his arm. As he does so, he feels a sudden stab of pain, says "Ouch!" and falls back into the chair. His attention drawn to his arm, he starts to bend it again, this time experimentally, again feels a stab of pain, and stops. He cannot move his arm past the point of pain, or he can do so only with a grim effort. This I will call a "negative bodily reaction." How are we to understand it?

If asked why he stopped bending his arm, the person may say, "I stopped bending it because the pain became too intense." But this answer does not force us into treating his action as something done as means to a further end (i.e., in order not to increase the pain). We are trying to elucidate the real relation underlying the "because" in "He stopped bending his arm *because* of the pain," and a purposive account, whether true or not, only returns us to the original impasse over explaining why someone should want to avoid pain. Moreover, representing his action as a means to some further end may blind one to the correct answer, that this movement's being "painful" in part consists in his being unavoidably caused to refrain from it.

Considered objectively, the fact is that a certain bodily movement somehow is blocked. The underlying mechanism is unknown. One possible hypothesis is that impulses traveling up peripheral fibers from the elbow operate *in the spinal cord* to inhibit or cancel any downcoming motor impulses that otherwise would activate the musculature of the arm, in effect disconnecting the arm from central control. But this hypothesis seems not to fit the subjective facts. It is not as though, as in paralysis, the subject's arm simply refused to obey his will. Rather, it is as though his "will" itself were paralyzed by the pain. As he starts to move his arm, his resolve to do so suddenly is replaced by an overwhelming contrary impulse. A more plausible hypothesis thus might be that as his arm starts to move, a volley of impulses from the elbow travels up certain spinal tracts, and the structure in the brain initiating and controlling this movement receives, directly or indirectly, a signal that causes the movement to be terminated or changed to its inverse. Thus the movement stops or is replaced with a contrary one. However, this deactivating signal is not the sole factor determining whether the movement will continue. Under special external circumstances and when certain central conditions exist, brain mechanisms will produce the movement despite the deactivating signal. Thus, under some circumstances, the subject will move his arm past the point at which this neural signal is generated.[51]

This hypothesis at least fits the subjective facts. It begins to explain why stopping the ("painful") movement seems both like a deliberate action and yet also strangely reflexlike and compelled. It seems deliberate because it is mediated by the same neural system that controls normal deliberate movements that are made after central computations. It also resembles deliberate action in that the person could do otherwise: the response is not under the total control of this signal, but would happen otherwise if different central conditions or different external stimuli were present. It is not bound by this stimulus. On the other hand, the response is reflexlike in that it is automatic, difficult to resist, and

51. If someone began pummeling him with her fists, we probably would observe the person in the armchair bend his arm in warding off the blows. And under certain other circumstances, even without such immediate external provocations, depending on his motivational state, he might bend his arm past the point of pain by a "pure act of will," as we say. But in other cases (e.g., a severely painful crick in the neck caused by a pinched spinal nerve), voluntary bodily movement past the point of pain is entirely impossible.

not made as a result of any higher-order computations or deliberations in the subject. (It is sometimes overridden, however, as a
result of such deliberations.) So it is neither completely compelled
nor altogether centrally controlled. This hypothesis thus at least
begins to explain these quasi-involuntary negative bodily reactions and to illuminate the peculiar intermediate area between
being compelled and being deliberate in which they lie. The reactions are as the foregoing hypothesis entails whether or not that
hypothesis is correct.

All of these reactions are, in an obvious way, *directed toward* a
bodily place. The positive bodily reactions of shaking, rubbing,
calming, and protecting, in the bee-stung man, for example, all
center around the injured finger. An abdominal point is the focal
point for doubling-up and sheltering reactions of someone hit in
the abdomen. The hands tend to go to the face of the person with
swollen sinuses. In each case, a set of automatic or semiautomatic
reactions focuses on some bodily place. There is no special difficulty in imagining neural mechanisms for this. Likewise, negative
bodily reactions also center around a bodily place. In the arthritis
victim the locus of compelled restraint was his elbow joint. This
point is the common element in an indefinitely large set of negative bodily reactions; every movement that involves the elbow is
blocked or restrained. These reactions, then, positive and negative, are all directed toward a bodily location. This undoubtedly
is part of what experiencing "pain" as located at a bodily place
consists in: having a set of positive bodily reactions that center
around that point, together with a set of negative bodily reactions
defined by it as their common element.

To complete the account, something further is required such
that a person who has it plus the foregoing reactions will experience pain at some location. The clinical separability of the
pain sensation from suffering shows this. The lobotomized or
drugged patient whom "pain does not bother" evidently has none
of these reactions yet still reports a pain sensation. So something
more than these reactions is required.

One additional requirement, although I do not know how to
account for it, may be a total body image state that is one way
when the subject has all these impulses, another way when he
does not. The suggestion then would be that, although the lobotomized or drugged patient no longer has the responses, he retains
a differential reaction in these two body-image states, one of

which formerly was associated with pain responses. On this hypothesis, it is possible that a lobotomized patient will distinguish "pain" apart from "suffering" only if he previously had both.

Another component of the phenomenon is the way pains tyrannize one's perceptual awareness. Most other sensations can be centrally controlled to a considerable extent. When a person is concentrating on what he is reading, for example, he may cease to hear the sounds coming to him from the street outside. But if his attention is called to them, he suddenly begins to hear them. If he starts carefully listening to them, he may become oblivious to the objects in his field of vision. Neural gating mechanisms probably are responsible for this.[52] Sound waves from the street were vibrating his eardrums even as he read, but he did not hear sounds because his brain was sending out signals that blocked impulses in the auditory tracts, diminishing their intensity or shutting them out completely. When he is told to listen, his brain stops blocking these impulses and perhaps starts blocking impulses from other sensory receptors. The result is a shift in perceptual attention from one sense modality to another. But this cannot be done equally well with impulses from injured tissue. Even if the victim tries to concentrate on something else, they break through and capture his attention. If he succeeds in getting his mind off his pain for a moment, soon he finds his attention back on it. His pain monopolizes his attention; he can focus well on nothing else. The explanation of this presumably is that the same gating systems that exist for other sensations either do not exist for pain or else do not operate in the same way. The brain can reject impulses in the auditory or optic tracts better than it can shut out impulses in the pain tracts.[53] Consequently, pain cannot be excluded from perceptual awareness in the way sights or sounds can. Furthermore, these pain impulses may themselves

52. See, e.g., Jerome S. Bruner, "On Perceptual Readiness," *Psychological Review*, 64 (1957), 138–141.

53. To some extent a person can shut out pain by focusing his attention elsewhere, so some gating for pain must exist. There are cases of soldiers wounded in battle who felt no pain from their wounds until brought back to the hospital. For physiological evidence of the existence of gating mechanisms for pain, see Ronald Melzack and Patrick Wall, "Pain Mechanisms: A New Theory," *Science*, 150 (November 1965), 971f. These gating mechanisms evidently, however, cannot be centrally controlled as effectively as the gating mechanisms for other sensory input.

tend to activate the gating mechanisms that shut out other sensory inputs. Thus the sick man lies in bed dwelling on his pain, unable to ignore it or to concentrate on anything else.

Aggravating his plight, moreover, these ungatable neural signals tend to activate the automatic bodily reactions described earlier. Not only is the victim unable to focus his attention on anything else, but he may be caused to writhe, moan, or scream, or in other cases, simply to lie deathly still. He either relinquishes control and turns himself over to these reactions or he must put effort into restraining himself. Thus the victim not only is unable to concentrate on anything else, he also is unable to do anything else. This is another important part of the suffering associated with pain.

The above is not nearly a complete account of pain. As explained earlier, a complete account of pain should describe a set of realizable properties such that a system having these properties could experience what it and everyone else would agree was pain. Some such properties have been cited, but they certainly do not tell the whole story. As more such pieces are added and fit together, a total picture should emerge of a system that would be capable of experiencing pain. It is important to recognize, however, that to a considerable extent, the problem of pain cannot be solved in isolation from a number of other problems. The solution must include an account of how the postulated pain mechanisms are related to various other bodily systems. As discussed earlier, for example, pain cannot be understood apart from an explanation of its relationship to motivational states, volition, and passive perceptual consciousness. Indeed, in a sense, no mental phenomenon can be understood apart from its relationship to many other mental phenomena. This point emerges clearly in the general theory developed in the next chapter.

CHAPTER 3

Completion of the General Model

1. Review of the Problem

Chapter 1 presented a characterization describing interrelationships among three things, M, L, and u, and hypothesized that when 'M' ranges over the class of humans and 'L' is taken to be some language, utterances of pure mental self-descriptions in that language satisfy the resulting open sentences. But this characterization also was satisfiable by certain utterances intuitively not categorizable as expressions of mental self-descriptions (for example, 'I have stimulated C fibers' said by a man in pain). We want a "complete" characterization of mental self-descriptions—one satisfiable by instances of all and only the mental self-descriptions. In Section 2 of this chapter, "physical" self-descriptions are excluded by adding to the characterization a further principle which they fail but mental descriptions satisfy, revealing the difference between these two kinds of description. With the addition of a fifth principle in Section 4 to handle certain borderline cases, the hypothesis is advanced that the model provides a complete characterization of the distinctive features of mental self-descriptions and, derivatively, of mental phenomena themselves. Consequences for psychology and neuropsychology develop in Chapter 4.

2. Addition of Principle 4 and Statement of the Hypothesis of the Model

Were this exposition addressed solely to an audience of impatient mathematicians, I might proceed next by pointing out that the *nature* of the "states" referred to in the earlier definition of a state table, and again in the principles stated in the general characterization of nontransitional self-description (in the last section of Chapter 1) was left unspecified. One obvious possibility is that they might be "structural states"; these are states that are expressed by a "structural state description," which individuates and defines a system's "states" in terms of various configurations or arrangements of its constituent internal concrete parts or subparts. In this case, one configuration of the system's parts corresponds to one "state," and in another configuration, the system may be considered to be in a different state.[1] Another altogether different possible interpretation of the "states" mentioned in such tables is that they are defined in terms of external *functional* rather than internal structural distinctions. To give this interpretation, the various "states" mentioned in the state table are taken to be *implicitly defined by that table itself* (and nothing else). Such states will be called "F-states." An F-state is defined by the table in which it appears. For individual a to be in F-state S_i, for instance, it is necessary and sufficient that a be in a state in which it would respond to all the same possible sequences of inputs by producing all the same sequences of outputs as would a realization of this state table when in state S_i. (Notice that no other reference is made to the system's internal properties or structure.) When the states mentioned in a table are understood to be F-states, the table will be called a "functional state table" (FST). (Whether or not these definitions coincide with those given by others, the author asks readers here to understand these terms in this sense.) For the systems (e.g., organisms) under study, FSTs will operate as our state-equations. Were this book addressed solely to mathematicians, F-states and FSTs having been thus defined, readers next would be given the axioms of the full model stated later in this section. However, since making these crucial concepts clear to everyone is desirable, I begin instead by retracing the longer route that led to these ideas and indicating the motivations for these axioms.

The problem of characterizing the essential difference between 'I have a pain' and 'I have stimulated C fibers' will be approached

1. Many students of machine theory almost always automatically interpret as *structural* the states machine theory actually discusses *abstractly* (i.e., without reference to the exact nature of their definition). This must be avoided here.

In a *"machine (state) table,"* the nature of the definition of the states is unspecified; they even may be interpreted as structural states. In what I call a *"functional state table,"* as explained in this chapter, the states are taken as implicitly defined by the table itself.

by developing a corresponding distinction for a nonhuman analogue. To this end, some preliminary remarks are required.

The concept of a functional state table (FST) first must be
introduced. As this concept is used here, an FST is conceived as a
description true or false of some system. In particular, it is an
instance of a very general mode of representation that characterizes certain operational properties of a system in abstraction from
its internal concrete structure. The crucial distinction between
structural and functional descriptions best is explicated with the
aid of an example of a simple physical system characterized by an
FST. (Later, FSTs describing humans will be introduced to solve
the problem of characterizing the difference between, e.g., 'I have
a pain' and 'I have stimulated C fibers'.) Consider Smith's manual
typewriter. Like most such machines, pushing its a-key causes a
token of the character 'a' to be printed; if the b-key is pushed, a
'b' is printed; and so on. Also it has a "shift-lock" button which,
pushed and latched, lowers the type-panel, causing the machine
to type in capital letters. When the shift-lock is pulled up, the
machine again types in lowercase letters. Let 'Sm_1' designate the
internal structural state of Smith's typewriter when it has its
shift-lock button up and its type-panel in raised position. (Thus,
by definition, the state description 'x is in Sm_1' is supposed to be
satisfiable only by the typewriter owned by Smith and only when
its shift-lock button is up and its type-panel is in raised position;
hence, Sm_1 is *not* an F-state.) Let 'Sm_2' designate this typewriter's
state when the shift-lock button is down and its type panel lowered. (Thus the shift-lock button simply functions to move the
machine back and forth between the two states, Sm_1 and Sm_2.)
His typewriter is then described by Table 3–1.

| | States | |
	Sm_1	Sm_2
Inputs		
push a-key	Sm_1 *(type 'a')*	Sm_2 *(type 'A')*
push b-key	Sm_1 *(type 'b')*	Sm_2 *(type 'B')*
.	.	.
.	.	.
.	.	.
push z-key	Sm_1 *(type 'z')*	Sm_2 *(type 'Z')*
pull shift-lock	$Sm_1(\Lambda)$	$Sm_1(\Lambda)$
push shift-lock	$Sm_2(\Lambda)$	$Sm_2(\Lambda)$

Table 3–1.

Since by definition, 'Sm_1' and Sm_2' designate specific structural
states of Smith's machine only, *this* table characterizes only that

particular machine (and so is not an FST). Jones, on the other hand, has an electric typewriter. Pushing a key on it closes a circuit activating electromagnets moving the type-ball and causing the appropriate letter to be printed. Pressing the shift-lock button causes the type-ball to be angled so that the machine types in capital letters; pulling it changes the angle so that lowercase letters are typed. Let J_1 be the structural state of Jones's machine when the shift-lock button is up, the circuit open, and the type-ball in a position to type lowercase letters. Let J_2 be the structural state of his machine when the shift-lock button is pressed, current is flowing through that circuit, and magnets are tilting the type-ball so that capitals will be printed. Then Jones's electric typewriter is described by Table 3–2.

	States	
	J_1	J_2
Inputs		
push *a*-key	J_1 (type 'a')	J_2 (type 'A')
push *b*-key	J_1 (type 'b')	J_2 (type 'B')
.	.	.
.	.	.
.	.	.
push *z*-key	J_1 (type 'z')	J_2 (type 'Z')
pull shift-lock	$J_1(\Lambda)$	$J_1(\Lambda)$
push shift-lock	$J_2(\Lambda)$	$J_2(\Lambda)$

Table 3–2.

Since by definition, 'J_1' and 'J_2' designate specific structural states of Jones's machine only, this table characterizes only his typewriter and also is not an FST.

In the overall way they function or behave, these two systems obviously have something in common. This is manifested in the fact that the table describing Smith's typewriter looks exactly like the table describing Jones's typewriter except for the names of the states (i.e., if 'Sm_1' and 'J_1' both were replaced throughout by some third symbol, and likewise for 'Sm_2' and 'J_2', the result would be identical tables). Both machines have similar input-output characteristics and can perform the same jobs; if they are started in corresponding states, pressing the same sequence of keys produces the same printed output on both machines. This similarity exists even though the two devices have different internal physical arrangements or configurations. What these two machines have in common is characterized by an FST. Prescinding from the particularities of the two typewriters and referring to their states only in an abstract functional way, the FST shown in Table 3-3 provides an overall input-output description that *both* machines satisfy.

	States	
	State 1	*State 2*
Inputs		
push a-key	*State 1 (type 'a')*	*State 2 (type 'A')*
push b-key	*State 1 (type 'b')*	*State 2 (type 'B')*
.	.	.
.	.	.
.	.	.
push z-key	*State 1 (type 'z')*	*State 2 (type 'Z')*
pull shift-lock	*State 1 (Λ)*	*State 1 (Λ)*
push shift-lock	*State 2 (Λ)*	*State 2 (Λ)*

Table 3-3.

This table is supposed to differ from the previous ones in that the state descriptions in it have no independent specification but are defined solely by Table 3-3. To be "in *State 1*," for example, is just to be in a state with the functional properties specified by the table. Thus *both* typewriters can be in *State 1*, and one can say, for example, such things as, "When either is in *State 1*, it responds to a push on the a-key by printing a lowercase 'a' and remaining in *State 1*." This functional state has, of course, different structural correlates in the two machines.[2] The correlate of *State 1* is Sm_1 in Smith's machine, J_1 in Jones's. This FST, then, defines a "Form" or pattern that various "concrete realizations" with different internal structures can instantiate or possess. It says, in abstraction from an instance's particular specific internal structure, configuration, or constitution, how that instance or realization would behave under various external conditions. State descriptions defined by an FST will be called "*F-states.*" In the FST above, *State 1* and *State 2* are F-states.

Being in a certain F-state may be logically sufficient for the true application to the system of certain ordinary-language predicates or phrases of description. For example, for something to be in *State 1*, as defined above, is logically sufficient for it to "be ready to print in lowercase letters." This fact will be represented graphically as in Table 3-4.

2. In "Minds and Machines," Putnam notes the possible analogy between, on the one hand, human mental states and the "logical states" of an abstract machine versus, on the other hand, human physical states and the "structural states" of a realization of an abstract machine (in *Minds and Machines*, ed. Alan R. Anderson [Englewood Cliffs, N.J.: Prentice-Hall, 1964], p. 84). The further exploration of this analogy that he urges is accomplished, with modifications, by the present chapter.

'is ready to print in
lowercase letters'

	State 1	State 2
Inputs		
push a-key	State 1 (*print 'a'*)	State 2 (*print 'A'*)
push b-key	State 1 (*print 'b'*)	State 2 (*print 'B'*)
.	.	.
.	.	.
.	.	.
pull shift-lock	State 1 (Λ)	State 1 (Λ)
push shift-lock	State 2 (Λ)	State 2 (Λ)

Table 3–4.

Any term of description for whose true application some F-state is a logically sufficient condition will be said to be *"functionally determined"* or *"functionally specified."* So '*x* is ready to print in lowercase letters' (as a description of a typewriter) is functionally determined. Obviously, a description is functionally determined only in relation to some FST (and, perhaps, some state within that FST); it makes no sense to ask independently of any FST whether or not a given description is functionally determined.[3] Obviously, too, in order that a description be functionally determined, its application to a system must depend logically on properties of the kind reflected in an FST and not on the arrangement or composition of the internal concrete parts of its realizations. [Below, it is posited that the true difference between (a) "physical" (structural) state descriptions of someone, and (b) "mental" state descriptions is that the latter are functionally determined.] Both F-states and the states determined by them will be called "abstract functional states," or "functional states" for short.[4]

A crucial distinguishing feature of functional state descriptions

3. Of course, one could ask, "Is this description functionally determined?" simply meaning thereby, "Does there exist *any* FST by which this description is determined?"

4. This definition is different from (and, in fact, incompatible with) Putnam's concept of a "functional state." For Putnam, a "functional state" of an organism is *not* (as it is on my account) a state entailed by some F-state; for Putnam, instead, a realization of a state table is in a certain "functional state" when *inputs* of a certain sort are present to it. See Hilary Putnam, "Psychological Predicates," in *Art, Mind, and Religion*, Sixth Oberlin Colloquium in Philosophy, 1965, ed. W. H. Capitan and D. D. Merrill (Pittsburgh: University of Pittsburgh Press, n.d.), pp. 42, 46, and 47–48, reprinted under the title "The Nature of Mental States," in *Materialism and the Mind-Body Problem*, ed. David M, Rosenthal (Englewood Cliffs, N.J.: Prentice-Hall, 1971), pp. 155–156, 159, and 161. In "What Psychological States Are Not," *Philosophical Review*, 81 (1972), p. 165, Ned J. Block and Jerry A. Fodor mistakenly attribute a different definition to Putnam.

is the possibility of systems being arranged so that, as long as they do nothing more than operate in accordance with a certain FST, they will produce these descriptions only when true, never when false. With some modifications, a typewriter can be used to illustrate this modest "incorrigibility" and its relationship to the difference between state descriptions that are functionally determined and those that are not. Imagine added to Smith's manual typewriter a button (marked 'Query') connected to a key on which is engraved (in tiny letters) a whole sentence, D_1, such as 'My type-panel is in the raised position' or 'I am ready to type in lowercase letters'; above this (on the same keyhead) let there be inscribed another sentence, D_2, such as 'My type-panel is lowered' or 'I am ready to type in all capital letters'. Now if the type-panel is in the raised position, pushing the query button will cause the bottom sentence, D_1, to be printed; otherwise pushing the same key will cause the top sentence to be typed. This addition to Smith's typewriter allows an outsider to learn its state at any time simply by hitting the query button and reading off the answer. Let a query button also be added to Jones's electric typewriter, this time by adding the necessary wiring and electromagnets and placing the same additional expressions, D_1 and D_2, on the typeball. The FST in Table 3–5 describes both systems now.

	STATE 1	STATE 2
Inputs		
push a-key	*STATE 1 (type 'a')*	*STATE 2 type 'A')*
push b-key	*STATE 1 (type 'b')*	*STATE 2 (type 'B')*
.	.	.
.	.	.
.	.	.
pull shift-lock	*STATE 1 (Λ)*	*STATE 1 (Λ)*
push shift-lock	*STATE 2 (Λ)*	*STATE 2 (Λ)*
push Query	*STATE 1 (type D_1)*	*STATE 2 (type D_2)*

Table 3–5.

In Chapter 1, the reader will recall, two different situations were distinguished: Situation I, in which a subject produces a description true of something he observes and Situation II, in which he does not describe an input but instead produces a description true of himself when in a state he is in when in the state as a result of being in which he produces that description, a state of affairs hypothesized to correspond to the situation in nontransitional mental self-description. A decisive difference between instances of Situation II, a difference corresponding to that existing between "mental" and "nonmental" state descriptions, now is modeled by the typewriter example. For depending on the *meaning* in the language of the sentences D_1 and D_2—in particular, whether their truth conditions are functionally determined—two different possible cases arise. (1) It may be that the descriptions expressed by these sentences would be true of *some* but false of *other* systems having the same FST. This would occur, for example, if D_1 were 'My type-panel is raised' and D_2 were 'My type-panel is lowered.' These self-descriptions would be true of Smith's manual if it produced them (as above) but false of Jones's electric if it did so (since it has no type-panel). Or (2) D_1 and D_2 might be such that they would be true whenever produced by any realization of this FST. Prereflectively, it might seem implausible that systems can be arranged so that (as long as they operate in accordance with a certain FST) they never can produce certain descriptions falsely, but in fact this easily happens if the descriptions are functionally determined. Suppose that D_1 is 'I am ready to print in lowercase letters' (as written in tiny letters by a single impact of the query key). This is shown in Table 3–6.

	'is ready to print in lower-case letters'	
	STATE 1	STATE 2
Inputs		
push a-key	STATE 1 (type 'a')	STATE 2 (type 'A')
push b-key	STATE 1 (type 'b')	STATE 2 (type 'B')
.	.	.
.	.	.
.	.	.
pull shift-lock	STATE 1 (Λ)	STATE 1 (Λ)
push shift-lock	STATE 2 (Λ)	STATE 2 (Λ
push Query	STATE 1 (type 'I am ready to print in lowercase letters')	STATE 2 (type D_2)

Table 3–6.

Then the description expressed by this output *will be true when produced by any system operating in accordance with this FST*, since any realization of this FST when in *STATE 1 is* "ready to print in lowercase letters." Hence, any system acting in accordance with this FST never will output an instance of D_1 when false. (Understanding the possibility of a system's being arranged so that, as long as it does nothing more than operate in accordance with a certain FST, it will produce a certain kind of output only when the description it expresses is true, never when false, is fundamental to all that follows. I am unable to explain this point more perspicuously than I just have. If the idea seems elusive, it is perhaps best grasped by reflecting on the truth conditions of the output sentence in relation to what it means to realize an FST.)

The above statement assumes, of course, that the other output, D_2, is not also 'I am ready to print in lowercase letters' (i.e., that $D_2 \neq D_1$). For if it were, a system operating in accordance with that FST could produce an instance of this description when false (namely, when in *STATE 2*).[5] The possibility of an FST *in several different places* calling for the production of instances of the same description does not affect the basic principle although it necessitates its restatement: If D is a functionally determined self-description (and there is no contradiction in its being produced by a system of which it is true), then there can exist an FST, F, *containing a state S_i* in which instances of D may be produced, such that *any* realization of F producing an instance of that description when in that state S_i, will produce it only when true. In simple cases where the FST does not in some places call for the production of an instance of the description when false, restriction to a particular state in the table is unnecessary.

Shortly the hypothesis will be formulated that nontransitional self-description of the "physical" sort corresponds to the first of the two cases described above ('My type-panel is lowered'), whereas nontransitional self-description of the "mental" sort corresponds to the second ('I am ready to print in all capitals'). That is, it will be posited that "physical" self-descriptions (such as 'I have stimulated C fibers') are distinguished from mental self-descriptions (such as 'I have a pain') by the fact that the latter are functionally determined whereas the former are not. According to this hypothesis, mental state descriptions are related to a person's body and its internal components (neural or otherwise) in the same way that abstract functional state descriptions of a typewriter are related to the machine and its concrete internal constitution. First, however, to assure understanding of the idea,

---

5. A situation like this obtains generally in the human case since most people are so arranged that they can be gotten to produce false instances of mental self-descriptions, For example, if the average person is told "Repeat after me, 'I am in pain'," he will accommodate by saying (even when false) 'I am in pain'.

let us consider some additional illustrations of functionally determined descriptions.

Example 1: Suppose we are dealing with currently manufactured computers, that L is English, and that F is an FST which demands that a certain input item (say, 'Where did you come from?') be responded to by printing out 'I was manufactured by IBM'. Then if F is realized by an IBM product, the result of inputting this item will be the production of a true self-description. If it is realized by a machine manufactured by Burroughs, however, the result of inputting 'Where did you come from?' will be the production of a false self-description (viz., 'I was manufactured by IBM'). Thus this description is not "functionally determined," since whether or not its self-application is true when produced depends on factors other than those fixed by an FST.

Example 2: Suppose that any realization of F is capable of computing the decimal expansion of π and that there is some functional state that it is in only when doing this. Suppose, moreover, that there is an input (e.g., 'What-are-you-doing?') to which the response called for when in this state is 'I am computing the decimal expansion of π' (and that this output is called for nowhere else in F). Then any realization of F will produce this output only when the description it expresses is true, since by hypothesis any realization of F in a state in which this description is produced is computing the decimal expansion of π.

Example 3: Consider a particular computer employing vacuum tubes which engineers have arranged so that if vacuum tube 312 fails, the machine will print out 'Vacuum tube 312 has failed'.[6] Any FST describing this antique and mentioning this operation must include somewhere the contents of Table 3–7:

	States	
	S_j	
. . .		. . .
.		
.		
.		
i	$S_k(print\ 'Vacuum\ tube\ 312\ has\ failed')$	
.		
.		

Table 3–7.

6. Putnam gives this example ("Minds and Machines," p. 83).

(where i may be the null input). But then, e.g., a transistorized realization of this FST that received i as an input when in S_j would produce the falsehood, 'Vacuum tube 312 has failed'.[7] So this description is not functionally determined.

If a self-description is determined relative to some FST (or certain states within that FST), any system that operates in accordance with that FST will produce instances of it only when true. So if some system produces an instance of this description when false, we know that it is not a realization of this FST (in one of these states). It is also clear that if some *possible* realization of an FST could, being in a certain state of it, produce a given description when false, then this description is not determined relative to that state in that FST. So a given description can be shown *not* determined relative to a certain state in a certain FST by showing that a system could be a realization of that FST in that state and yet the description be false of it. One way of showing this is to take a system that *does* realize the FST and then modify it so that it still realizes the same FST but no longer satisfies the description. (For instance, in example 3 above, one can imagine all vacuum tubes replaced with equivalently functioning transistors.) And it may be shown that there exists *no* FST by which a given description is determined by showing that for *any* FST, a system realizing it and producing the description only when true could be altered so that it still realized the same FST but the description, if produced, now would be false of it.

These ideas will be used to characterize human mental self-description as follows: For every "mental" description, the existence will be postulated of an FST containing a state (or sequence of states) that determines it. The corollary follows that for each subjectively reportable mental state, there exists an FST whose realizations necessarily will produce instances of the corresponding mental self-description only when true. (Although none of the FSTs postulated need describe the speaker himself, generally some will, and for the purpose of grasping the basic idea of the theory, the reader initially may imagine this so.) The upshot of this hypothesis is that the F-states of these FSTs determine *mental* states. The nature of these FSTs, how they relate to a

---

7. I am assuming that a vacuum tube that has failed is not listed among the *inputs* in this FST. If it were, it would be a case of Situation I—i.e., description by transition.

person's linguistic, ratiocinative, and perceptual abilities, as well as their other properties, will be considered in more detail later. Explicit reference to an FST in the axiomatization below necessitates slightly rewording part of the general characterization on p. 67 before supplementing it; specifically, the reference to "input" and "output," which remained indefinite in the earlier formulation, is now, in Principles 1 and 3, made explicitly relative to the postulated FST. The newly added Principle 4 expresses the postulate that the description is functionally determined. A fifth principle will be added later.

MODEL OF NONTRANSITIONAL MENTAL SELF-DESCRIPTION

General Characterization

There exists a functional state table, F, such that:

1. If $\underline{M}$ produced $\underline{u}$ after receiving some input in F, it is not the case that the statement expressed in $\underline{L}$ by $\underline{u}$ is true in virtue of this input's presence.

2. $\underline{M}$ produced $\underline{u}$, the description expressed in $\underline{L}$ by u is true of M, and it is true of $\underline{M}$ in virtue of M being in a state he was in when he produced $\underline{u}$.

3. The descriptive statement expressed in $\underline{L}$ by $\underline{u}$ is not, if true, true of $\underline{M}$ in virtue of the production by $\underline{M}$ of any output in F which $\underline{M}$ happens to produce.

4. There is a state (or sequence of states) in F such that being in this state (or passing through this sequence) is logically sufficient for satisfying the state description expressed in $\underline{L}$ by $\underline{u}$.

Corollary: (If no contradiction exists in the supposition that $\underline{u}$ is produced by a subject when the description it expresses in $\underline{L}$ is true, then) there exists an FST containing a state, or sequence of states, from which utterances of a description of the same type as $\underline{u}$ can be produced only when true, never when false. (Note that the restriction in the conditional's antecedent allows for such mental states as being "panic-stricken," "paralyzed with fright," or "completely hysterical" in which it may be impossible for the subject to issue a report.)

This characterization is applied to someone producing an utterance by substituting the person's name for 'M', a term designating the utterance for 'u', and the name of the language for 'L'. As applied to humans, an FST of the postulated sort takes as "inputs" different possible environmental situations and describes as "outputs" various pieces of behavior. It can be imagined set out in tabular form as in previous examples. The decision to interpret the inputs and outputs in this way is not based on any absolute or intrinsic distinction found in nature, and is "arbitrary" in the sense that a theory alternatively could regard, say, peripheral afferent neural events as the "input" (as, e.g., Putnam does) and, say, firings of motor neurons as the "output." My specified interpretation of "inputs" and "outputs" (rather than any of the other possible interpretations) is chosen ultimately because it provides a better and more fruitful theory. It should perhaps also be pointed out that, in the general case, the description of each individual "input" and "output" may be very lengthy and complex. Each distinct possible "input" may be a total environmental situation such as might confront a human (e.g., a surrounding room filled with miscellaneous objects). The full linguistic description of a single input, therefore, might be more detailed even than a novelist's five-page description of one particular room. A similar room with, say, one of the books on the shelf moved a just-noticeable-distance to the right or left might constitute a separate and distinct possible input. A single "output" might be represented as a small space-time segment of a total bodily response: its description might characterize the configuration of the entire musculature, including posture, motions, and accelerations of movements.[8] Of course, since the FSTs shown in these pages are only simple examples to illustrate various points, the input and output descriptions in them will be much less complicated. FSTs of the postulated sort are conceived as descriptions (in particular, monadic predicates) true or false of a subject depending on

8. For a simple illustration of an FST describing a human, see the first part of Appendix IV. In the general case, the (a) "inputs" and (b) "outputs" in FSTs describing humans may be thought of as given by *vectors* whose various components specify or describe (a) different features of possible environments and (b) the (simultaneous) movements of various bodily parts. For an excellent analysis of how such inputs and outputs may be specified completely and rigorously, see the first part of James G. Taylor, *The Behavioral Basis of Perception* (New Haven: Yale University Press, 1962). (However, the formalism of the "behavioristic" perceptual theory subsequently presented in that book inadvertently entails that [except for "drives"] the perceiving organism has only *one* functional state.)

whether the subject would behave as they predict, and not something to which recourse is made in planning or executing his actions. Every person with a life chronology satisfies *some* FST-description (indeed, indefinitely many different ones).[9] This is a trivial fact[10] and prejudges no theory of mind; it would hold whether humans were probablistically operating mechanisms or bodies activated by Cartesian souls. Many theories of mind, however, are excluded by the hypothesis (formulated below) that FSTs exist whose realizations, ipso facto, have "a mind." Although for anyone, many simple FSTs describe him, those postulated below are not simple. The highly complex rational (and sometimes irrational) procedures and patterns of behavior they characterize are such that, if the hypothesis is true, their realizations will be capable, for example, of reasoning, perceiving, having sensations, thinking, making judgments, feeling emotions, and speaking the language.[11]

By characterizing (1) a certain class of specific historical events of utterance production, this hypothesis aims at indirectly characterizing (2) the class of "mental" descriptions conceived as sentence-forms in abstraction from their utterance. Directly, the model describes what happens when, on a particular occasion, someone produces nontransitionally a true mental self-description; if the hypothesis is correct, the characterization's open sentences are true of this person, utterance, and language on that occasion. But indirectly, it characterizes a class of sentence-forms. For it picks out a class of utterances (namely, those utterances produced in a way that satisfies the characterization) which in turn determines a class of sentence-forms (the class of sentence-forms with tokens in this class of utterances), and this class, the theory hypothesizes, is the class of mental self-descriptions.[12] In this way, a characterization of particular utterance-events indi-

9. By a "life chronology" is meant a serial history, not necessarily complete or exhaustive, of certain situations that might have confronted the person during his life and his probable responses to them. Given this, an FST with which his actions accord is easily constructible.

10. "Everything is a Probabilistic Automaton under some [functional] Description," remarks Putnam in "Psychological Predicates," p. 42 ("The Nature of Mental States," p. 156).

11. The theory does not entail that creatures with no language have no mental states. They may, however, be incapable of undergoing all the mental states of which linguistic speakers are capable.

12. Other-person mental descriptions (e.g., '*He* is in pain') are assumed obtainable by simple grammatical transformations—e.g., replace the first-person pronoun with the third-person pronoun and change the verb accordingly.

rectly characterizes a class of sentence-forms or descriptions. This is formulated precisely below.

Consider the utterances that satisfy the characterization when 'M' is replaced by people's names and 'L' by the name of some language. The "Hypothesis of the Model" (or "my functionalist hypothesis," as it also will be called) is that, so restricted: (1) every utterance satisfying the characterization expresses a mental self-description in that language; and (2) every mental self-description has[13] tokens satisfying the characterization. Alternatively, the hypothesis may be expressed as follows: If all the principles are conjoined, 'M', 'L', and 'u' regarded as variables, and the range of 'M' restricted to the class of humans and 'L' to some particular language, then the extension of 'u' in the resulting open sentence is a class containing utterances of all and only *mental* self-descriptions in that language. (For variable 'L', the extension of 'u' is the totality of mental descriptions in all languages.)

Let ϕ be some subjectively reportable mental state (such as pain or even just being conscious). Then the hypothesis implies that an FST, F, exists containing a functionally defined state, S_j, in which, necessarily, any realization of F is in mental state ϕ and from which utterances expressing this fact may be produced. Thus a realization of F (in S_j) cannot make a mistake in reporting its mental state. The situation as portrayed by the model is represented in Table 3–8, where the horizontal bracket between 'ϕ' and 'S_j'

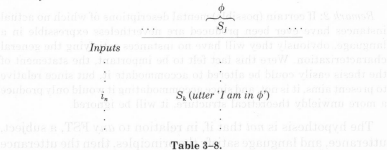

Table 3–8.

signifies the logical sufficiency of functional state S_j for mental state ϕ, and i_n (if not the null input) is some external stimulus that would elicit the verbal response 'I am in ϕ'. Since it posits a similar situation for each pure mental description, the hypothesis entails that organisms' "mental states" are simply FST-determined

13. Or "can have." See Remark 2 later.

abstract states of them. So not only does it explain how correct mental self-descriptions are produced, it also shows the general nature of their truth conditions.

Remark 1: Part 2 of my hypothesis does not assert that *every* utterance expressing a pure, present-tense mental self-description satisfies the characterization. Some do not. For example, if someone requests of someone who is *not* in pain, "Repeat after me: 'I am in pain',", and he does so, the case fails Principle 2 because the description expressed by the utterance is untrue of the speaker. (The case of someone who obeys this request when in pain trivially satisfies this principle.) Likewise, the model is unsatisfied by someone who lies when producing a mental self-description.

Please note that nowhere in this book is it said or implied that subjects cannot produce false mental self-descriptions! As everyone knows, this is almost a daily occurrence, and any theory incompatible with this fact is false. The present theoretical aim is to understand how, or in what sense, mental descriptions can be such that subjects *can* be arranged or programmed so as to produce them only when true, never when false—that is, one aim is to understand the actual facts behind the so-called "incorrigibility principle" (which claims that it is, in principle, impossible for subjects who understand the language and have made no verbal slips to make a mistake or to be mistaken in their sincere reports or beliefs about their own subjective mental phenomena). To say that a certain state of affairs *can* exist is not to say or to imply that it *does* exist.

Remark 2: If certain (possible) mental descriptions of which no actual instances have ever been produced are nevertheless expressible in a language, obviously they will have no instances satisfying the general characterization. Were this fact felt to be important, the statement of the thesis easily could be altered to accommodate it, but since relative to present aims, it is not, and since accommodating it would only produce a more unwieldy theoretical structure, it will be ignored.

The hypothesis is *not* that if, in relation to *any* FST, a subject, utterance, and language satisfy the principles, then the utterance expresses a mental description in that language. Rather, the hypothesis is that there exists a certain class, α, of FSTs such that a subject, utterance, and language satisfy the principles in relation to an FST in α if and only if the utterance expresses a true mental self-description in that language. (Thus, exhibition of some FST relative to which some nonmental self-description would satisfy the general characterization would not refute my hypothesis; instead, it would show only that the exhibited FST was not in the postulated class α.) A canonical formulation of the hypothesis clarifies this. Writing '$C(①, ②, ③, ④)$' for the predicate

> ① is an FST & ② is a system & ③ is an utterance & ④ is a language & ①, ②, ③, and ④ satisfy the general characterization

the hypothesis of our model is expressed in quantificational notation as follows:

$$(\exists \alpha) \{ \alpha \text{ is a class of FSTs } \&$$
$$(u) [(\exists F) (\exists M) (\exists L) (F \, \varepsilon \, \alpha \, \& \, C(F, M, u, L))$$
$$\text{if and only if}$$
$$u \text{ is a (true) instance of a}$$
$$\text{mental self-description}] \}^{14}$$

This says that there exists a class of FSTs relative to which all and only mental self-descriptions satisfy the principles (and not that mental self-descriptions are the only descriptions satisfying the characterization relative to some FST).

So, in particular, nonmental state descriptions (such as functional state descriptions of typewriters and some of humans discussed in Section 4) can satisfy the general characterization without refuting my functionalist hypothesis. The typewriter case simply *models* the relationship between "mind" and "body": mental state descriptions of an organism are related to structural state descriptions of its internal concrete constitution (e.g., its brain states) as abstract functional state descriptions of a typewriter are related to descriptions of its physical or mechanical states.

Note that *nowhere* in this book is it said or implied that mental states are identical to F-states! The hypothesis is only that F-states *determine* mental states (that is, for each ordinary-language

---

14. If we assume that every possible mental self-description (conceived as a sentence-form) has had a true instance produced, i.e.,

> (d) [(d is mental self-description). ⊃.
> (∃u) (u is an instance of d & u is true)]

then from the hypothesis one may infer that every mental description has instances satisfying the general characterization, i.e.:

> (d) [(d is a mental self-description). ⊃ .
> (∃M) (∃u) (∃L) (∃F) (u is an instance of
> d & C(F, M, u, L))].

This is identical to Part (2) of the basic hypothesis as originally formulated.

mental state, being in certain F-states is alleged to be a logically sufficient condition for being in that mental state). The postulated relationship between mental states and F-states is not one-to-one, but many-to-many. To each ordinary-language mental-state predicate, $M_i(x)$, in general there will correspond (perhaps infinitely) many F-states that determine it, and *each* of these F-states, in general, simultaneously will determine (perhaps infinitely) many separate and distinct mental states. So the postulated relationship is a complex many-to-many correlation, and *not* identity between the states.

Notice too that the hypothesis is expressed by a biconditional giving *necessary and sufficient* conditions for an utterance's being a "true mental self-description." Obtainable from these conditions, in the manner explained earlier, are necessary and sufficient conditions for a predicate's being "mental" (as opposed to "nonmental"). Readers must not be confused here by the fact that the new condition just added to the general characterization, Principle 4, entails only that, for a given mental state, the realizing of certain F-states in the postulated class of FSTs is a *sufficient* condition for being in that mental state, and does *not* entail that being in this F-state is a necessary condition for being in that mental state. The question here is what makes a state description "mental." The recently postulated (sufficient) condition for a concrete system (e.g., an organism) to be in some particular mental state (such as pain or hunger) actually functions, in the present theoretical context, primarily as a necessary condition (for a state description's being "mental") that *non*mental state descriptions (such as 'I have stimulated C fibers') cannot satisfy. This *sufficient* condition is employed by the hypothesis in attempting to state *necessary and sufficient* conditions for a state or state description's being "mental."

Remark 3: The hypothesis, if true, appears to be a statement whose truth is due partly to the meanings of words and partly to empirical facts about the natural world. (Some philosophers might prefer, for this reason, that it to be stated in terms of unqualified possibilities rather than in terms of logical sufficiency.) The same may hold, of course, of its corollaries.

Although the hypothesis does not actually supply the FSTs it posits, the postulate of their existence is of fundamental importance to the scientific investigation of mind. It gives a normal form for theory construction in psychology and neuropsychology; detailing these FSTs becomes psychology's task,[15] while neuropsychology's is uncovering the neural mechanisms by which they are realized in sentient creatures. It entails, moreover, that a system need only realize a suitable FST (i.e., have a certain overall input-output characteristic) to be capable of experiencing sensation, emotion, thought, intention, etc., a consequence of obvious importance to those interested, for example, in computer simulation of mental phenomena. And since it entails that there is nothing "left over" relevant to an organism's mental phenomena unreachable by a functionalist approach, it permits investigators to study an organism's abstract functional states, interrelationships among these, conditions affecting them, their behavioral consequences, and the underlying mechanisms by which they are realized, confident that no feature of its mental life thereby has been overlooked. That is, it assures researchers that they can gain access to everything relevant to an organism's mental phenomena simply by attending to its functional characteristics (there being, for example, no inaccessible private objects or events to worry about). It shows, furthermore, how speakers' "subjective reports" about their own mental states can be accepted and employed in psychological studies without thereby committing oneself to anything like the traditional introspectionist interpretation of this procedure. More specific empirical applications of this functionalist theory are developed in Chapter 4, while the next section of this chapter shows some philosophic implications of the hypothesis, including the falsity of various traditional theories of the mental-physical relationship and explanation of the so-called "incorrigibility" of mental self-knowledge and of the apparently privileged and unique epistemological relationship of a subject to his own mental states. Before developing these consequences, however, certain basic considerations more directly supporting the hypothesis are presented.

Note first that, as the hypothesis implies, an intuitively nonmentalistic self-description like 'I have stimulated C fibers' whose exclusion has been sought indeed does not satisfy the supplemented general characterization. Because it is a structural rather

---

15. This conception of psychology is consistent with Putnam's. See "Robots: Machines or Artificially Created Life?" *Journal of Philosophy*, 61 (November 1964), 676–678; reprinted in *Modern Materialism: Readings on Mind-Body Identity*, ed. John O'Connor, (New York: Harcourt, Brace & World, 1969), pp. 247–248.

than a functional state description, no FST could exist such that any realization in a certain F-state of it necessarily would satisfy this description. It is logically possible for something to realize any FST, and to be in any state of it, without having stimulated C fibers. Thus it fails Principle 4. It also fails to satisfy the corollary—no FST could exist such that any realization when in a certain F-state of it would be capable of producing this self-description nontransitionally only when true. This can be seen by a permutation argument. Consider any FST with provision for producing this self-description nontransitionally; for example, the one in Table 3–9.

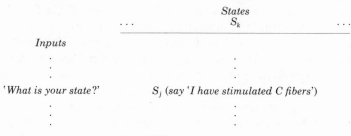

| | | *States* | |
		S_k	
Inputs	...		...
		.	
		.	
		.	
'What is your state?'		S_j (*say 'I have stimulated C fibers'*)	
		.	
		.	
		.	

Table 3–9.

Suppose (a) that Mr. Brown concretely realizes this FST and (b) that, as it happens, he has stimulated C fibers whenever he is in S_k and (c) that production of this output is called for nowhere else in this FST. Then whenever he is in the state as a result of which he produces this self-description, it is true of him. Now imagine Brown permuted as follows: remove his C fibers and replace them with equivalently functioning other elements (e.g., artificial neurons) similarly connected. Everything else will remain unchanged, the permuted Brown still will realize the same FST, yet the self-description 'I have stimulated C fibers' now will be false when he produces it. But this is any FST. Hence there is no FST with provision for outputting 'I have stimulated C fibers' nontransitionally such that by merely operating in accordance with it, a realization necessarily always would produce the description 'I have stimulated C fibers' only when true. (Notice that this demonstration depends only on the highly plausible assumption that there is no *logical* contradiction in the supposition that any FST could be realized by a system having no C fibers.)

A more concrete expression of the same idea is this. Assume

that a person's linguistic and other training is part of the process by which the person comes to have a certain FST. Then for "mental" self-descriptions, the hypothesis implies that a child can be trained so that, as long as he acts in accordance with the FST this training is designed to inculcate, regardless of what else happens, he never will produce these descriptions when false. (This perhaps explains the intuition that children who produce mental self-descriptions when false need *linguistic* retraining.) But with 'I have stimulated C fibers in my nervous system', no amount of training could make someone produce this utterance only when true for all permutations of him (including alterations in his neural wiring) that do not change the ratiocinative procedures induced by that training. That is, 'I have stimulated C fibers' fails to satisfy the characterization because, for any set of computational procedures infixed in him, a subject could act in accordance with them and yet produce this self-description when false (e.g., due to the replacement of his C fibers with artificial neurons).

Remark: This way of expressing the point needs qualification to make it clear (as was explicit in the more formal statement that preceded it) that it is made in the context of *nontransitional* self-description. For someone might be trained to pass from observations (made, say, during surgery on himself while conscious) of stimulated C fibers in his body to the statement, 'I have stimulated C fibers'. That is, a functional description might include a step like that shown in Table 3–10, or some

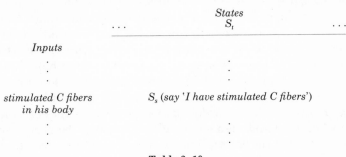

Table 3–10.

other in which the input "stimulated C fibers" leads to the utterance, 'I have stimulated C fibers'. In this event, as long as someone operated in accordance with this FST he never mistakenly would say, 'I have stimulated C fibers' because as long as he said this only when there was something satisfying the input description *"stimulated C fibers in his body,"* he never would say it falsely. But this case is *not* one of knowledge without observation, and the performance would fail Principle 1 because when (if) the speaker says 'I have stimulated C fibers' after observing stimulated C fibers in his body, the statement expressed by this utterance *is* true in virtue of the presence of this input (viz., the stimulated C fibers he observes). In fact, the case would now be an instance of Situation I fitting the Transition Model.

The other nonmental self-descriptions that satisfied the general characterization in Chapter 1 similarly are excluded by Principle 4. Consider someone who produces the self-description, 'I am six feet tall', not from self-observation but, say, purely from memory. An FST for this might appear in part as in Table 3–11.

	States
	S_m
Inputs	
'How tall are you?'	S_k (say '*I am six feet tall*')

Table 3–11.

His performance satisfies Principles 1, 2, and 3, but it fails Principle 4 because a different realization of the same FST (e.g., a shorter person) could produce the description when false. Merely operating in accordance with this FST would not guarantee that one would produce the description only when true. It is not functionally determined. Other examples include: 'I am blond'; 'I am handsome'; 'I weigh 150 pounds'; 'I have blue eyes'. For any FST, we can show that these descriptions fail Principle 4 by starting with a realization of it who does happen to produce the description only when true and then showing that he could be permuted in such a way that the description becomes false of him even though he is still a realization of that same FST. (For example, we imagine him with a different hair color, changed physiognomy, a few pounds added, different eye pigmentation, etc.) [Generally, for any nonmental description and any FST, either a falsifying permutation can be made or if not, such a permutation is blocked by something in the input or output columns and the case fails to satisfy Principles 1 through 3.] Thus, nonmental self-descriptions of the kind discussed above fail to satisfy the general characterization and to this extent, the first half of the hypothesis is confirmed. (Other nonmental self-descriptions will be considered later.)

The second half of my functionalist hypothesis (postulating that mental self-descriptions *do* satisfy the general characterization) entails that the applicability of mentalistic descriptions is logically independent of the nature of the particular mechanisms that enable subjects to realize these states, i.e., that these descriptions characterize subjects in abstraction from the concrete occurrences underlying the F-states that determine them. One consideration supporting this hypothesis is its congruity with the basic natural exigencies that prompt and surround language games of mentalistic description. To understand how, in accordance with the hypothesis, such descriptions may be introduced into the language, used, and finally taught to subjects themselves, let us imagine, first, watching a mother in a primitive linguistic community as she trains her two young children to identify various fruits by name. The initial configurations of their untutored nervous systems are, of course, unknown to her (indeed, each may have come into the world with a different prewiring), and in a sense, of no interest to her or to the community. Her goal is simply to get each to say 'Papaya' when presented with a papaya, 'Pineapple' when presented with a pineapple, etc., and her task will be completed when both can do this. If the technique of child training she employs succeeds, presumably it does so by altering something in each child's nervous system so that, when put into the appropriate state (perhaps by the verbal cue 'What's this?'), he will, when confronted with a fruit, make the appropriate verbal response. But again, she need not know the neural details. Even if, as may be the case, the underlying processes that enable it to make the transition correctly are different in each child, this fact is of no importance to her. From her point of view, as long as both children can do the same thing, her objective has been accomplished. This being so, it easily can be supposed that her linguistic community has some special description that characterizes, independently of the particular physiological processes underlying their ability, this "same thing" that both successfully trained children now can do (e.g., that both can "identify fruits by name").

Similarly useful would be a name for the *state* that trained children are put into when asked, "What's this?" It might be called the native-language equivalent of 'a-state-of-expecting-to-be-given-something-to-describe' or 'a-state-of-waiting-to-identify-the-next-object-shown-him', a description predicable of subjects in similar functional states (in which they will respond to the next exhibited object by saying its name) whether or not their underlying structural states are identical.[16] Such terminology would enable members of the linguistic community to discuss different children in a common general way, fitting the children's behavior into broader contexts and refining their expectations of them without, e.g., knowing the children's internal neurological states. Told, for example, that a child "expects to be given something to describe," they can predict the child's probable response if handed a fruit (that he will describe it and not, e.g., grab and eat it, as he might in a hunger state). An abstract functional state description of this sort suits their needs perfectly; given their knowledge of the children and their practical concerns, it conveys precisely the information they require.

The utility of such a state description would be greatly increased if the children themselves could be trained so that, in response to some preestablished input (the native-language equivalent, perhaps, of 'What are you up to?') *they themselves* would produce an utterance expressing it. This would enable speakers arriving late upon the scene and others ignorant of preceding events quickly to learn a child's state by inputting this query and noting his output. Moreover, if children throughout this society were shaped to similar FSTs and taught the same replies, never-before-encountered children likewise could be dealt with easily on the basis of self-produced state descriptions. Happily, as the present theory shows, there is no special difficulty in teaching children to report their own subjective mental states.[17] For responding 'Orange' when in this state and confronted with an orange does not differ operationally or mechanically from responding, 'I'm expecting to be given something to identify' when in this state and confronted with the words, 'What are you up to?' In an FST that showed these operations, as in Table 3–12, the only difference between Row X and Row Y is that the outputs have different interpretations in the language. To someone who did not

16. Putnam discusses this idea. *Ibid.*

17. On the introspectionist account, there are famous special difficulties over how a child could ever be taught to describe his own mental state correctly.

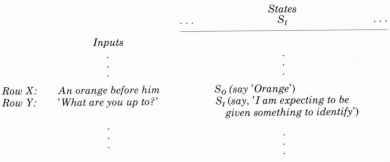

		States S_I	
Inputs		.	
		.	
Row X:	*An orange before him*	S_O *(say 'Orange')*	
Row Y:	*'What are you up to?'*	S_I *(say, 'I am expecting to be*	
		given something to identify')	
		.	
		.	

Table 3–12.

know the language, this table would appear as Table 3–13 does to us.

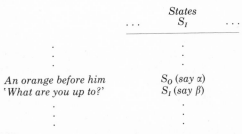

	States S_I	
.	.	
.	.	
An orange before him	S_O *(say α)*	
'What are you up to?'	S_I *(say β)*	
.	.	

Table 3–13.

He could not tell whether in saying α or β the speaker was describing himself or describing something outside himself. For the speaker in both cases simply passes from an object (an orange or an utterance) to an utterance; the cases are considered "different" only because in our language different interpretations are accorded to the outputs. Thus, since similar internal processes occur in both cases, there is no special difficulty in understanding how a child could be brought to produce this mental state description when it is true of himself.

As long as the child performs in accordance with the FST this training is intended to inculcate, he will produce this description only when it is true of him. For he will produce it only when in S_I, and when in S_I he is in a state of "expecting to be given something to identify." So he will produce the description only when true.

Hence this mental self-description also satisfies the corollary to the hypothesis.

Additional considerations supporting the hypothesis arise in response to the following *challenge*:

Earlier it was argued that the self-description 'I have stimulated C fibers' fails to satisfy Principle 4 because for any state in any FST, there could be realizations of that FST in that state which did not satisfy this description. This was shown by arguing that for any F-state and person in it, he could be "permuted" so that he would remain in the same F-state while the description now would become false of him. But what prevents this in the case of mental descriptions? What prevents "permuting" a child so that he would be in the same state of the same FST but no longer be in a state truly describable, e.g., as "expecting to be given something to identify"?

A short answer is: this is impossible because the truth conditions of 'I expect to be given something to identify' are tied to the F-state in a way that the truth conditions of 'I have stimulated C fibers' are not. For, according to the hypothesis, the truth conditions of the mental description are such that if anyone is in a certain state of the postulated FST, then this description is true of him and its negation is incompatible with his being in this F-state. Unfortunately, because I do not possess this child's (or anyone's) complete FST description, I cannot prove this claim directly. But I can adduce evidence against its denial and so, support it indirectly.

Falsity of the hypothesis would entail that given any FST, any F-state in it, and any mental state, the supposition that someone has that FST and is in that F-state is logically consistent *both* with the supposition that he is in that mental state *and* with the supposition that he is not in that mental state.[18] In other words, his

---

18. Thus, for example, in "The Mental Life of Some Machines," Putnam appears to affirm a denial of the hypothesis as follows: "Quite different combinations of computing skills, beliefs, and rational preference functions can lead to exactly the same behavior, not only in the sense of the same actual behavior but in the sense of the same potential behavior under all possible circumstances" (in *Modern Materialism*, ed. O'Connor, p. 278).

being in that mental state is not completely determined by his F-state. If the hypothesis is true, then this is not so.[19]

More concretely, in the case of the child trained in fruit identification, denial of the hypothesis would entail the following: Although this child, competent in fruit identification, was told to identify the next object shown him, and as a result was put into such a state that if presented with an orange, he would say 'Orange', with a papaya, 'Papaya', etc., and when asked his state responded, 'I'm expecting to be given something to identify', nevertheless it is possible to conjecture that he did *not* "expect to be given something to identify." The claim must be then that the applicability of this state description depends on some additional variable (a private object?) that the conjecturer would vary on a permutation. For unless one supposes that mental descriptions are indeterminate in their truth value,[20] to refute the hypothesis one must isolate some parameter, independent of any FST, that affects which mental description is true of the subject (i.e., variation of which varies the truth value of the ascription). The hypothesis implies that no such variable exists. In discussing this conjecture, I will speak as though I possessed a complete FST-description of the child supporting the attribution in question and including any behavior relevant to it. The conjecturer will try to suppose a permutation that changes the truth value of the attribution, and I will argue against the possibility of doing this.

Notice first that the conjectured permutation must involve no change in what the child will say or do under any circumstances. For if a permutation changed the child's behavior, it would either (a) change his behavior so that it no longer accorded with the FST and hence would not refute the hypothesis, or else (b) change his behavior in some respect *not* mentioned in the FST and hence, by the assumption in the preceding paragraph, be irrelevant to the

19. The bearing of the hypothesis on the philosophical problem of skepticism about other minds here becomes obvious. The hypothesis is inconsistent with the skeptic's assumption that different incompatible mental state descriptions are compatible with the totality of possible outward manifestations. In another respect, however, the hypothesis perhaps vindicates the skeptic's position. For as will be shown later, the hypothesis entails that there is no procedure by which others can *conclusively* ascertain a subject's F-state (and hence, his mental state) by any amount of behavioral or input-output observation.

20. In the unlikely event that mental ascriptions are never determined in their truth value by anything, the hypothesis is false because no mental self-descriptions can satisfy Principle 2 or Principle 4.

truth of the attribution.[21] Not only must the child's actually exhibited behavior remain unchanged, but so must what he *would* have done under various unrealized hypothetical conditions. For an FST describes not only a person's actions in the situations that were actualized, but also what the person would have done in other circumstances. The hypothesis, in other words, has a monopoly on all relevant behavior, actual or possible. So I shall assume that in every circumstance, past, present, or future, actual or possible, the child acts as if he "expected to be given something to identify" at that time. And the conjecture is that somehow, in spite of all this, the child was *not* in this state.

Two facts immediately emerge. First, the conjecture is prima facie implausible. We are to suppose that this child who has been told to identify the next object shown him and as a result is in such a state that he will say 'Orange' when presented with an orange, etc., and who *says* he "expects . . . to identify," nevertheless is *not* "expecting . . . to identify." Certainly this is contrary to what anyone would be inclined to say of the child on the basis of these facts. Second, it is difficult to see what remains for the conjecturer to permute (with the desired effect). Behavior is excluded, as shown above. He might change the child's nervous system, but the alteration would have to produce no change in the operation of the child in accord with his FST—either some minor neural change or else a major one whose overall outcome is still a system fitting the same FST. But such a change, eventuating in no difference in what the subject says or does in any possible situation, would constitute no reason to claim that the child did not "expect . . . to identify." The change in the operation of his nervous system might have no bearing at all on his mental state; indeed, since, by assumption, the change makes no difference in what he says or does, the most tenable claim would be that the subject is not even sensitive to it. In any case, the conjecturer would have no justification for a claim that this permutation would affect the child's mental state. Similar difficulties would beset a permutation of "private objects." Even positing something beyond the subject's functional state (perhaps something to which only he has access), what reason is there to think that permutation of it would affect the subject's mental state? This is especially so since noth-

21. This assumption is completely fair. The discovery of relevant behavior not mentioned in the FST only shows that *this* FST is inadequate. The conjecturer is supposed to be showing that *no* FST is adequate.

ing said or done varies, including all the mental reports he gives. The child still would look exactly like someone who "expected . . . to identify," and no evidence indicating otherwise ever would arise. So even if this "something" were permuted, there still would be no reason why we should suppose then that the child did not "expect to be given something to identify."

The case against the conjectured permutation actually rests on more than its prima facie implausibility and the impossibility of giving reasons in support of it. There are positive reasons for thinking such a permutation impossible. Since the only mental change mentioned in the conjecture is that the child no longer "expect to be given something to identify," I ask whether *all other* mental descriptions previously true of him would remain so after the permutation. If, for example, before the permutation it was true to say that the child "heard and understood his mother's request," "believed he was going to be given something to identify," "wanted to get it right," "was waiting and watching for something to be shown him," etc., then do all these other mental descriptions still apply? If so, we are being asked to suppose that the child heard and understood his mother's request, believed he was going to be given something to identify, wanted to get it right, and was waiting and watching for something to be shown to him— and yet was *not* expecting to be given something to identify! It is very difficult to see how this could be so (indeed, the supposition may even involve a contradiction).

This conflict arises because many different interlocking mental state descriptions usually are applicable to a person at the same time. Diagrammatically this is illustrated in Table 3–14.

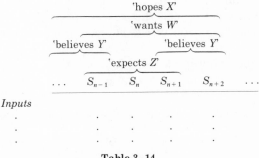

Table 3–14.

As represented in this diagram, the descriptions, e.g., 'hopes X', 'wants W', and 'expects Z' (but evidently not 'believes Y') are true of a realization when it is in state S_n. These different mental descriptions can be so interrelated in their meanings or implications that whenever certain of them are true of a subject, certain others also must be true of him.[22] (For example, limiting consideration only to the portion of FST shown in the illustration above, necessarily, if a realization "wants W," then it either "Believes Y" or "expects Z.") This explains the difficulty in supposing that the child "heard and understood his mother's request, believed he was going to be given something to identify, wanted to get it right, and was waiting and watching for something to be shown him," and yet was *not* "expecting to be given something to identify." If those descriptions (or those descriptions plus others) are true of him, then it *must* be true to say of him, "he expects . . . to identify." If the expectation description does not apply, then neither can all those other mental descriptions.

Thus anyone proposing an alternative mental description of the subject also must revise many other mental descriptions formerly accepted as true of him at that time. This becomes extremely complicated because each further change may necessitate more changes, which necessitate further changes, and so on. In fact, in order to achieve an overall mental description consistent with the originally proposed permutation, the conjecturer must, in general, give a *radical mental redescription* of the subject, changing intention descriptions, desire descriptions, belief descriptions, sensation descriptions, etc. And not only must all these descriptions fit with each other, they must also be compatible with all the behavior in his FST. This adds further difficulties because each of these other descriptions may carry, by itself or together with others, additional implications about the subject's behavior in other circumstances. Yet the redescription must involve no change in the operation of the subject in accordance with the FST.

To appreciate how quickly difficulties multiply, let us watch the conjecturer try to construct a radical mental redescription. He

22. In "Robots: Machines or Artificially Created Life?" Putnam remarks: "Psychological states are characterizable only in terms of their relations to each other (as well as behavior, etc.), and not as dispositions which can be 'unpacked' without coming back to the very psychological predicates that are in question" (in *Modern Materialism*, ed. O'Connor, p. 244).

proposes that the child in this F-state does not "expect to be given something to identify." But the child still *says* that he expects to be given something to identify. How is this fact accommodated? Perhaps the conjecturer will attempt to reconcile it by supposing that the child *believes* that he expects to be given something to identify but is *mistaken* in this belief. However, this encounters immediate difficulties. The child appears to understand all the words he uses, he can explain what his mother meant, he showed no signs of surprise when presented with something for identification, and he will, in fact, identify the next object shown him in the appropriate way. So how, in this case, is his belief that he "expects to be given something to identify" mistaken? Perhaps, then, the conjecturer will begin his radical mental redescription by supposing that the child does *not* believe he will be given something to identify and hence does not expect it. But then why did he *say* otherwise? "Well, he was lying." But is this the same child who *trusts* his mother and *wishes* to please her? (Evidently the conjecturer must now change motive and belief descriptions.) Why did the child lie? "Perhaps he thought his mother was going to trick him and would not really give him something to identify, so he did not expect it; but he lied and said that he did expect this because he believed that doing otherwise would infuriate her and he wanted to avoid this." (Our original child seems to have turned a bit neurotic.) But what is his attitude toward such a deceit? If he likes being tricked, one would expect him to seek out such situations (which, by hypothesis, the original child does not do). "Well, conjecture then that he dislikes it." But if that is so, how would he react if his mother said, e.g., "I'm sorry, I know I've been treating you dreadfully; forgive me and I won't do it again"? Presented with this sentence, the original child would not know what his mother was talking about and (as I shall suppose we see from his FST) respond with incomprehension (e.g., say, "I don't know what you mean"). In contrast, a child satisfying the new radical mental redescription presumably would know what his mother meant and respond affirmatively. But this diverges from the FST. So this redescription is blocked.

The above does not prove conclusively the impossibility of a radical mental redescription compatible with the imagined FST. Perhaps further suppositions could reconcile the conjecture with the behavior cited. Without possessing a complete functional description of the child, the question cannot be decided with certainty.[23] But although not conclusive, the argument does *support* the claim that only one overall mental description is compatible with the FST-description. The options open to the conjecturer narrow rapidly, and he is forced to suppositions of ever-increasing intuitive implausibility. By extrapolation, it seems likely that no radical mental redescription compatible with the FST can be formed. And if this is so, then mental descriptions can satisfy Principle 4, supporting part (2) of the hypothesis.

The similarity between the reasoning used above and that used in daily life to decide between alternative mental descriptions of someone further confirms the hypothesis. In a courtroom, the question arises: What was the assassin's state of mind? The defense claims the act was unpremeditated: the defendant had been studying mysticism and was thrown into a wild and irresponsible state by the mirrors in the room. But then, asks the prosecution, how did he happen to be carrying a gun at the time and why on the previous day had he practiced rapid firing on a pistol range and asked the rangemaster for ammunition "that must not misfire"? The defense answers with another set of motive and belief descriptions: he was carrying a gun because he believed his life in danger, he was pistol shooting because he had decided to take up the sport, and he asked for this ammunition because misfires irritated him. The prosecution challenges by asking about past inputs: What happened to put him in fear of his life, what made him decide to take up this sport, and why was he concerned about misfires since none had occurred that day? And why had he written in his diary that he must kill the victim? How can these facts be reconciled with the psychological descriptions proposed by the defense? The deliberating jurors entertain similar questions. Would the defendant have acted the same way with no mirrors in the room? If he had been unable to shoot the victim that day, would he have made a similar attempt another day? And so on. They treat his behavior in various circumstances as evidence of the nature of his FST and use mentalistic words as theoretical terms to abstract and discuss various aspects of "what he would have done if. . . ."[24]

23. If we had a complete FST, the matter would be simpler to decide because we then could employ a strategy of searching through it for responses incompatible with each new supposition. Whether there could be a decision procedure here I do not know. If not, defeating an alternative general mental description simply would be a matter of ingeniously asking the right questions.

24. I am not suggesting that the jurors would recognize this description of their activity.

The mentalistic descriptions offered by the defense suggest that his FST has one configuration while those offered by the prosecution suggest that it has another, and after hearing the arguments, the jurors try to decide who is correct.[25] That inquiries into someone's state of mind proceed in this way corroborates the hypothesis; it is exactly what one would expect if it is true.

The states for which confirming the hypothesis is most difficult are those of sensation.[26] This is largely because no one yet knows what a perception-FST would look like (that is, an FST such that a realization of it would have all the properties of something having sensory consciousness or awareness).[27] An FST of this sort would amount to a theory of perception, and my present inability to exhibit one does not invalidate the theory. Partial confirmation of the present hypothesis provides reason to think that such FSTs exist, but only subsequent research in perceptual psychology can substantiate this.

Readers desiring further elaboration and defense of Principle 4 should turn next to Appendix IV.

3. Some Philosophical Implications of the Hypothesis

This section develops some important logical implications of the hypothesis of the model (or "functionalist hypothesis," as I shall also call it, intending by these words to refer always, of

25. Lest theoretical uncertainty about the uniqueness of fit of mental state descriptions to F-states undermine faith in the judicial process, I note that it can be independently argued that all that is really important here *is* the defendant's functional state, something that is a perfectly determinate matter and one of the sort fixed by publicly observable kinds of things. Certainly I do not claim that there is any automatic procedure leading step-by-step from observations of inputs and outputs to full and totally certain knowledge of a subject's functional states. (Indeed, in Appendix II it is proved that there can exist no such procedure.) But even if my hypothesis were false, and mental state descriptions had different truth conditions from those postulated (or no truth conditions), functional descriptions true of the subject still would exist and be determined exclusively by reference to facts of the externally observable sort.

26. In Chapter 2, certain perceptual phenomena were discussed specifically to show that the existence of apparent objects in these cases does not require postulating private objects. These phenomena were treated as degenerate cases of full-blown perception, but no account of full-blown perception was given.

27. A system capable of perception presumably has many properties uncaptured in any of the simple example FSTs given here. For instance, a perceiver often is able still to respond appropriately to things no longer present to his senses without recalling a verbal description derived at the time (e.g., someone says, "Tell what it looked like," and he does so).

course, only to my version of the hypothesis as formulated previously). In this section it is demonstrated that, far from being trivial or cognitively vacuous, this hypothesis has many fundamental theoretical and philosophical implications. (Empirical and experimental consequences are developed in Chapter 4.)

A widely endorsed view holds that a person cannot be mistaken in his belief about his mental state.[28] According to this view, a person who affirms 'I have a pain' either cannot be wrong or, if he is wrong, his error always can be attributed to a verbal slip or to not understanding the meaning of the words he uses. Necessarily, a subject who understands the words he is using and who sincerely reports that he is in a certain mental state is in that state.[29] Some philosophers have taken this incorrigibility as the distinguishing mark of the mental; others have denied that it even exists.

My hypothesis illuminates this question by showing that although as stated, the incorrigibility thesis probably is false, it only narrowly misses the truth. Thus while its opponents are right in detail, its proponents are right in substance. The incorrigibility thesis entails that for any mental self-description, if a subject (a) understands the language, and (b) speaks sincerely, then (c) he never will produce this mental self-description when false. The hypothesis entails that for any mental self-description, there is an FST such that if a subject (a') is a realization of it, and (b') is in certain states of it, then (c) he never will produce this mental self-description when false. These two claims are closely parallel but slightly dissimilar. The consequent, (c), is the same in both assertions but the antecedents differ. Realizations of the postulated FSTs can speak and understand the language, so having the postulated FSTs entails mastery of the language. But the postulated FSTs also include nonlinguistic behavior: for example, bodily reactions to nonverbal stimuli. So the postulated FSTs incorporate more than the rules of the language. Condition (a') entails condition (a) but not vice versa. So (a') is a stronger condition than (a).

28. Here the claim is not that a subject could not misobserve or misrecognize the contents of his mind, but that he could not hold a mistaken belief about it.

29. Many philosophers have asserted this. See, for example, Norman Malcolm, *Knowledge and Certainty* (Englewood Cliffs, N.J.: Prentice-Hall, 1963), pp. 84–85; Sydney Shoemaker, *Self-Knowledge and Self-Identity* (Ithaca: Cornell University Press, 1963), p. 168; Robert C. Coburn, "Shaffer on the Identity of Mental States and Brain Processes," *Journal of Philosophy*, 60 (1963), 91.

Second, although *some* of the ways in which a person may come to produce a false mental self-description are handled *both* by condition (b) of the incorrigibility thesis and by my hypothesis, *others* are accommodated only by the hypothesis. On my hypothesis, there is no difficulty over the possibility that, in addition to the states in which, necessarily, a given mental description truly applies, a subject's FST also may contain other states in which the speaker produces it when false. For example, a subject's FST may provide for outputting some mental self-description in both state S_n and state S_m, as shown in Table 3–15,

	S_n		S_m	
$\ldots$	$\ldots$	$\ldots$	$\ldots$	$\ldots$
i_k	S_o (*utter 'I am ϕ'*)		S_p (*utter 'I am ϕ'*)	

Table 3–15.

where the self-description 'I am ϕ' is true of a realization when in S_n but false of him when in S_m. This can happen in a variety of ways. (1) Most simply, when in certain states (e.g., a cooperative mood), the FST may call for repeating verbatim any given verbal input. So if someone says to a realization of this FST when in one of those states, "Repeat after me: 'I am in pain'," the realization may produce that self-description when false. The incorrigibility thesis handles this case successfully by requiring that the subject be sincere or honestly believe what he says. (2) The FST may be such that a realization of it could produce a false mental self-description with intent to deceive (i.e., tell a lie). For example, just as he can perform other actions as means to some end, a realization may be able to compute the social effects of his utterance and so produce a mental self-description (e.g., 'I have a headache') when false, as a means to some result (e.g., releasing himself from some obligation). The incorrigibility thesis also accommodates this case by its requirement that the subject believe what he says. So cases (1) and (2) both are handled by condition (b) of the incorrigibility thesis.

Where it works, condition (b) of the incorrigibility thesis succeeds because generally when a subject is in the mental state of "*believing that* he is in mental state ϕ," he is also in mental state ϕ. That is, for most F-states in which the mental state description 'p' is true of him, the mental state description 'believes that p' also is true of him. For most F-states in which 'he has a pain' is truly predicable, for example, so is 'believes that he has a pain', and vice versa. For this reason, generally if someone "believes that he is in mental state ϕ," he is in mental state ϕ. But this rule fails in at least two kinds of cases, providing counterinstances to the incorrigibility thesis. (3) In Chapter 1, the example was given of a hypnotized man who, as all the evidence indicated and as he subsequently agreed, for a time believed that he had a pain although he did not. Here he was put into a state that had properties qualifying it for the mental description "believes that p is true" but did not have properties qualifying it for the mental description 'p'. Similar cases can arise with complex mental states. For example, it is notorious that a person sometimes can believe that he acts from a certain motive but later agree that his motive was different. In such states, a subject could (a) with understanding of the language and (b) speaking sincerely, produce a false mental self-description. So such cases are counterinstances to the incorrigibility thesis. But they do not refute the claim entailed by my hypothesis. For such a subject obviously is not in one of the states of a postulated FST in which the self-description is always true.[30] (4) Another counterinstance is the following. In the computational process by which he constructs a certain mental self-description, a subject may go astray or err with the result that he arrives at a false mental self-description. This was illustrated in Chapter 2 with the example of the awakened dreamer who made a truncated mistake in recalling and recounting the apparent events of his dream, and so gave a false dream self-description. One also could make a truncated mistake in describing the apparent object in a complex hallucination, and this could result in the production of a false mental self-description. There seems to be no reason why the subject should not "be sincere" or "honestly believe" this description to be true. So unless these mistakes in description somehow are attributed to incomplete mastery of the language, these cases also constitute counterinstances to the incorrigibility thesis. So although normally when condition (b') obtains, so will condition (b), and vice versa, this is not invariably true. There are cases

30. One should remember that the important thing about the hypothesis is its postulating that such F-states *exist*. (Otherwise, this reply might seem empty.)

that satisfy condition (b) but falsify the consequent (c). For the reason given, however, none of these cases satisfies condition (b').

Strictly speaking, then, the incorrigibility thesis is refuted by cases consistent with the hypothesis. Nevertheless, I think it is reasonable to regard the incorrigibility thesis as an attempt to underscore those features of mental self-description characterized by the present account. The property of mental self-descriptions that philosophers inaccurately have termed their "incorrigibility" is really their FST-determinedness. Subjects are not necessarily correct in their mental self-descriptions, but they would be if they had the proper functional organization. In this sense, I think it can be said that the hypothesis explains the facts underlying the ill-named "incorrigibility" of mental self-descriptions.

The hypothesis also illuminates the facts behind the frequent and familiar claim that subjects stand in a "unique" or "privileged" epistemological relationship to their own mental states. In the first place, as has been explained, the procedure by which a subject arrives at a mental description of himself generally differs from that employed by anyone else. Others obtain the description by observation of that of which it is true (viz., the subject himself), which is not how he obtains it. In his case the description issues directly from the state it describes.[31] While everyone else arrives at it transitionally, the subject arrives at it nontransitionally. In this respect, then, the subject's epistemological position vis-à-vis his mental state is *unique*. In judging that the subject is in a certain mental state, moreover, others must depend on observed behavioral manifestations (including the subject's report). This procedure is fallible, and they may judge erroneously. Not only is it possible (although unlikely) for them to misobserve his behavior, but no series of behavioral observations conclusively establishes someone's FST or functional state.[32] The subject himself, however, need not fear incorrect observations as a source of error, since he does not arrive at his self-descriptions by observation.[33] He is *in* the state at issue, and as already explained, if suitably programmed, automatically

31. No detailed account has been offered of the exact processes by which most kinds of mental self-descriptions (intention descriptions, belief descriptions, etc.) are obtained. As explained in Chapter 2, in some cases a subject obtains the description by truncated observation and description, but many mental self-descriptions are obtained in other ways.

32. This is proved in Appendix II.

33. See Chapter 1, Section 5.

will produce only true mental self-descriptions. In *this* sense, his epistemological position is "privileged." So without positing the existence of something that can be observed only by the subject, the theory explains respects in which the subject's epistemological relationship to his own mental states is privileged and unique.

The logical relation of functionalism to "mind-body dualism" depends on the exact claims made by the latter.[34] My hypothesis is *formally* consistent with the following two dualistic contentions: (1) A person is composed of two nonabstract entities, one physical and the other spiritual or immaterial in substance ("dualism"), and (2) causal processes can propagate in either or both directions between these two entities ("interactionism"). Nothing in the functionalist hypothesis as I have formulated it precludes a compound entity of this sort from satisfying the general characterization in relation to mental self-descriptions. To be sure, on my application of the model, the *inputs to* and *outputs from* the realizing system are physical, but nowhere has it been postulated that realizations of FSTs determining mental descriptions are entirely constituted of physical parts. It still could be hypothesized, for example, that causal processes originating in external stimulus objects affect an incorporeal part of a person through that person's physical sense receptors, thereby leading to other changes (called, perhaps, "acts of will") that activate bodily mechanisms causing behavioral output, the entire process, including all changes of state in both physical and nonphysical subcomponents, taking place in a manner satisfying the mind-determining FSTs postulated by the hypothesis. With arrows representing the propagation of causal processes, this uneliminated dualistic possibility is flow-charted in Figure 2. Nothing in the principles so far contradicts the supposition that Mr. Smith, for example, to whom we apply the characterization is a system of this sort. So the hypothesis is logically compatible with claims (1) and (2).[35]

Of course, the *denial* of dualistic postulates (1) and (2) also is compatible with my hypothesis. In fact, its account of mental phenomena is extremely well suited for development into a pure

---

34. For an exposition of various dualisms, see C. D. Broad, *The Mind and Its Place in Nature* (1925; London: Routledge & Kegan Paul, 1968), chapter III.

35. Perhaps I should remark here that I know of no sound justification for these two claims, however.

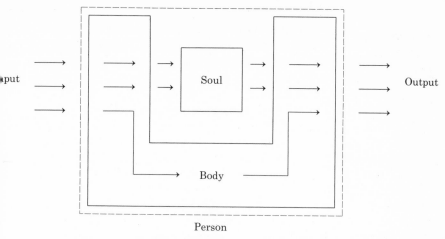

Input

Output

Figure 2. Dualistic conception of realizing system

physicalism. The model may be transformed into a completely materialistic theory of mind simply by adding to it the very plausible assumption that in humans the postulated FSTs are entirely realized by the nervous system and associated bodily mechanisms. This view I shall call "physicalistic functionalism" or "functional-state materialism." According to it, FSTs of the postulated kind are realized in each person by a giant, astronomically complicated switching network whose frequent changes from one overall excitation configuration to another are modulated by stimulations from the outside environment (input arriving in the form of complex patterns of neural impulses delivered simultaneously over millions of afferent channels from various sense organs) and whose output signals are transmitted through efferent pathways to effector organs generating overt bodily behavior. The conclusion that this material system in its successive physicochemical states is the concrete mechanical realization of the subject's successive mental states only requires, on the hypothesis, assuming that both the next state of the central net and the efference it generates are determined, at least probabilistically, by its current sensory input plus its own overall structural state at the time it receives that input. (Notice, too, that the "mass action" of the brain [i.e., the involvement of much of the whole brain in the performance of each function] as postulated, e.g., by Karl Lashley, is rendered intelligible by this wholistic model of

the neuropsychological relationship.) The evidence presently
available for these physicalistic assumptions appears in standard
sources.

That FSTs of the postulated kind can be implemented neurally
will not seem implausible to anyone acquainted with the theory
of formal neural networks, and readers who familiarize themselves in greater detail with its beautiful theoretical analysis will
be rewarded with a far deeper appreciation of the meaning and
implications of my hypothesis.[36] Abstracting from the many physiological characteristics that distinguish neurons found even in
different parts of the nervous system of a single individual within
a species, the McCulloch-Pitts theory formally studies the properties of neural networks whose elements, called "formal neurons," are idealizations of actual neural fibers or cells. A formal
neuron is assumed to have a certain number of input surfaces
capable of receiving signals and a certain number of output
branches with endbulbs capable of transmitting impulses to affect
other neurons to which they are connected. A *receptor neuron* is
assumed to carry an action potential or "fire" if and only if it is
stimulated by an environmental influence (e.g., light, heat, pressure) of the proper sort and intensity. The conventional sche-
matics of Figure 3 show such a cell with five *excitatory endbulbs*
at the end of its axonal arborization.

· impulse flow

→

Figure 3. Receptor neuron   *Figure 4.* Effector neuron

Effector neurons, conventionally represented as in Figure 4, are
elements connected to nonneural structures such as muscle fibers
or glandular cells that are activated when an impulse traveling
down the neuron reaches them. Receptor cells are indirectly connected to effector cells by an intermediate network of *central cells*
or "interneurons." Interneurons are assumed to be connected
only to other neurons and to fire if and only if they receive input

36. For a readable introduction, see James T. Culbertson, *The Minds of Robots*
(Urbana, Ill.: University of Illinois Press, 1963), chaps. 3 and 4.

signals or stimulation exceeding their "thresholds." (A cell with a threshold of n requires a total of at least n impulses simultaneously synapsing on it to be triggered.) Figure 5 is a schematic representation of a simple circuit consisting of two receptors synapsing on a central cell with a threshold of 2. Cell c will fire if and only if impulses reach it from both input cells, a and b, at approximately the same time, so it functions as what computer scientists call an "AND gate." Neuron f in Figure 6 fires if either

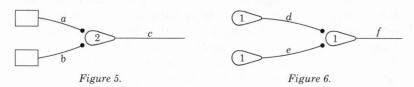

Figure 5.   Figure 6.

cell d or cell e fires (as well as if both do), so it functions as an "OR gate." Synaptic connections between neurons can be inhibitory as well as excitatory; conventionally, inhibitory endbulbs are schematically represented by a hollow circle, and excitatory endbulbs by a solid circle. Figure 7 shows the synapse of cell k which has an inhibitory endbulb and cell p with an excitatory endbulb on cell m which has a threshold of 1. Where '1' represents

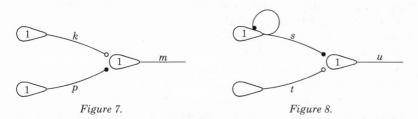

Figure 7.   Figure 8.

"fires" and '0' represents "is quiet," the input-output characteristics of this circuit viewed as an isolated structure are given by Table 3–16, which, it will be noted, has the form of a logical truth-table.

k	p	m
0	0	0
0	1	1
1	0	0
1	1	0

Table 3–16.

The characteristics of this network correspond to the logical truth function "p and not k" (i.e., $m \equiv (p \ \& \sim k)$). The network in Figure 8 features a small "*reverberating loop*"; once activated, firings on cell s continue to trigger successive firings on the same cell. So cell u will fire if and only if cell t does not fire ($u \equiv \sim t$). Thus neurons with inhibitory endbulbs can perform essentially the same function as what computer terminology calls an "inverter"—that is, an element that can be used to compute the logical function of negation. Since, as every logician knows, any finite truth-functional compound is expressible using only the simple truth-functional relationships already distinguished (negation and conjunction, or negation and alternation), it follows that for every possible finite truth function, a neural net can be formed that implements it. Like vacuum tubes or transistors, formal neurons are "universal elements": any prescribed input-output characteristics can be obtained from some network built out of them. The theory of formal neural networks studies complicated circuits built up from these elements with their input and output surfaces suitably interconnected with arbitrary complexity. Such a system's "functioning" is defined by singling out some of the inputs to the entire system, and some of its outputs, and then describing what original stimuli on the former are to cause what ultimate behavior of the latter. The analysis by McCulloch and Pitts shows that any "functioning" in this sense that can be specified logically, strictly, and unambiguously in a finite number of words also can be realized by such a formal neural network.[37] This means, in other words, that for any specified stimulus-response characteristics, a neural net can be designed mediating that behavior. Since a finite FST (whose "inputs" are objects or events capable of affecting the organism's sensory receptors and whose "outputs" include motor movements) is such a specification, it follows that FSTs of the postulated sort can be realized or implemented by neural networks.

(This possibility shows that if my functionalist hypothesis is true, it indeed solves the classical mind-body problem. For the hypothesis entails that a neural network (plus associated bodily

---

37. John von Neumann, "The General and Logical Theory of Automata," in *The World of Mathematics*, ed. James R. Newman (New York: Simon and Schuster, 1956), IV, 2089–2090; also Culbertson, *Minds of Robots*, p. 43; also Donald M. MacKay, "Mentality in Machines," *Aristotelian Society, Supplementary Volume 26* (1952), 85.

mechanisms) can be in the mental or psychological states determined by the implemented FST.[38] So the theory explains how a completely physical or material structure could undergo mental states, including any state of consciousness. The theory's ability to explain how a purely physical system could be the subject of any mental state shows that it indeed solves the "mind-body problem" as traditionally conceived.)

To return for a moment to the topic of the hypothesis's logical relationship to various forms of dualistic interactionism, although, as shown earlier, my functionalist axioms (without the additional physicalistic assumption) are *formally* compatible with a (weak) dualistic interactionism, the foregoing physiological facts show that the postulate of a special spiritual or immaterial subcomponent now is completely gratuitous and unnecessary, and so, for this (and other) reasons, therefore ought not to be made. For reconsider that nonspatial, immaterial "mind" or "soul" whose postulation Figure 2 represents. Consider this entity itself in isolation simply as an input-output system. The physical events in the body (e.g., excitations of neural fibers in secondary sensory projection areas) to which this entity allegedly responds (or by which it allegedly is affected) can be viewed as "inputs" to it. And the physical events that this entity by its operations allegedly causes or produces in the body can be regarded as its "outputs." (Various dualistic interactionisms differ, of course, in their conception of the modus operandi of the coupling between the two postulated components, but on one specific theory the successive inputs might be, for example, the series of differently configured ensembles of impulses on the totality of afferent peripheral neural fibers, and the postulated immaterial subcomponent (the "mind") might guide or affect the body indirectly by raising or lowering the thresholds or "resistances" at various synaptic junctions.) Thus, presumably, for any possible immaterial subcomponent ("mind"), an FST would exist specifying, for each possible sequence of such inputs, the sequence of such outputs it would produce. But then, as was explained earlier, a *physical* neural network also could be formed that implements this same FST and performs all the same operations as the postulated immaterial subcomponent. That is, for any "mind" or

38. Thus Locke was correct as well as candid when he confessed that he did not see why a thinking substance must be immaterial.

"soul" S_i, considered simply as an input-output system (i.e., a black box with certain input-output characteristics), there can exist a completely physical system, $Phys(S_i)$, that satisfies the same input-output function (i.e., would respond to all the same possible sequences of inputs from the original brain and body by producing all the same sequences of neural output effects). Thus, if the postulated immaterial subcomponent somehow were disengaged or causally detached from the body and the neural surrogate network attached in its place, not only would the resulting body behave in all the same ways in all the same circumstances as the original person, but it also would, if my hypothesis is true, be capable of undergoing all the same mental states as the previously dualistic person. Combining this conclusion with the fact (demonstrated in Chapters 1 and 2) that if the hypothesis is correct, a nonspatial subcomponent need not be posited as a harbor for "introspectively revealed private mental objects," the conclusion follows that a dualistic hypothesis now is unnecessary. And since, as is agreed universally, the hypothesis of dualistic interactionism involves special theoretical difficulties that do not arise for purely physicalistic theories (e.g., problems in understanding how a material body and an incorporeal spirit could interact), the conclusion is strongly supported that even the weak hypothesis of dualistic interactionism should be rejected.

We have seen that if my functionalist axioms (*minus* physicalistic assumptions) are correct, then although a modest dualistic interactionism *could*, logically, still be true, such a postulate seems unwarranted and unlikely. However, my axioms are strictly and *formally incompatible* with a *stronger dualism* positing, in addition, (3), that the truth or falsity of the attribution of mentalistic descriptions to a person depends only on the state of that person's nonphysical subcomponent ("mind" or "soul"), and that if no such subcomponent exists, the system cannot be in mental states. The theory composed of dualistic claims (1), (2), and (3) will be called "supplemented dualism." Since supplemented dualism postulates that mental states are states of a nonphysical *subcomponent* of a person while my hypothesis postulates that they are states of the entire system realizing the FST, perhaps it is not surprising that each should exclude the other. The incompatibility of supplemented dualism with our functionalist hypothesis is seen as follows. If supplemented dualism were true, then an entity could, logically, have or be the subject of

mental states only if it had a nonphysical or immaterial subcomponent. Thus, if supplemented dualism were true, then a
system without a nonphysical subcomponent could not have
mental states. But if our functionalist hypothesis is correct, then
a system could have mental states without having a nonphysical
subcomponent. Thus, it is not the case that both our functionalist
hypothesis and supplemented dualism are correct. Therefore, if
the hypothesis is correct, supplemented dualism is false.

A currently popular version of the "mind-body identity theory"
known as *central state materialism* claims that mental or psychological states are identical to "brain states" or "central states."
What is the logical relationship of this claim to physicalistic
functionalism? Debaters of central state materialism tend to be
vague about the exact nature or definition of the "brain states"
or "central states" whose alleged identity with mental states
they discuss, but as illustrations they cite such state descriptions
as "stimulation of the C fibers,"[39] the "brain state in which the
nocioceptive neurons in the thalamus and the cortex are firing,"[40]
"physico-chemical workings of the central nervous system,"[41]
"physico-chemical states of the brain,"[42] and even just "patterns
of electrical discharge in space."[43] So a specific example of a
psychophysical state-identity claim of the form in question apparently would be, e.g., "Pain is identical to activation of the
C fibers."

From their illustrations, it seems clear that the "brain states"
or "central states" whose identity with psychological states is
posited by central state materialists are what I have been calling
"structural states" (of the brain or body). (Whatever they are,
"central states" certainly are not functionally defined.) In general, a *structural state* of a system can be defined or specified by a
list of some or all of the system's parts or subcomponents, a
description of some of their individual states or properties (e.g.,
"excited," "quiet," "charged," "conducting"), and a specification
of some set of causal connections, interactive couplings, or other
relationships between these parts. Each of the following thus

39. Putnam, "Minds and Machines," pp. 85f.
40. Jaegwon Kim, "Properties, Laws and Identity Theory," *Monist*, 56 (April
1972), 183.
41. Armstrong, *Materialist Theory*, p. 89.
42. *Ibid.*, p. 90.
43. *Ibid.*, p. 76.

qualifies as an example of a "structural state description" of an entity of the indicated kind: a blueprint of a house, an "exploded diagram" of a typewriter, and the circuit diagram of a neural network specifying the neurons active at an instant, some of their individual properties, and their synaptic junctions or other interactive relationships. Thus a specific "structural state" of a nervous system might be conceived of as a configuration in space and time of its various anatomical components, each in its own momentary individual physiological state (e.g., firing, quiet), coupled together in synaptic or other connections having certain thresholds or other specific properties. When impulses are on different neurons, or interconnective relationships are changed, the system is in a different structural state. The specification or definition of a "structural state of the body" presumably then can be given by a list of anatomical components, a description of their individual states ("excited," "quiet," etc.), and a description of their physical interrelationships. Various distinct simultaneous structural states of the body are definable by listing different bodily subcomponents, different individual states, or different interrelationships.

Assuming the "central states" or "brain states" discussed are indeed structural states of the brain or body, central state materialism then asserts or implies that mental or psychological states are identical to structural states of the realizing system. Notice that an *identity of states* is here postulated: the relationship alleged is *identity* (' = '), and the objects or entities claimed to be "identical" are certain *states*. On this point, central state materialism and functional state materialism diverge. Both theories agree that "mental" or "psychological" states are actually states of nothing other than a material body, but the two theories conflict regarding the nature of these states. My hypothesis implies that psychological states are functionally determined, while central state materialism maintains that a material system's psychological states are identical to certain of its structural states.

In general, to assert "*A* is identical to *B*" (or *A* = *B*) is to use '*A*' and '*B*' as if these symbols named objects. In particular, to postulate that "*State X* is identical to *State Y*" is to treat the terms '*State X*' and '*State Y*' as if they designated entities. But if "states" are going to be treated as entities, what sort of entities should they be treated as, and what are the criteria for their identity? Whatever they may be, "states" clearly are *not* what metaphysics calls "concrete particulars." A concrete object or particular (typewriter, person, or whatever), in the course of time, may pass into and out of the *same* state on many separate occasions (e.g., a flipflop can be "set" or "reset," a neuron can be "excited" or "quiet," a substance can be in a "solid" or "liquid" state, an automobile transmission can be "in gear" or "in neutral"), but its *state*, considered as an entity in linguistic or metaphysical abstraction from the system or object which is "in" that state, is not a concrete particular. In this respect, "states," in fact, seem similar to "properties" when these are hypostatized. To say, e.g., that "*x* is in a liquid state" seems hardly different from saying "*x* has the property of being liquid" or just "*x* is liquid." (Nominalists might complain that to talk of "states" as entities [e.g., "anger"] is simply to reify the corresponding linguistic state predicate ['*x* is angry'], just as similar treatment of adjectives ['hard', 'feminine', 'conscious'] yields abstract singular terms ['hardness', 'femininity', 'consciousness'] supposedly denoting the properties or qualities that concrete objects satisfying the adjectival description are said to "have.") If this is correct and "states" when reified resemble properties, then "states" as entities are *abstract entities* or *platonic objects*, i.e., abstract Forms or "universals" which concrete individuals can pass "into" or "out of" on various occasions.

Assuming that states are indeed abstract objects, for it to be true that mental states are identical to certain structural states of the brain and body, this claim must satisfy the truth conditions appropriate to claims of identity between abstract objects. Although it is unclear what the identity conditions appropriate to such entities in general are, the following seems plausible as a *necessary condition* for state identity: State X = State Y only if it is *not* physically possible for a system or structure to be in one of these states without being in the other. (By "physically possible" I mean "not in conflict with the [true] laws of nature"; a state of affairs is physically [or "naturally"] impossible if its existence would contradict or violate the true laws of nature.) This principle seems reasonable. For after all, if it is physically possible for an entity to be in *State X* without being in *State Y* (or vice versa), then *State X* and *State Y* hardly could be the same identical state. If they were identically the same state, then it would not be physically possible for something to be in the one state without being in the other (or to satisfy the one state description without satisfying the other). Talk of "possibilities" here is important. For example, one plausible candidate for ("contingent") state identity might be (a) the macrostate of having a high temperature ("being hot") with (b) the microstate of having its constituent molecules have high mean kinetic energy. Such an identification presumably would require, at minimum, a lawlike connection in nature between the two states. Just as the fact that every animal with a heart has kidneys, and vice versa, does not entail that the *property* of having a heart and the *property* of having kidneys are identical properties, so too if every hot object that ever has existed or will exist merely *happened* to consist of molecules with high mean kinetic energy, this fact would not suffice to establish the identity of the states. Mere coextensiveness of the associated state descriptions is insufficient for state identity. At the very least, coextensiveness of the state descriptions "in all physically possible worlds" is necessary. This being so, it follows that to refute a claim of state identity, it is unnecessary actually to *exhibit* a system which is in the one state without being in the other. Rather, it suffices simply to show that the laws of nature entail the (physical) *possibility* of something being in one of the states without being in the other. Identity of "the state of having a high temperature" with "the state of being composed of molecules having high mean kinetic energy," for example, certainly would be disproved if it were shown to be physically possible to create a hot object whose molecules did not have high mean kinetic energy. Strictly and logically speaking, it is *not* requisite for such a proof that an instance of such an object ever actually be produced or exist (laboratory requirements might exceed our resources, or we might simply choose to spend our time otherwise). To refute the identity claim, it would suffice simply to show that such a state of affairs is physically possible (even if it never has existed). *If* in some physically possible world, hot gases exist whose constituent molecules do not have high mean kinetic energy, then the state of having a high temperature and the state of having high mean kinetic energy of constituent molecules are not the same state. Similarly, identity of *State X* with *State Y* entails at least the physical impossibility of something being in the one state when not in the other. This metaphysical premise (for our subsequent reasoning) also could be expressed in a different mode: *State X* is identical with *State Y* only if the two corresponding linguistic state descriptions ('is in *State X*', 'is in *State Y*') are coextensive in all physically possible worlds. The important implication of this is that state-identity claims in some cases are refutable by purely theoretical reasoning. In particular, *if* it can be deduced from the laws of logic and nature that for any state P_k of the class or kind of states P, it is physically possible for a system to be in state M_i without being in state P_k, then this will prove that state M_i is not identical with any state of the kind P. Even a claim of only "contingent identity" is refuted if the laws of logic and nature can be shown to entail such a possibility.

In the paragraphs below, my version of a functionalist hypothesis, together with certain plausible additional assumptions about the natural world, is shown to entail that mental or psychological states are *not* "identical" to structural states of the realizing system (i.e., the body with nervous system, according to physicalistic functionalism). Loosely overviewed, the argument is basically that the hypothesis plus these assumptions entails that any given mental state can be realized by system hardware in a potential *infinity* of different structural states. Hence, for any given mental state and bodily structural state, it is physically possible for a system to be in the given mental state without being in that structural state (i.e., it is possible for an individual to satisfy the corresponding or associated mental state description *without* also satisfying the corresponding bodily structural state description). Therefore, this bodily structural state is not identical to the given mental state. But this was *any* bodily structural state; therefore the given mental state is not identical to any bodily structural state. The argument perhaps is best elucidated by an analogue with the simple typewriter model developed earlier.[44] In the case of typewriters, an identity statement corresponding analogously to the sort endorsed by central state materialism in reference to conscious systems would be the claim that "the state of being ready to type in all capital letters" is identical to some typewriter structural state (such as "the state of having its typewriter panel latched in the low position relative to its chassis"). Such an "identity thesis" could be refuted, of course, by showing that typewriters can exist that are "ready to type in capitals" without being in the latter state (as the physical possibility of constructing, e.g., an electric typewriter with a type-ball

44. This analogy functions purely and entirely as a heuristic aid to comprehension. The argument being illustrated is *not* an "argument from analogy," nor does the typewriter model play any other essential role in it.

instead of a type-panel demonstrates). Since indefinitely many concrete systems or mechanisms *in diverse structural states* all can implement the same functional state and since no unique structural state description is satisfied by all and only systems in this functional state, therefore this (typewriter) functional state is *not* identical to any (typewriter) structural state. Likewise, it follows from my hypothesis that "mental" or "psychological" states are realizable by infinitely many possible systems or mechanisms each in different structural states. Hence, for any bodily structural state P_k such that being in P_k is sufficient for being in mental state M_i, it is also physically possible to be in mental state M_i without being in bodily structural state P_k. Therefore, bodily structural state P_k is not identical to mental state M_i. (Readers with a distaste for details can skip to p. 176 without loss of continuity.)

Additional specific assumptions about the exact nature of the definition or specification of central state materialism's "brain states" or "central states" facilitates a more detailed and rigorous development of the foregoing basic argument. In particular, consider the implications of assuming that these "brain states" or "central states" are specifiable by what will be called "atomic structural state descriptions." An *atomic structural state description* of a system consists of:

(a) a finite list of component subparts or elements of a system or structure;

(b) a specification of interrelationships among some or all of these elements;

(c) a specification of properties of some or all of these individual elements.

One example of an "atomic structural state description" of a system would be a Newtonian description of an ensemble of bodies specifying their relative positions, momenta, and interactive relationships. Another example would be any typical schematic diagram of an electronic circuit showing the components (transistors, tubes, resistors, capacitors, etc.), some of the properties of these individual components (their resistance, capacitance, inductance, voltage, etc.), and their connective interrelationships (hard-wired connections, field effects, etc.). An instance closer to the present concern would be a complete (or partial) diagram of a nervous system showing constituent neural fibers, their individual physical properties or states at an instant (e.g., "firing," "in a refractory period," "quiet"), and relationships among them (e.g., excitatory synaptic junctions, inhibitory synaptic junctions, synaptic threshold values). A labeled circuit diagram of a neural network at one instant in time would constitute an "atomic structural state description" of it; at another instant, with impulses on a different subset of neurons in the net or changes in their interconnective relationships, the same network could be in a different atomic structural state. What will be called a "basic structural state description" is any finite disjunction of atomic structural state descriptions (e.g., 'x is in P_1 or x is in P_3'). (Notice that the term 'atomic' here is used in a logical rather than physical sense; the disjuncts are called "atomic" *not* because they describe the system at the level of molecules, atoms, or fundamental particles—although that, of course, is not precluded either—but rather as a way of distinguishing them from more complex logical compounds built up from them by means of truth-functional connectives.) Basic structural state descriptions of the body and nervous system will be called, for short, "basic bodily structural state descriptions."

As remarked earlier, the theory of neural networks, or more generally, circuit theory, assures us that any FST of the postulated sort can be realized by some neural network. (In this event, of course, the realization's passing from one F-state to another is made possible by the underlying circuitry's passing from one atomic structural state to another.) Thus, for any F-state in a postulated FST, there exists at least one basic structural state description such that a system's satisfying it (i.e., a net's being in this structural state) is sufficient for the system's being in that F-state. Assuming, moreover, the FST to be in the postulated class α, my hypothesis implies that being in this structural state is sufficient for being in the *psychological* state(s) determined by this F-state. Clearly, if central state materialists propose to "identify" a given psychological state, M_i, with some structural state, P_k, of the realizing system, then this structural state must be such that being in it suffices for being in M_i. So if there exists only one atomic structural state such that being in it is sufficient for being in M_i, M_i will be identified with it; otherwise, if M_i can be realized by several distinct atomic structural states (e.g., P_1, P_2, ..., and P_n), then presumably mental state M_i will be identified with the basic structural state defined by the logical disjunction of these atomic structural states (e.g., "a is in $M_i \equiv a$

is in P_1 or a is in P_2 or . . . or a is in P_n."). The falsity of any such identification now will be shown.

Proof that basic bodily structural states are not identical to mental states is easily accomplished by adding to our other contingent assumptions about the natural world the following corollary from the theory of circuits: If a neural network satisfying atomic structural state description P_k which lists n subcomponents can realize a given set of FSTs or F-states, then so can *another network* which (a) satisfies atomic structural state description P_j which lists m component parts, where integer m is greater than integer n, but which (b) does not satisfy the original state description P_k. In effect, this principle asserts that for any system that can be in a given F-state, it is physically possible for there to exist a different system containing, in an essential way, more component parts yet realizing the same FST (i.e., having the same input-output characteristics). This assumption is highly plausible. To illustrate it very simply, suppose that a given neural circuit contains somewhere in it three interneurons joined together in series with the synaptic thresholds indicated in Figure 9.

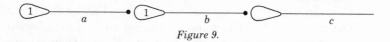

Figure 9.

Then an impulse on fiber a will cause b to fire, which in turn will excite neuron c. This simple structure, which functions to relay signals from a to c, is equivalently replaceable in the net by the subcircuit in Figure 10 which employs five neurons.

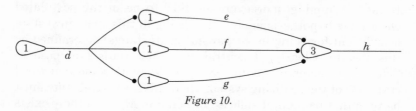

Figure 10.

In this subcircuit, an impulse on fiber d will trigger simultaneous impulses on the three neurons e, f, and g, which in combination will fire cell h. Notice that although this subcircuit contains more components than the first, it relays exactly the same information from the leftmost cell to the rightmost as did the first, and any network in which the first subcircuit was embedded would function identically if the first subcircuit were replaced by the second. Also notice that each of the five elements in the second circuit is *contained essentially* (in the strict sense that if it were removed or rendered inoperative, the system no longer would function in the same way). The second circuit contains essentially more elements or components than the first but still performs exactly the same input-output function. This is a very simple illustration of the general principle that for any neural network satisfying a given FST, there can exist another network containing more subcomponents that also satisfies it.

This principle (together with the assumption that FSTs determining mental states can be realized by a neural net) entails that each mental state M_i is realizable by infinitely many different neural networks in distinct atomic structural states. It follows that for each mental state M_i, there are infinitely many different possible atomic bodily structural states, whose descriptions mention ever-increasing numbers of components, such that if a system satisfies any of these atomic structural state descriptions, then it is in mental state M_i. From this it follows that for any *basic* bodily structural state description and any mental state M_i, it is physically possible for something to be in mental state M_i but *not* satisfy that basic bodily structural state description (i.e., not be in that basic bodily structural state). This is seen as follows. Consider any basic bodily structural state, say P_k, which central state materialism might postulate to be identical with mental state M_i. Since its associated state description is a finite disjunction, there must be a disjunct listing a number of parts greater than or equal to the number listed by any other disjunct state description. Consider a neural circuit satisfying the structural state description given in this disjunct. By the assumed principle, there exists an atomic structural state description whose satisfaction is sufficient for realizing the same F-state and being in the same mental state, M_i, that lists a number of essential components greater than the number listed in this disjunct, and so, therefore, greater than the number listed by any disjunct of the description expressing P_k. A system that satisfied this larger state description would be in mental state M_i without being in bodily state P_k. But this argument is quite general; P_k is any basic bodily structural state.[45] Therefore, for any basic bodily structural state P_k and any mental state M_i, it is physically possible for a system to be in mental state M_i without being in structural state P_k.

But the metaphysical principle assumed earlier (viz., that *State X = State Y* only if it is not physically possible for something to be in one of the states without being in the other) entails, in particular, that if it is physically possible for something to be in mental state M_i without being in basic bodily structural state P_k, then mental state M_i is *not* identical to structural state P_k. (In other words, if the two state predicates 'x is in M_i' and 'x is in P_k' are not coextensive in all physically possible worlds, then *State $M_i \neq$ State P_k*.) The conclusion of the preceding paragraph entails that for *any* mental state M_i and *any* basic bodily structural state P_k sufficient for it, it is physically possible for something to be in M_i without being in P_k. Therefore, no basic bodily structural state is identical to mental state M_i.

Although the exact general nature of the "brain states" or "central states" that they allege to be identical with mental states seems nowhere precisely to be specified by central state materialists, the examples they cite, as explained earlier, all seem to be instances of basic structural states of the body in the sense defined above. If so, and states of the sort that central state materialism postulates to be identical with mental states are, or are equivalent to, basic bodily structural states, then the conclusion follows (assuming my hypothesis true) that central state materialism's identity thesis is false. Psychological states are not identical to "central states" or "brain states."

From physicalistic functionalism's standpoint, of course, the basic fault in central state materialism is not its physicalism or materialism, but its misrepresentation of the true nature of the relationship between mental and physical-structuralistic systems of description, i.e., its misconstruction of the psychophysical map. The general form of neuropsychological correlations it supports is mistaken; the *fundamental* psychophysical invariances obtain

45. The same reasoning still applies even if the disjunct state description characterizes only a proper subpart of a neural circuit. The principle in question entails that there can be constructed another subcomponent containing essentially more parts which (a) does not satisfy the same structural state description, but which (b) has the same input-output characteristics. Thus, a system in which this functionally equivalent larger subpart replaced the original one would not satisfy the original disjunct structural state description, but by the functionalist assumptions, it would be capable of being in mental state M_i.

not between psychological and structural states of an organism, but rather between psychological and *functional* states of it. Appreciation of this crucial truth, unfortunately, too easily escapes experimentalists in laboratory situations where (at least at the level of gross anatomy) distinct specimens of the same species usually possess similar neural structures. For, since structural similarity entails functional equivalence (although not conversely!), it easily can *appear* that fundamental correlations have been discovered between a given psychological process or state and some structural state or change in structural state (e.g., the firing of certain neurons in a certain anatomical sub-region of the brain), when actually the crucial invariance relates these structural events to the mental process via functional states of the system. So a full and proper understanding of even these basic experimental data ultimately requires the functionalist insight. For only functionalism *explains*, what it is about, say, a certain midbrain process that makes it part of the neural correlate or realization of one psychological state rather than another. After all, one neural impulse, for example, qua action potential, more or less resembles another, and the neural processes in which it figures, qua physiological events or changes of state, appear much like any other (each involving, as it might be, a series of impulses traveling through some neural circuits). What is it about one of these neural processes that makes it underlie mental phenomenon *A* while another structural process, perhaps occurring at the same time in a neighboring circuit (or even at a different time in the same circuit), underlies some entirely different psychological state *B*? What is it about the members of one set of neural events, for example, that makes them underlie the psychological state of "feeling frightened" while the members of a different set of neural events are associated with, say, "feeling hungry"? The identity thesis provides no hint of an answer to this fundamental question. Central state materialism, in particular, leaves it a *mystery* (in the thickest sense) why a certain neurophysiological process underlies mental state *A* rather than *B*. To the same question, in contrast, functional state materialism offers a definite and plausible answer (namely, that different structural events or neural processes underlie different psychological phenomena because of their differing relationships (a) to certain kinds of possible *inputs* or external stimuli, (b) to certain kinds of possible *outputs* or behaviors, and (c) to *other structural states* having their own characteristic special relationships to inputs, outputs, and other states). The neural processes in one group, for example, may have a certain special relationship to perceivable dangerous external environments and escape behavior, while the neural processes in the other group normally are related directly to the pursuit and ingestion of food.

To conclude this contrast of the two materialisms, it also may be relevant to observe that functionalism's implication that mental states are variously realizable is confirmed empirically. Good indirect evidence indicates that the same psychological capacities and states in fact sometimes *are* diversely realized in different individual systems (and even in the same individual at different times). It is well known, for example, that in most people the primary neural mechanisms underlying linguistic ability are situated in the left cerebral hemisphere, but that in some people they are located in the right cerebral hemisphere. Here, at even the grossest level of anatomy, different bodily structures (and hence different bodily structural states) are known to underlie the *same* mental ability. It has also been observed widely that individuals who have suffered a mental impairment or "loss of function" due to brain damage eventually may recover the original ability completely. Since brain tissue is not regenerative, different neural components must be taking over the same function. So here, apparently, even within a single individual, the same psychological phenomena are realized by different structural processes at different times. Countless other observations of the celebrated "plasticity" of the nervous systems of higher animals also strongly support my functionalist hypothesis.

This hypothesis entails that logically sufficient conditions for the true application of any pure mental predicate can, in principle, be expressed entirely in behavioristic terminology. This is established in Appendix II (to which some readers may now wish to turn) where a formal metalinguistic proof too detailed to exhibit here shows that an F-state ascription (e.g., 'x is in F-state S_i') is logically equivalent to an indexed, dispositional, input-output characterization. From this, together with my hypothesis, the behavioristic conclusion follows. Appendix II also shows that although my hypothesis entails logical behaviorism, the two are not equivalent, and hence not identical theories.

This entailment may be surprising to some. For, as seen above, the hypothesis is compatible with some forms of mind-body dualism. And from this fact, together with the entailment, it immediately follows likewise that *analytical behaviorism is compatible with some forms of mind-body dualism*, a conclusion obtained by absolute and unconditional argument independent of the truth of my hypothesis. (Although incidental, this corollary is important because standard texts invariably have assumed its negation. Analytical behaviorism apparently advances a much less consequential thesis than many writers have supposed.)

Strict operationism (often confused with logical behaviorism), however, is incompatible with my version of the functionalist hypothesis, as Appendix II also shows. That is, accepting my hypothesis requires violating the demand of some theoreticians that all terms used in psychological theorizing be "operationally definable." For as Appendix II shows, no sequential procedure of behavioral manipulation and observation can exist for deciding the truth or falsity of F-state ascriptions. Hence, since F-state ascriptions are not operationally definable, acceptance of the hypothesis entails rejection of strict operationism.

4. The Addition of Principle 5 to Handle Certain Borderline and Other Cases

Let us now consider the relationship of the hypothesis to certain self-descriptions lying on the fringe of the class of mental state descriptions. Grouped under various rough headings, some examples are:

Group I: *Intellectual Capabilities*
   "I can speak English."
   "I can identify goldfinches."
   "I can reason."
   "I know how to follow directions."
   "I know how to do long division."
   "I can produce mental self-descriptions."

Group II: *Pure Qualities of Character, Personality,
         or Mental and Emotional Health*
   "I am vain."
   "I am honest."
   "I am ambitious."
   "I am sane."
   "I am schizophrenic."

Group III: *Qualities of Character Mixed
        with "Physical" Qualities*
"I am beautiful."
"I am strong."

Group IV: *Intellectual Capabilities Plus
        Specific Motor Skills*
"I know how to swim."
"I can fix cars."
"I can play squash."

Group V: *Pure Motor Skills*
"I can swing my arms."
"I am physically capable of X-ing" (where X is a simple
physical action).

Group VI: *General Metaphysical Self-descriptions*
"I am a concrete particular."
"I am in some state or other."

The distinctions among some of these groups are not sharp, which, as will be seen, creates problems.

Consider first the self-descriptions in Group I. They are seen to satisfy Principle 4 of the Model of Nontransitional Self-Description by the following reflections. If true of a subject, these descriptions are so in virtue of the subject's facility in various rational operations, such as identifying goldfinches, speaking English, reasoning, etc. To say, for example, that someone "can identify goldfinches" is to say, among other things, that the ability to move from goldfinches to correct descriptions of them is within his repertoire. This ability would be reflected in an FST description of him showing how, in appropriate circumstances, he would pass from a goldfinch to a correct description of it, and the ascription 'can identify goldfinches' is true of him in virtue of his having an FST of this sort. But any realization of the same FST would have the same ability and the description 'can identify goldfinches' also would be true of it. Hence this self-description (like all those in Group I) can satisfy Principle 4. It also can satisfy Principles 1–3.

A problem thus is created for the hypothesis because, intuitively, "being able to identify goldfinches" or "being able to speak

English" while perhaps "mental" descriptions, are not "mental state" descriptions. They seem better categorized as descriptions of intellectual capabilities than as descriptions of mental states. Whether this intuition is correct need not concern us, however, because such cases easily are controlled by adding to the general characterization a further principle:

5. It is not the case that the description expressed by $\underline{u}$, if true, is true of $\underline{M}$ simply in virtue of $\underline{M}$ being a realization of some FST.

Descriptions in Group I fail this condition, for if they are true, their truth is entailed simply by the subject's being a realization of a certain kind of FST. Thus these cases can be excluded or admitted, as desired, by adding or omitting Principle 5. As long as the cases are under control in this manner, our intuitions regarding them perhaps need not be debated.

Similar considerations apply to descriptions (such as 'I am vain') in Group II. Intuitively these are character descriptions, and again it would seem strange to say that they describe mental states. They, too, are controlled by Principle 5, for they depend on the subject's FST having a certain overall configuration rather than on his being in a particular state of it. Thus supplemented, the model accounts for both the affinity and also the contrast between mental states (such as pain, fear, and expectation), on the one hand, and qualities of character and intellect (such as intelligence and honesty), on the other. The "mentalistic" quality of all these descriptions is reflected in the fact that all can satisfy Principles 1–4 of the general characterization; their dissimilarity is captured in the fact that only mental state descriptions satisfy Principle 5.

The situation is slightly different for the "mixed" descriptions in Group III, such as 'I am beautiful'. They are not functionally determined if their truth conditions depend on characteristics of the subject other than those reflected in his functional description. Depending, for example, on exactly what was meant by the attribution "beautiful," someone might no longer qualify if his physiognomy were changed on a permutation. If not, the description 'I am beautiful' fails Principle 4 because it would be falsified by a permutation of the subject that leaves his functional organization unaffected. (So the characterization, we observe, detects the difference between "beautiful bodies" and "beautiful souls.")

One strong reason for adding Principle 5 is that without it the descriptions in Group IV and V (such as 'I can play squash' or 'I can swing my arms') also can satisfy the general characterization. For since the output is physical behavior, any realization of the same FST can exhibit the same physical behavior, and consequently the only permutation that would falsify one of these descriptions is a permutation changing the subject's FST. These self-descriptions thus satisfy Principle 4. So, since clearly they refer to physical abilities rather than to mental states, it seems best to add to the model Principle 5, which these descriptions do not satisfy, and in the remainder of this book, this addition will be assumed.[46]

The following query may now arise: Why could there not exist *nonmental* state descriptions defined in such a way that they too would be functionally determined? That is, what prevents defining some *"physicalistic"* state description purely in terms of input-output considerations of the sort involved in an FST-description? Why can one not define, for example, some description 'ϕ' as true of a system whenever it is in a *"physical"* state such that it will produce a specified behavioral output if it receives an input of a certain sort? For example, suppose it is stipulated that 'ϕ' is true of individuals whenever they are in a state such that if a sudden noise is made in their proximity (the input), they will exhibit a startle reaction (the output). This simple state description now has been defined in terms of input-output considerations of the sort expressible in an FST-description. It would be true of any physical realization of a certain FST (who is in the appropriate F-state), i.e., it is functionally determined, and thus it can satisfy Principle 4 and the other principles of the general characterization. But if it is a *"physical"* state description, does this not refute the hypothesis?

In response, several points must be made. First, the mere existence of an FST relative to which some nonmental self-description satisfies the general characterization does not refute the hypothe-

---

46. Gilbert Ryle's analysis of mental phenomena in *The Concept of Mind* (London: Hutchinson, 1949), consisted essentially in assimilating mental descriptions in general to those in Groups I and II, and then "showing" that these referred to abilities and traits no more ghostly than those in Groups IV and V. One flaw comes in the first assimilation; another comes in his analysis of "dispositions" and their relationship to states.

sis. For the hypothesis does not assert that every functionally determined state description is a mental description, but only that every state description *determined by some member of the postulated class of FSTs* α is a mental description. The FST in the example might not belong to this class. So even if 'ϕ' were a functionally determined nonmental state description, it would not refute the hypothesis.

Second and more illuminating, it is not obvious that 'ϕ' will be "nonmental." Merely stipulating that it be "physical" does not make it so. (Indeed, on a sufficiently liberal interpretation of the term 'physical', even mental states could be counted as "physical" if functional state materialism is true.) The description 'ϕ' was defined as true of anyone when in a state such that if confronted with a sudden noise, he would exhibit a startle reaction. A word in ordinary English close in meaning to this is the adjective 'jumpy'; someone who is in a state like that described is said to "be jumpy." Now is this a nonmental state? Intuitions may differ, but to me 'jumpy' seems more nearly a mental description than not. When we say, "Jones is jumpy today," we perhaps are not talking about him in quite the same way as when we say he is happy or irritable, but we are talking in a way close to it. The main difference is that being jumpy is a much simpler state than happiness or irritability. The inputs and outputs relevant to the attribution are much less complicated and it lacks the complex interconnections with other states that, e.g., happiness has. If sound, the intuition that this very simple functional state description, tailor-made to fit the general characterization, has mentalistic overtones further supports the hypothesis.

A predicate like 'is jumpy' possibly lies near the lower limit of state descriptions intuitively categorizable as "mental." For one certainly can define simpler functional state descriptions that clearly are nonmental. An example is, 'My patella response is operative now', a description true of a subject whenever the subject is in a state such that if tapped below the knee in a certain fashion, his leg will jerk. Not only is this state description definable solely in terms of input-output characteristics without reference to the subject's internal physical constitution, but there are possible FSTs such that any realization of them would produce this description only when true. Part of such could appear as in Table 3–17.

	S_1	S_2
tap below knee 'How's your patella response?'	S_1 (*leg jerk*) S_1 ('*My patella response is operative*')	$S_2(\Lambda)$ S_2 ('*My patella response is not operative*')

Table 3-17.

(Assumed irrelevant to the present discussion is the fact that humans happen to be so constructed that they cannot report nontransitionally the status of their patella response—i.e., the contingent fact that this FST is humanly unrealized.) Relative to this FST, 'My patella response is operative' can satisfy Principle 4 even though it is not a "mental" self-description. This does not refute the hypothesis, of course, since this FST need not be in the postulated class, α, but it prompts speculation on the difference between abstract functional state descriptions that are "mentalistic" and those that are not. One important difference, probably, is complexity. The description 'My patella response is operative' is simpler than the description 'I'm jumpy today' in two ways. First, the inputs and outputs relevant to the former are much more narrowly circumscribed than those relevant to the latter. Second, the interrelationships between the former description and other abstract state descriptions are much simpler than those connecting the latter with other functional states. Likewise, 'I am jumpy' is a much simpler state description than, say, 'I am in pain' or 'I believe that p' or any of the other paradigmatic mental state descriptions. This suggests that the difference between functional state descriptions that are "mentalistic" and those that are not is one of degree. Some, like 'I am in pain', clearly are mentalistic; others, like 'My patella response is operative', clearly are not; and some, like 'I'm jumpy today', are intermediate or borderline. If so, the hypothesis perhaps may be criticized on the grounds that it suggests there is a sharp line between mental and nonmental state descriptions when, in reality, there is a gray or indeterminate region between the two, with the difference being one of degree. Thus one might seek to bring the hypothesis into closer accord with the facts by introducing some weighting factor and speaking of various abstract functional state descriptions as "more" or "less" mentalistic, but such an addition, desirable as it might be in other circumstances, here is unneeded. For present purposes, the hypothesis that mental descriptions are functionally determined suffices. It may encounter some difficulty at the lower end of the spectrum of functional state descriptions, but as long as the model fits the central core of cases, deviation at the periphery can be tolerated. In this respect it is comparable to the Ideal Gas Laws in thermodynamics which fit the central core of cases well but deviate at extremes of temperature. Its slight idealization of the situation will not vitiate the model or destroy its usefulness.

Experimental Applications and Empirical Confirmation of the Theory

This chapter relates the model to various theoretical problems in the behavioral sciences. Topics treated include the knowledge of one's own actions, perception, and certain issues in theoretical psycholinguistics.

1. Knowledge of Actions

An "action self-description" is an utterance produced by someone stating that he is performing a certain action or exhibiting certain behavior. A pure example is uttering 'I am swinging my arms' while one is swinging one's arms.[1] The epistemology of such utterances has puzzled philosophers. For although action self-descriptions sometimes are produced as a result of self-observation, usually they are not. Instead, people often *know without observation* what actions they are performing. As G. E. M. Anscombe put it, usually "I can say what I am doing without looking to see."[2] But if so, *how* does one know this? How, moreover, can a subject know without observation the *same* fact (e.g., that he is opening the window) that can be known by others only through observation?

> The difficulty is this: What can opening the window be except making such-and-such movement with such-and-such result?

---

1. A "pure" action self-description is one whose truth is independent of context; the truth of a "mixed" action self-description (e.g., 'I'm signing a will') depends not only on the subject's muscle actions but also on other external factors. See Chapter 1, Section 5.
2. G. E. M. Anscombe, *Intention* (Oxford: Blackwell, 1958), p. 51.

And in that case what can *knowing* that one is opening the window be except knowing that that is taking place? Now if there are two *ways* of knowing here, one of which I call knowledge of one's intentional action and the other of which I call knowledge by observation of what takes place, then must there not be two *objects* of knowledge? How can one speak of two different knowledges of exactly the same thing? It is not that there are two descriptions of the same thing, both of which are known, as when one knows that something is red and that it is colored; no, here the description, "opening the window," is identical, whether it is known by observation or by its being one's intentional action.[3]

This might be thought to lead to the conclusion that "if there are two ways of knowing there must be two different things known,"[4] but, as will be seen, there is no need to say this. The same analysis that accounts for nontransitional mental self-description also explains how a person can have knowledge without observation of his own actions and explains this without positing any additional objects of knowledge.

The explanation is quite simple. Recall first, that in applying an FST-description to a human, the "outputs" are taken to be actions or pieces of behavior like swinging one's arms or opening the window. For example, a particular FST might include the operation shown in Table 4–1.

Inputs	$\cdots$	S_c	$\cdots$
.	.	.	.
.	.	.	.
.	.	.	.
'Please swing your arms'	.	S_a (*swing arms*)	.
.	.	.	.
.	.	.	.

Table 4–1.

A subject in state S_c of this FST (associated, perhaps, with the mental description 'in a cooperative mood') presented with the request 'Please swing your arms' will begin swinging his arms and pass into state S_a. (A more complex action like opening a window would require a more complicated FST—e.g., told to open the

3. *Ibid.*
4. *Ibid.*, p. 53.

window, the subject first would have to locate the window, then walk to it, grip it, and lift—but this does not affect the present general analysis.[5])

This being possible, there is no difficulty in also supposing that for state S_a in his FST there appears, for the input query, 'What are you doing?' the output 'I am swinging my arms', as shown in Table 4-2.

	S_c	S_a
'Please swing your arms'	S_a (*swing arms*)	
'What are you doing?'		S_b (*continue swinging arms and utter,* '*I am swinging my arms*')

Table 4-2.

There obviously is no difficulty in imagining a system so arranged. Having begun to swing his arms upon hearing the request, 'Please swing your arms', a realization of such an FST would, on the query, 'What are you doing?' respond by uttering, 'I am swinging my arms'. And he would, thereby, produce a true action self-description. In order to describe correctly his own actions, someone need only be organized in this general way. Notice that no transition from observation of himself is involved; the subject needs no input of swinging arms to make this report. He can "say what he is doing without looking to see." He is able to do this because he is arranged so that he is in a certain state, S_a, only when producing this action, and when in this state he will produce, on an appropriate query, an utterance that expresses in the language the statement that this output has been produced. Thus, even with no information fed back from the arm into the system through any sense modality, the subject still can give a correct description of his output. This, then, explains how a subject can report his own actions without observation.[6]

This analysis also explains how the subject can have knowledge

5. Even the action of swinging one's arms would involve a complex subroutine on a more detailed representation (e.g., "first swing arms to right until they stop; then swing left until they stop; repeat until . . ."). The coapplicability of FSTs varying in descriptive detail is discussed in Appendix I.

6. In fact, it provides a general blueprint for a mechanical system capable of reporting its own outputs without feedback from its sensory receptors.

without observation of the *same* fact that others can know only through observation. For his being the source of these actions enables him to produce action self-descriptions without a transition, whereas others cannot produce correct descriptions of the subject's actions in this same way for the simple reason that they are not the subject in this state. The information contained in the description must come to others through sense observation, but for the subject himself, this information already is "stored" implicitly in his state. The fact that the subject and others have this knowledge by different processes, however, does not mean that their knowledge is not "of the same thing." Obviously it is: under normal circumstances when swinging his arms, both the subject and others know the same thing (namely, that he is swinging his arms). Here as earlier (contra Ryle) the sorts of things one can find out about himself are the same as the sorts of things he can find out about other people, but his methods of finding out are different.

The analysis also shows that this nonobservational self-knowledge requires no special processes. It is a simple product of the same kinds of processes that underlie all other operations of the system: namely, that when in a given state, a given input elicits a given output. The difference between "knowledge by observation" and "knowledge without observation" is simply a function of the interpretation assigned in the language to the output; no special process or occurrence in the subject makes the difference. If the utterance produced by the subject ('I am swinging my arms') happened to have the same meaning in the language as the sentence 'That's a question' has in English, this identical sequence of operations might constitute making a transition from an object to a description true of it.

Remark: The relationship between pure action self-descriptions and the general characterization of nontransitional self-description is as follows. When produced nontransitionally as described above, action self-descriptions can satisfy Principle 4 of the general characterization. For there can exist FSTs containing F-states which, for each listed input, call for either the (continued) production of that output-action or else passage into some other state. Any realization while in this state, then, will be in the process of performing this action so the action self-description will be true of it. In this case, however, a nontransitionally produced action self-description fails Principle 3 because, if true, it is true of the subject in virtue of his production of one of the listed outputs, which contradicts Principle 3.[7] The failure of action self-descriptions to satisfy the general characterization further confirms Part 1 of my hypothesis (which claims that only *mental* self-descriptions satisfy the model).

In considering actual cases, it is important to distinguish between (1) a subject's being able correctly to say, e.g., 'My knee is bent', *because he has bent it* as an action of his own, and (2) a subject's being able correctly to describe the same situation when he has not produced it. The former case is analyzed as above. The latter occurs, for example, if while the subject's eyes are closed, someone else moves his leg and he later reports its position. This sort of case is represented as involving a transition (from leg to description) as in Table 4–3.

$\cdots$	S_j		$\cdots$
.	.	.	.
.	.	.	.
.	.	.	.
subject's leg and knee	.	S_k (*'My knee is bent'*)	.
when bent and query			
'What's the position			
of your knee?'			

Table 4–3.

In such cases, he knows the status of his knee by observation. The observation is kinesthetic, involving not vision or any of the other classical four senses, but the subject's bodily sense awareness of the configuration of his limbs and torso. Physiologically, it probably depends on the operation of special proprioceptive receptors in his muscles, joints, and tendons.

Only when the position of his limbs is the result of his own action can a subject know it without observation.[8] Some theorists have maintained

---

7. An FST-description will portray the nontransitional production of pure and mixed action self-descriptions in the same way. However, producing certain behavior in a certain state of some FST does not suffice to guarantee that a mixed action self-description is true of a realization, since its truth also depends on factors outside the subject.

8. Empirical evidence presented later confirms this by showing that, in fact, people can have this knowledge even when their proprioceptive receptors are not functioning normally.

that knowledge of bodily position usually is nontransitional; this may be correct, but not for the reasons they give:

> a man usually knows the position of his limbs without observation. It is without observation because nothing *shows* him the position of his limbs; it is not as if he were going by a tingle in his knee, which is the sign that it is bent and not straight. Where we can speak of separately describable sensations, having which is in some sense our criterion for saying something, then we can speak of observing that thing; but that is not generally so when we know the position of our limbs.[9]

But why can one not speak of a "separately describable sensation" associated with the position of one's leg (e.g., "the sensation that one's leg is bent") just as much as, say, with observing a red object (e.g., "the sensation of something red")?[10] The same holds for the claim that a sensation is not "in some sense our criterion for saying" that our knee is bent. Why can the same not be said with regard to the sensation of redness in the matter of telling the color of a red object? It obviously can. The real source of antipathy to the idea of kinesthetic observation probably is not these reasons but rather a prejudice in favor of restricting the term 'observation' to the five senses enshrined by Aristotle. But the opposition is still groundless. In the first place, even allowing modern Aristotelians a monopoly on the word 'observation', the distinction between transitional and nontransitional cases still can be retained. In the second place, contrary to the Aristotelians, it can be urged that application of the term 'observation' should be extended to include kinesthetic awareness. After all, the operations of this bodily sense and the operations of the other "five senses" are similar in relevant ways. In each case, special sensory nerve systems respond to particular distal stimuli and transmit information centrally, making it possible for the subject correctly to describe an objectively existing situation. It is possible, moreover, to experience hallucinations and illusions of a kinesthetic sort just as with any other sense modality. So there seems to be no good reason not to extend the term 'observation' to this means of knowledge as well.

Remark: As explained above, bodily knowledge gained through kinesthetic observation is treated by the model like any other knowledge gained by transition. When the situation described by the report is *not* represented as one of the subject's *outputs* (e.g., when another person has placed the subject's limbs in that position), his report may satisfy

9. Anscombe, *Intention*, p. 13.
10. For further discussion of this point, see David Braybrooke et al., "Some Questions for Miss Anscombe about Intention," *Analysis*, 22 (1962), 49f.

Principle 3. But it then fails Principle 1, because the truth of the self-description depends on the nature of the *input*. Consequently, the possibility of bodily knowledge by kinesthetic observation is consistent with my hypothesis.

According to this analysis, there are two different possible ways in which a person might come to know, e.g., that one of his limbs is bent. He might know this nontransitionally because he bent it as one of his own actions, or he might know it through kinesthetic observation. If this is correct, then at least in principle, the two should be separable.[11] It should be possible for one of the two modes of knowledge to cease functioning, leaving the subject with only the other. For example, the sensory system involved in the kinesthetic perception of limb position might become dysfunctional, leaving the subject no longer able to tell the position of his limbs by kinesthetic observation. But if the efferent system requisite to moving the limb remained intact, he still might be able to tell its position in those cases in which he placed the limb in that position by his own action, assuming he realized an FST like that shown in Table 4–4.

	S_c	S_h
'Place your hand on your head'	S_h *(Place hand on head)*	
'Where is your hand?'		S_d *(Continue to hold hand on head and say 'My hand is on my head')*

Table 4–4.

A realization of such an FST requires no input from his arm in order to report its position when he has placed it there. He can report its position nontransitionally. The present analysis would be confirmed, then, by the discovery of subjects who can correctly describe the whereabouts, e.g., of their limbs when *they themselves* have placed them there, but who (unlike the rest of us) cannot do this when their limbs have been arranged in the same position by someone else. For example, with his hands behind his back such a person could tell that his hand was formed into a fist when *he* had

11. The distinction between these two means of knowledge is theoretical. Normally, the two probably operate jointly in a person's knowledge of his own actions.

so clenched it, but unlike the rest of us, would be unable to tell this if someone else had so formed it.[12]

Syndromes in which one, but not the other, of these ways of knowing has ceased to function are observed in neurally damaged subjects. A patient who has lost all sensation, e.g., in an arm but is able still to move the afflicted limb can report its position correctly without the aid of his eyes or other sense modalities.[13] Since his arm is numb, he must be gaining this information non-transitionally. He can tell the position of his arm because he is a realization of an FST like the one described above. There is a certain state into which he passes during or after production of the arm movement, and when in this state he can produce utterances saying that this action has been produced. Thus the subject can report correctly the position of his arm even though it is devoid of sensation. The correctness of this analysis and the absence of feedback of sensory information is confirmed by a famous experiment. William James reports observing that if such a patient is asked to put the affected hand on top of his head while his eyes are closed, and at the same time this action is prevented by holding his arm still, he will report that he has done so and be astonished on opening his eyes to find that the movement has not taken place.[14] This observation, baffling on many theories, is understood on the present analysis. Since his arm is numb, the subject cannot tell its position by kinesthetic observation. He

12. This effect might be produced surgically by interrupting selected afferent pathways from sensory receptors in the muscles, joints, and tendons. It may seem obvious that this could be done peripherally, but this might not be so, because the same peripheral pathways also might be involved in feedback control of voluntary action, so that interdiction of these fibers would affect both functions. If so, the interruption would have to occur higher up, in the spinal cord or even in the brain. In the spinal cord, peripheral proprioceptive receptors from muscles, joints, and tendons snyapse both with fibers running to the cerebellum and with fibers running to the cerebral cortex (Stephen W. Ranson and Sam L. Clark, *The Anatomy of the Nervous System* [Philadelphia: Saunders, 1959], pp. 391f). On the assumption that the cerebellum handles the coordination of action and that the fibers going to the cortex are not requisite to completion of the action, one possible place to make the lesion would be in the medial lemniscus of the pons where it would stop only those impulses going to the cerebral cortex. However, it also is possible that interconnections between the cortex and the cerebellum higher up would necessitate a more complex set of lesions. Some evidence also exists that this disruption of the body sense would produce unconsciousness. See J. Purdon Martin, "Consciousness and its Disturbances," *Lancet*, 256 (1949), 50.

13. This is well documented. See, e.g., Martin, "Consciousness," p. 51.

14. William James, *Principles of Psychology* (New York: Henry Holt, 1890), II, 105. Quoted in G. N. A. Vesey, "Volition," *Philosophy*, 36 (1961), 352.

knows its position only nontransitionally. Normally, when he receives an order to put his hand on his head, he executes this action and passes into a state in which he "knows" and can say that his hand is on his head. But here, by restraining the subject's arm, the experimenter prevents the occurrence of the output. The subject, however, still has been caused to pass into the same state (or one very similar to it). Thus if asked, while his eyes are closed, he will say that his hand is on his head, and when he opens his eyes, he is surprised to find that it is not. By preventing the occurrence of the output, the experimenter nullifies one of the conditions requisite to the success of the nontransitional method here (viz., that the output issue from the state) and so causes the subject to come to an erroneous belief.

2. Experiments with Inverting Spectacles

Kepler and Scheiner, in the seventeenth century, first established that the image formed on the retina of the human eye is inverted. Since that time, many theoreticians who have considered this fact have wondered why we do not, as a consequence, perceive the visible world as upside down. The question was discussed by Descartes,[15] Berkeley,[16] Lotze,[17] Müller,[18] and Helmholtz,[19] among others. The history of this debate is available elsewhere, however, and will not be repeated here.[20] Against the background of this question, Roberto Ardigo in 1886, and George M. Stratton in 1897, conducted now-famous experiments in which they wore continuously, for extended periods of time, special eyeglasses which inverted, and reversed from left to right, the retinal image. That is, these lenses had the effect of rotating the retinal image through 180° so that the visible world appears

15. René Descartes, *Dioptrique* (1637).
16. George Berkeley, *A New Theory of Vision* (1709), secs. 88–116.
17. Rudolph Hermann Lotze, *Medicinische Psychologie oder Physiologie der Seele* (Leipzig: Weidmann'sche Buchhandlung, 1852), pp. 360–371.
18. Johannes Müller, *Handbuch der Physiologie des Menschen für Vorlesungen* (Coblentz: J. Holscher, 1837–40).
19. Herman V. Helmholtz, *Helmholtz's Treatise on Physiological Optics*, translated from the third German edition, ed. J. P. C. Southall (New York: Optical Society of America, 1925), III, 154–232, 242–270.
20. For a history of the dispute before this century, see Gordon L. Walls, "The Problem of Visual Direction: I. The History to 1900," *American Journal of Optometry* 28 (1951), 55–83. For a review of the history of the problem in this century, see Ian P. Howard and William B. Templeton, *Human Spatial Orientation* (New York: John Wiley and Sons, 1966), pp. 367–418.

upside down and reversed to the wearer. Seen through them, for example, a room's furniture seems to hang upside down from the floor above while light fixtures float like balloons at the end of chains anchored to the ceiling extending beneath the viewer's feet. Objects appearing visually high and to the right can be grasped only by reaching low and to the left, and vice versa. Rotating one's head to the right makes visible objects appear to pass by going also to the right. And so on.

Stratton wore such glasses for seven days and recorded his experiences during that time.[21] On the first day, he reports,

> The entire scene appeared upside down. When I moved my head or body so that my sight swept over the scene . . . the visual picture seemed to move through the field of view faster than the accompanying movement of my body, although in the same direction. It did not feel as if I were visually ranging over a set of motionless objects, but the whole field of things swept and swung before my eyes.
>
> Almost all movements performed under the direct guidance of sight were laborious and embarrassed. Inappropriate movements were constantly made; for instance, in order to move my hand from a place in the visual field to some other place which I had selected, the muscular contraction which would have accomplished this if the normal visual arrangement had existed, now carried my hand to an entirely different place. . . . At table the simplest acts of serving myself had to be cautiously worked out. The wrong hand was constantly used to seize anything that lay to one side. In pouring some milk into a glass, I must by careful trial and correction bring the surface of the milk to the spout of the pitcher, and then see to it that the surface of the milk in the glass remained everywhere equally distant from the glass's rim. . . .
>
> Relief was sometimes sought by shutting out of consideration the actual visual data, and by depending solely on tactual or motor perception and on the older visual representations suggested by these. . . . In order to write my notes, the formation of the letters and words had to be left to automatic muscular sequence, using sight only as a guide to the general position and direction on my paper. When hesitation occurred in my writing, as it often did, there was no resort but to picture the

21. George M. Stratton, "Upright Vision and the Retinal Image," *Psychological Review*, 4 (1897), 182–187; also "Vision without Inversion of the Retinal Image," *ibid.*, pp. 341–360, 463–481. Stratton's papers are reprinted in part in *Readings in General Psychology*, ed. Wayne Dennis (New York: Prentice-Hall, 1949), pp. 24–40.

next stroke or two in pre-experimental terms, and when the movement was under way, control it visually as little as possible. . . .

Objects were, however, taken more or less isolatedly; so that inappropriateness of place with reference to other objects even in the same visual field was often, in the general upheaval of the experience, passed by unnoticed. I sat for some time watching a blazing open fire, without seeing that one of the logs had rolled far out on the hearth and was filling the room with smoke. Not until I caught the odor of the smoke, and cast about for the cause, did I notice what had happened.[22]

But during the next six days, Stratton found himself adapting to his new perceptual experiences. By the second day, he already was beginning to be able spatially to relate seen objects to unseen objects:

Unseen objects could, by force of will, be represented in harmony with things in view, more easily than on the preceding day. I could, for instance, voluntarily bring before me, in consistent relation to the visual field, the general outline of the room in which I was sitting. My own body, however, was much less tractable; at best I could get only my legs and arms appropriately represented, and this only by an effort not required by other objects. . . .

There was much evidence of a rigid interconnection of experiences, by which the place or reality of one thing decided the place or reality of something else. The vividness with which a part of the body could be localized by visual representation, was influenced to some extent by the consistency of this representation with the actual perceptions of sight. . . . In walking through the room, the disappearance of a low-hanging electric globe toward the space in which my chin and neck were represented, and the immediately following contact of the globe with the top of my head, tended to disturb the place of representation of both my chin and scalp; while attention to the ceiling disappearing, as I walked along, in what was normally the lower part of the visual field, weakened the connection of the image of my feet with this place in the field. . . .

As to the uprightness or inversion of things, the general feeling was that the seen room was upside down; my body, represented in pre-experimental terms, was felt as standard and as having an upright position. But different circumstances pro-

22. Stratton, "Vision without Inversion of the Retinal Image," pp. 343–345.

duced a different feeling. When I looked out over a wide land-scape, the position in which I felt my body to be and the position of the scene before me were surely discordant and unnatural. Yet I could not, as I had the day before, take either the one or the other unreservedly as standard. . . . The very expanse of the landscape in comparison with the size of my body no doubt tended to subordinate the position of my body and render it less reservedly a norm for judging of correctness of position. But even when, indoors, the view was almost completely filled with the dining-table and its furnishings, there was no striking and obvious feeling that the scene was upside-down.[23]

By the third day, vision was more frequently leading to correct movements:

I was now beginning to feel more at home in the new experi-ence. . . . Walking through the narrow spaces between pieces of furniture required much less care than hitherto. . . .

Contacts in walking past objects had hitherto for the most part been surprising, because the contact was felt in a different place from the one anticipated. But today I noticed that ex-pectation was coming more into harmony with the actual experience. . . .

In this way and from other influences, there was coming to be a more vital connection between my actual perceptions and the larger visual system of merely represented objects. It was becoming easier to follow a line into the field of sight and, con-tinuing the line into this larger system of things, to know what it would lead to. The rooms beyond the one I was in, together with the scene out of doors, could be represented in harmonious relation with what I was actually looking at. Such representa-tions, however, were more or less a matter of voluntary effort; the spontaneous pictures were usually on the pre-experimental basis.[24]

By the fourth day, passage from vision to appropriate motor ac-tivity was beginning to become automatic:

During the day, actions appropriate to the new visual percep-tions frequently occurred without any conflict or apparent ten-dency to react by a misinterpretation of visual positions. My hands, in washing, often moved to the soap or to the proper

23. *Ibid.*, pp. 347–348.
24. *Ibid.*, pp. 349–351.

position in the basin, without premeditation or any need of correcting the movement. . . .

The feeling of contact of things on one side of my body was likewise becoming more spontaneously referred to the proper place in the new visual representation. Hitherto the proper lateral reference had probably always been an afterthought, or reflective reconstruction; the wrong localization was first suggested and then rejected. Now the wrong localization, it is true, still came, but often no sooner than the correct one, and in subordination to this.

The feeling of the inversion or uprightness of things was found to vary considerably with the strength and character of the representation of my body. When I looked at my legs and arms, or even when I reinforced by effort of attention their new visual representation, then what I saw seemed upright rather than inverted. But if I looked away from my body and gave exclusive force to its pre-experimental image, then everything in sight seemed upside down. Especially was it noticeable that during active movements of the body . . . the feeling of the uprightness of the scene was much more vivid than when the body was quiet.[25]

On the fifth day, actions that formerly required conscious planning were beginning to become automatic:

At breakfast, with the lenses on, the inappropriate hand was rarely used to pick up something to one side. The movement itself also was easier and less wayward; seldom was it in an entirely wrong direction. When hand and object were both in sight I did not, as a rule, have to calculate or try to find the direction and extent of movement necessary to reach the object, but merely fixed my attention on the thing, and the hand was laid upon it without more ado, except for an occasional slight correction of the direction.

In walking I did not so often run into obstacles in the very effort to avoid them. . . . When the doors were open I could walk through the entire house by visual guidance alone, without holding out my hands in front of me to warn in case of a misinterpretation of the sight-perception. . . . My movements were of course still cautious and awkward. And often the question of right and left was troublesome; for example, I wished to grasp the handle of the door beside me, and must hesitate a moment before it was clear which hand to use. But I found that the

25. *Ibid.*, pp. 352–354.

appropriate hand often came to the appropriate side of the
visual field directly and without the thought (frequently necessary before) that *that* visual side meant the *other* side in motor
or older visual terms.[26]

On the seventh day he reports that when moving actively, "I felt
that I was more at home in the scene than ever before. There was
perfect reality in my visual surroundings, and I gave myself up to
them without reserve and without being conscious of a single note
of discord in what I saw."[27]

From the time of these early experiments to the present, this
question has puzzled theoretical psychologists: Will a person
wearing upside-down spectacles ever come to see the world as
rightside up, and if so, how? Ardigo, in 1886, appears to report
that objects eventually were seen as rightside up by him. Likewise, on the final day of his experiment Stratton reported: "As
long as the new localization of my body was vivid, the general
experience was harmonious and everything was rightside-up."[28]
He was completely at home in his new visual world except for an
occasional feeling of viewing it from an inverted body:

> But when, for any of the reasons already given—an involuntary
> lapse into the older memory-materials, or a willful recall of
> these older forms—the pre-experimental localization of my body
> was predominantly in mind, then as I looked out on the scene
> before me the scene was involuntarily taken as the standard
> of right direction, and my body was felt to be in an inharmonious
> position with reference to the rest. I seemed to be viewing the
> scene from an inverted body.[29]

Since the time of Stratton, others have repeated the experiment with similar results. When Frederick Snyder and Nicholas
Pronko asked their subject, after several days of wearing the
glasses, whether things still looked upside down to him, he
replied:

> I wish you hadn't asked me. Things were all right until you
> popped the question at me. Now when I recall how they *did* look
> *before* I put on these lenses, I must answer that they do look
> upside-down *now*. But until the moment you asked me I was

26. *Ibid.*, p. 355.
27. *Ibid.*, p. 463.
28. *Ibid.*, p. 469.
29. *Ibid.*

absolutely unaware of it and hadn't given a thought to the question of whether things were rightside-up or upside-down.[30]

James G. Taylor and Seymour Papert performed a similar experiment in 1953.[31] Papert, who wore the glasses and apparently adapted to them completely, reports that his reaction to the question, "Do things still look upside-down to you?" came simply to be one of annoyance at its irrelevance.[32]

Despite these reports, many investigators have continued to doubt that these subjects ever came to see the world as rightside up. Their basic objection is theoretical, stemming from implicit adherence to a representative model of perception[33] (for which the work of Stratton and his successors constitutes practically an *experimentum crucis*). If one posits that a perceiving subject is directly aware not of external physical objects but only of subjectively experienced representations or sensory images of those objects, then it is very difficult to understand how anyone in these experiments could have come to see the world as rightside up again. For on a representative model, the initial effect of putting on the glasses must be an inversion of this subjectively experienced visual picture; wearing the glasses causes it to be upside down. A wearer could come to see things as rightside up again, then, only through a reorientation of this object. His subjective visual field would have to turn over or reverse itself in some way. That such a momentous subjective event could escape notice seems unlikely, yet none of the subjects in whom reinversion occurred reported an experience of seeming to see anything rotate, turn over, or otherwise shift. Since apparently no such experiences occurred, many psychologists therefore have concluded that, despite the subjects' reports, they never did come to see things rightside up but instead only "adapted" to their upside-down visual fields. One writer puts the argument in terms of an analogy between the subjective visual field and a table:

> For analogy, let me suppose that I am standing at a small table (the subjective visual field) on which a number of checkers

30. Frederick W. Snyder and Nicholas H. Pronko, *Vision with Spatial Inversion* (Wichita, Kansas: McCormick-Armstrong, 1952), p. 113.

31. James G. Taylor, *The Behavioral Basis of Perception* (New Haven: Yale University Press, 1962), pp. 198f.

32. Lecture, Massachusetts Institute of Technology, 1967.

33. Notice that representative theories of perception involve an application of the Transition Model analogous to Application I which was rejected in Chapter 1.

(visual objects, present or ideated) are strewn in a random manner. I "take in" their arrangement. If, now, I am to come to be able to see the checkers in a 180°-inverse of this arrangement, there are three things that I can do:

1. Lift the table a bit and rotate it 180°, and set it down again.
2. Push each checker across the table, either "upward" or "downward" as need be for each, until the arrangement of all is the inverse of what it had been.
3. Walk around the table and look at it from the opposite side.

The first case would accomplish an inversion (or a re-erection) through a rotation of the oculocentric field. This could not have happened to Stratton, for he describes no "intermediate" appearances of objects as lying on their sides, etc. The second case violates the known permanence of relative oculocentric directions, and could be peremptorily dismissed as a topological impossibility even if we did not know that Stratton had observed no such reciprocal infiltrations. The third case would compare with a successful inversion of the body image. But to keep the changing visual situation from being identical with #1, I should have to shut it out while I walked around the table. But Stratton experienced no period of *blindness* "psychic" or what-have-you, after which things seemed oriented otherwise than before.[34]

(The author overlooks the possibility of flipping the table over twice completely, first end-to-end and then sideways, but one notes that Stratton likewise records no period during which he saw the backside of his visual field.)

But if one resists such theoretical prejudice and accepts the subjective reports of the subjects in these experiments, it is hard not to conclude that they did eventually come to see the world rightside up while wearing the glasses (or at any rate, were on their way to doing so when the experiment ended). But how should this phenomenon be understood? What is the relation between the subject's behavioral adaptations and his coming to see the world as rightside up again? And how could a subject experience a reinversion of his visual field without undergoing any rotations, inversions, or migrations in his visual experience? My hypothesis answers these questions by showing how a set of behavioral recoordinations could result in reinversion of the subject's visual field and why no experience of things seeming to rotate, invert, or migrate in the visual field need be involved. This congruence of

34. Gordon L. Walls, "The Problem of Visual Direction: III. Experimental Attacks and Their Results," *American Journal of Optometry*, 28 (1951), 199–200.

experimental results with the hypothesis further supports it in opposition to private object theories.

On the hypothesis, the experiment is understood as follows. Before donning the glasses, the subject is capable of visual perception and sees things normally: opening his eyes to surrounding objects in good illumination, he is caused to pass into a sensory state of a visual kind, a state in which, among other things, he "sees things rightside up." Now the reasoning goes as follows. The subject can see things rightside up. Whenever he does, mental state descriptions like 'is now seeming to see things rightside up' are true of him. Moreover, mental capacity descriptions such as '(generally) sees things rightside up' are true of him in virtue of the fact that he is capable of passing into such sensory states. (These latter assert a capability and like the description 'knows English', they are truly predicable of him even when he is not exercising the capability—e.g, when he is sitting with his eyes shut or sleeping.)[35] Although none of these is a frequently used mental description, all are mental descriptions nonetheless, and it follows from my hypothesis that FSTs exist upon which their predication depends. Assume the subject realizes one of these. Then these mental state descriptions are true of him when he is in certain states of this FST and in virtue of his being in them, and the mental capacity descriptions are true of him in virtue of the fact that he is a realization of an FST with such states in it.

Since it is less cumbersome, the analysis will be developed in detail only for the appropriate mental capacity descriptions; the argument for mental state descriptions goes analogously. The part of an FST reproduced in Table 4–5 will be used as an illustration. Notice that the table shows only a small part of an imagined entire FST; for many operations shown, the subject passes into states not listed in the part of the FST given.[36] Needless to say, this is only an illustration and is not to be taken as a serious

---

35. Mental capacity descriptions were discussed in Chapter 3, Section 4.

36. Often an input will leave a subject in a state that is essentially identical to his original state, differing only in that the subject now has a memory of that input. For example, a man who desires an apple is not generally caused to pass out of this desire state by the sound of a horn, although after the horn has sounded, he probably will remember and be able to report it. He will pass into a different F-state, but one that also falls under many of the same mental state descriptions. This is sometimes indicated by the subscripts attached to the names of F-states. For instance, state S_{dh} is much like S_d, a state associated with desiring an apple, except that when in S_{dh} the subject also will be able to report the past occurrence of the sound of a horn.

INPUTS	"Desires an apple" S_d	"Expects to be given something to identify" S_i	"Listening (eyes closed) with intent to identify what is heard" S_l	"Looking with intent to say whether a thing is rightside up" S_r	"Prepared to describe visual impressions" S_{ri}
illuminated apple hanging high and to the left, pointed to by someone	S_a (reach & grasp, high & to the left)	S_b (utter 'Apple')	S_l (Λ)	S_{a2} ('Yes')	S_{ria} ('I see it as rightside up')
missile approaching right eye	S_m (duck left)	S_{mi} (duck left)	S_l (Λ)	S_{m2} (duck left)	S_{m3} (duck left)
rightside-up drawing before him of smiling face	S_{df} (Λ)	S_f (utter 'rightside-up smiling face')	S_l (Λ)	S_{f3} ('Rightside up')	S_{f5} ('I see it as rightside up')
upside-down drawing before him of smiling face	S_{df2} (Λ)	S_{f2} (utter 'upside down smiling face')	S_l (Λ)	S_{f4} ('Upside down')	S_{f6} ('I see it as upside down')
horn sounding	S_{dh} (Λ)	S_h (utter 'a horn')	S_{ld} (utter 'I hear a horn')	S_{rh} (Λ)	S_{rih} (Λ)
'Close your eyes and listen'	S_l (close eyes)	S_l (close eyes & utter 'OK')	S_{l1} (utter 'I am')	S_{r1} ('How would I tell with my eyes closed?')	S_1 (Λ)
question 'Is this rightside up?' coming from right side	S (turn head and eyes right)	S (utter 'What?' & turn gaze right)	S_{l2} (utter 'My eyes are closed')	S_{r2} (turn head & eyes right)	S_{rir} (turn head and eyes right)
'Tell me how this seems to you, rightside up or upside down?'	S_{r1} (Λ)	S_{ri} (Λ)	S_{l4} ('With my eyes closed?')	S_{ri} ('OK')	S_{ri} ('OK')

(truncation brackets appear across the S_r / S_{ri} columns for the rightside-up and upside-down drawing rows, each labeled "truncation")

Table 4-5.

attempt to characterize an actual human subject with an FST-description, a task no one is yet in a position to accomplish. (This ignorance does not affect the analysis, however, since it will be obvious how to generalize it to any other FST.)

Suppose, then, that the subject realizes an FST perhaps resembling the illustration and in virtue of this, "sees things rightside up." When he dons the glasses, the new system consisting of subject plus glasses immediately becomes a realization of a different FST. If his original FST resembled the illustration in Table 4–5, then part of the FST of the new system might appear as in Table 4–6.

	"Desires an apple" R_d	*"Looking with intent to say whether a thing is rightside up"* R_r	*"Prepared to describe visual impressions"* R_{ri}
Illuminated apple high and to the left. . . .	R_a *(reach and grasp, low and to the right*	R_{a2} *('No')*	R_{ria} *('I see it as upside down')*
Missile approaching right eye. . . .	R_{dm} *(duck right)*	R_{m2} *(duck right)*	R_{m3} *(duck right)*
Rightside-up drawing of smiling face. . . .	R_{df} *(Λ)*	R_{f3} *('Upside down')*	R_{f5} *('I see it as upside down')*
Upside-down drawing of smiling face. . . .	R_{df2} *(Λ)*	R_{f4} *('Rightside up')*	R_{f6} *('I see it as rightside up')*

Table 4–6.

This subject will report that a rightside-up drawing of a smiling face looks upside down, and that an upside-down drawing looks rightside up,[37] reach low and to the right for an apple high and to

37. Limitations of space as well as of the author's ingenuity have made this table oversimplistic as a new FST-description of a realization of the previous FST who has donned inverting spectacles. R_r, like S_r, is supposed to be associated, e.g., with the mental description, "Looking with intent to say whether a thing is rightside up." But realistically speaking, few people are so naive that when looking through inverting spectacles at, for example, a tree, they would assert that it was upside down. A more detailed and realistic FST-description would show the subject's general knowledge that no trees hang upside down in inverted orchards, together with his awareness that he has just put on inverting spectacles, from the beginning, entering into the series of computations between the first influences of the tree on his sense organs and his final statement. FST-descriptions can be made as realistic as one's patience allows, but for present purposes, the illustration's crudeness does not matter.

the left, and duck right (instead of left, as he should) to avoid a missile approaching his right eye. One may suppose the rest of his FST likewise shows the other new responses to visual environments that the subject plus glasses will have.[38] Operations unrelated to visual-motor coordination (e.g., purely ratiocinative operations such as correctly answering a question like 'What is 7 + 5?') will, of course, be unchanged in the new FST.

The nature of many states in the new FST obviously differs from what it was in the previous one since many states involve different, often opposite, responses to the same inputs. (Hence, functionalists are not surprised that different mental capacity descriptions should be true of the subject plus glasses afterward than were true of him before he donned the glasses. For, according to the hypothesis, a change in FST is a necessary condition for one mental capacity description becoming inapplicable and its contrary becoming applicable, and this necessary condition has been satisfied in the present case. So it fits with the hypothesis that the subject no longer sees things rightside up, but instead sees them upside down when he puts on the glasses.)

More importantly, the theory explains how the subject plus glasses again can come to see things as rightside up. For assuming the hypothesis is true, it logically follows that if with time and training, the subject with glasses comes to *have the same FST* as did the original subject without glasses, then the same mental descriptions that applied to him originally without glasses now will apply to him while wearing the glasses. In other words, the hypothesis entails that for the subject plus glasses again to become a realization of the original FST is a sufficient condition for the mental capability description 'sees things rightside up' again to apply to him. Hence, if the subject plus glasses changes in his internal functioning so that he produces all the same behavioral responses to every input as he did before donning the glasses, then if the hypothesis is true, he again will see things as rightside up. And this, of course, is approximately what appears to have

38. Notice that the new FST does *not* represent the situation as if the inputs themselves were inverted. The inputs are objects or events in the subject's external environment, and these have not been altered in the experiment. What are altered are his responses to these objective situations. (There are, of course, other ways of setting up an FST-description in which the inputs would be represented as affected by the glasses—for example, an FST-description in which images on the retina were taken as inputs to the central nervous system—but these are not employed in the present analysis.)

happened in the case of Stratton and the others. They gradually reacquired their original output responses to visual situations. As time passed, Stratton with glasses learned again to duck under overhanging obstacles, step over objects on the ground, reach for objects where they actually were, use his eyes in writing, and so on. The totality of his bodily responses .became appropriately recoordinated with all his visual inputs, and similar recoordinations took place in subjects in other experiments. Given this behavioral relearning, the so-called "reinversion of the subject's visual field" is accounted for by my hypothesis. For if it is true, this reestablishment of proper input-output correlations *itself constitutes* a "reinversion of the subject's visual field," so that once these correlations have been reestablished, the subject will ipso facto "see things rightside up."

The implication that properties of the visual field are determined by nothing other than the totality of the perceiver's dispositions to respond to the external environment may seem difficult to believe. One unconsciously retains the model of a privately perceived subjective visual field and feels (quite correctly) that if this entity is inverted, merely acquiring new sensory-motor correlations would not reinvert it. This, however, is exactly the point: as the hypothesis implies and this experiment confirms, no such entity exists! There is no privately experienced subjective visual image. Difficult as it may be for traditional theorists to accept, seeing the world as rightside up consists in nothing other than being in a state that involves a certain integrated totality of correct responses to it.

Some unconvinced readers still may believe that (in their own cases at least) they could imagine returning to the original FST and so making all the correct responses to visible objects, while still having an upside-down visual field. Therefore, let us consider the plausibility of this analysis from a subjective standpoint. Imagine yourself as the subject in the experiment. When you first put on the glasses, everything appears upside down. The ceiling appears below you, the floor above you with furniture hanging down from it. When you tip your head downward, your feet suddenly seem to appear above your head. The chair on which you bump your left knee appears above your head on the right. You start to walk and graze the top of your head on an object appearing from below. Your turn to the right to avoid a door edge appearing on your left and run into it. Someone shows you a drawing and asks its orientation: it appears rightside up but you realize it must be upside down. To get about in the world at all, each action must be prefaced with a conscious calculation. This you do, perhaps at first falteringly, then more readily. You form the rule that to grasp something appearing on the right, you must reach to the left. You make a note always to say that upside-down appearing objects are rightside up. You try always to remember to duck in response to objects appearing from below, to move right to avoid hitting edges appearing on the right, and to step over objects appearing above. As time passes, all these correct responses, originally made only after conscious calculations, begin to become automatic. When an object appears before you, the correct hand spontaneously goes out to the place where you see it. You automatically walk uneventfully through the doorways you see. When you see something on the rug, you step over it. Someone asks you to point to the chandelier, you stick your arm out, and observe your outstretched finger in line with it. When someone holds a picture rightside up and asks its orientation, the first thing that occurs to you is that it is rightside up. Suppose that all your other behavior likewise becomes, again, automatically appropriate. How now do things seem to you visually, rightside up or upside down? Well, why not ask *you*? We show you a rightside-up picture and ask you how it looks. You reply that it looks to be rightside up. "No," we say, "how does it look *to you*?" "It looks rightside up to me," you reply. "No," we say again, "we mean for you to describe your visual impression." "My visual impression," you answer, "is of a rightside-up picture." "Point your finger toward where the floor seems to you to be," we demand and you point downward. "No," we continue, "point your finger so that it seems to be pointing upward in your visual field," and you extend your finger in an objectively upward direction. All your behavior has returned to the old FST. What is left to be upside down? Nothing. As you yourself agree, you now see the world rightside up again.

"But what if I don't give the reports you've imagined or give some additional indication that I am still seeing the world upside down?" Then not all your behavior has returned to the original FST. If you have returned to the original FST, your verbal behavior, like all your other behavior (reaching, ducking, pointing, etc.), also will be as it was originally. And you will report that everything appears rightside up. "But even supposing my verbal behavior changes, might I not still inwardly believe that things still look upside down to me?" Surely, then, you can tell us what you believe. We will ask you what you inwardly believe and you can answer honestly. If, as we are supposing, you have fully returned to your original FST, then when we ask you, you will reply that you believe that things appear rightside up to you, for when you return to your original FST all your *beliefs* are also as they were before. You sincerely will report that things look rightside up to you, and you will be correct. (If something exists or occurs in you that affects none of your dispositions to behave, you must be unaware of it.)

My hypothesis has similar implications for other aspects of vision. Consider, for example, the infamous "problem of the inverted spectrum." Is it possible, philosophers have asked, that others subjectively experience a different color than I do when we look at the same visible entities, but that we have all learned to apply the same color words to the same objective things so that we agree in all our color judgments, and that all our other behaviors and dispositions to behave in relationship to colored external objects are also the same, so that consequently the subjective discrepancy is not recognized? On this supposition, it may be, for example, that what others experience when they look at a so-called "blue" sky is what I would call red if I could have their visual impressions, but since I never can have their visual impressions and we agree in all our reports, the fact never could be established. Putnam considers this a real possibility:

> Speaking *scientifically* rather than epistemologically (e.g. in terms of what physiology might disclose) I think it not impossible that someone's spectrum might be reversed, i.e. he might see blue where I see red and vice versa. Nevertheless he would use the color words "correctly" enough by ordinary standards.[39]

By "speaking *scientifically* . . . in terms of what physiology might disclose," Putnam presumably means something like the following. Physiology might discover, for example, that two neural channels, A and B, in most people are connected respectively to

39. Hilary Putnam, "Reds, Greens, and Logical Analysis," *Philosophical Review*, 65 (1956), 211.

two further channels, 1 and 2, and that reversing these junctions so that A is connected to 2 and B to 1 causes these people to report seeing red where formerly they saw blue, and vice versa. Now suppose a few people are discovered to have been born with A connected to 2 and B to 1. Would this not disclose that they see red where others see blue, and vice versa? No. If they have similar FSTs and the same responses to all external situations, then assuming the hypothesis is correct, all experience the same color sensations (i.e., are in similar color-sensory states) in the same situations.

Surprising as it may seem, this conclusion has received indirect empirical support. In a series of experiments, Ivo Kohler had subjects wear special color-distorting glasses.[40] The left half of each lens was tinted yellow, the right half blue. At first, of course, donning such glasses causes objects on the left to look yellowish, objects on the right bluish. As with the inverting spectacles, however, the effect disappears with prolonged wearing. In time, visible objects again look normally colored to subjects with glasses and appear no different on the left than on the right. Since light from a white object passing through the yellow side of the lens casts a yellowish image on the retina and yet after adaptation such an object seen on the left again elicits a "white" response (rather than yellow), adapted subjects (with glasses on) obviously correspond (in an imperfect but sufficient way) to Putnam's abnormals imagined born with transposed neural connections. For presumably when an adapted subject looks at an alabaster object through the yellow side of the glasses, certain neural fibers activated by yellowish images on the irradiated sides of the retinas (call these fibers "A") no longer activate a neural system (call it "Y") generating the report "yellow," but instead integrate with other signals to activate a system ("W") producing a white report (thus the acclimated subject with glasses now again describes white objects seen through the yellow lens as looking white). So in the adapted subject, fibers "A" evidently connect with W, whereas in normal people (as in subjects before adaptation) they connect to Y and if connected to W would cause them to report seeing yellow objects as white. Yet as acclimated subjects themselves agree, they now again see alabaster things as white. So as

40. Ivo Kohler, "Experiments with Goggles," *Scientific American*, 206 (1962), 5, 68.

the hypothesis implies, the existence of transposed visual channels does not mean that the person in whom they exist has subjectively different color experiences when looking at the same
things. This experiment has the nicety that the subject with the
reversed neural connections is identical to the person who earlier
had unreversed connections, so there is no problem about comparing the reports of different perceivers. He himself can tell
us that his postadaptation (i.e., posttransposition) sensory experience is identical in the same environments to his sensory
experience as a normally wired person. Moreover, the result is
independent of any worries about the possible association of the
same color word with dissimilar color experiences. For the subject can certify that now, after the adaptations and transpositions,
he sees everything as being the *same* color (whatever its name may
be) as he did before donning the glasses. So this experiment confirms the implication of the hypothesis that two people (or one
person at different times) can have different connections in the
internal neural structures underlying their perception of colors
and yet have the same color experiences. All that matters is the
overall functioning of the system, its FST, and if this is the same in
two subjects, they see the same colors in the same situations.
What exactly "seeing colors" consists in is, of course, not known
at this time, but if the hypothesis is true, it does not consist in the
inward reception of a privately perceived subjective color patch
or representation.

Returning to inverting spectacles, several points deserve further mention. First, notice that the present account does not
require that a subject with glasses who comes to see things rightside up again ever should undergo a period of blindness or have
the experience of seeming to see things rotate, migrate, or turn
over, as representative models require. (Indeed, the analysis suggests that seeing things rightside up is a matter of *degree* and not
an all-or-none matter as representative models imply.) The reinversion occurs by the subject's gradual reestablishment of correct
behavioral responses to external visible things, and this reestablishment need involve no experiences of seeming to see anything
shift, migrate, or invert. Of course, the hypothesis itself does not
preclude the possibility that, as a matter of empirical fact, humans
are so constructed that none ever will return to rightside-up
vision except by a process taking him through some intermediate

states in which he has such experiences (although experimental evidence indicates that this does not happen). The hypothesis merely does not *require* any such intermediate visual effects, as do representative models. For, as has been explained, according to it, nothing more need "go on inside" the subject, physically or mentally, again to "see things rightside up" than the reacquisition of correct behavioral responses to visible objects. So the hypothesis explains the fact that the subjects in whom reinversion occurred reported no experiences of seen things seeming to rotate, invert, or migrate.

Together with the assumption that subjects usually construct sensory-state self-descriptions by truncated description as explained in Chapter 2, this account also permits explaining how adapted subjects with glasses eventually come to produce new protocols (mental self-descriptions) reporting that they again see things rightside up. There is no difficulty, of course, in understanding why, immediately after donning the glasses, the subject should report that everything now looks upside down to him. For with the glasses on, normal external environments now cause him to pass into sensory states like those he formerly would have been put into by viewing an objectively upside-down scene. So naturally he says, "Everything looks upside down to me." But what causes these subjective self-descriptions to change as the subject adapts and forms new responses to the external environment? Why does he not end up with everything but his subjective reports changed and those remaining as they were when he first donned the glasses?

One possibility is that as part of acquiring new responses, he begins to learn again to give objectively correct descriptions of external objects. He begins to adapt so that, for example, when asked to describe an objectively rightside-up drawing, he will say the correct thing (namely, that it is rightside up). Similarly with all his other descriptions of visible objects: he learns again to give objectively correct descriptions of them. At this point, he still may maintain a distinction between how things look to him (upside down) and how they really are (rightside up) and say that rightside-up external objects *are* rightside up but *look* upside down. But as time passes and correct objective responses become more automatic, the subject begins to waver and become indecisive in his mental self-descriptions. For since his accustomed procedure for producing sensory self-descriptions is truncation, his automatic tendency is simply to engage in truncated description—that is, to go through the same descriptive operations he normally would go through in trying to arrive at a description of what he saw and then convert the result into a self-description. Thus as new correct responses to external objects become more automatic, the tendency will be to produce the corresponding self-descriptions—to say that things "look" rightside up. For example, once his automatic response to a rightside-up picture has become saying that it is rightside up, what is he to say in response to the question, "How does it look to you?" except that it looks rightside up? After all, the question presumably means something like, "Going by your visual impressions alone, would you be inclined to say that this picture is upside down or rightside up?" and the honest answer to this question is that, going by his visual impressions alone, he would be inclined to say that it is rightside up. To continue to say that it *looks* upside down would require a burdensome extra computational operation (he would have to remember to convert the derived truncated description, 'It's rightside up', to its contrary before incorporating it in a self-description), and this extra operation would have no point. What could he mean by doing this? What would he be saying if he said it looked upside down? Once his objective descriptions and all his other responses have returned to normal, in what respect could things be said to look upside down to him? If he continued to say that they did, he would be no different from a person with normal vision who went around absurdly saying that he saw things upside down but was unable to give any content to his statement. So a time comes when, as a matter of course, he again says that things look rightside up to him and no longer reports that things look upside down.[41]

3. Seeing with the Skin

In a striking and unexpected way, recent experiments in visual prosthesis appear also to confirm the theory. For the hypothesis seems to entail that, in a sense, the eyes, optic nerve, and other special neural structures usually associated with visual percep-

41. The observed fact that changes in objective descriptions (the grist for truncations) precede changes in these sensory self-descriptions provides empirical support for this analysis.

tion are not strictly necessary for it. If the same optical information from the environment were introduced into the nervous
system through any afferent channel (even one previously associated with a completely different sensory modality, e.g., touch)
and if the subject's nervous system adapted in such a way as to
become able to use this inflow of information appropriately to
guide its actions and behavior in environments of illuminated
objects, then the subject would have "visual experience" of the
sort enjoyed by normally sighted persons. If this implication is
true, the practical and theoretical applications stagger the imagination. For instance, persons blinded by disease or injury that
rendered their eyes or other normal mechanisms of vision inoperative might be enabled to "see" again (as before), by means,
say, of a miniature TV-camera-hat worn on the head like a miner's
cap and attached through amplifiers to an array of small buzzers
or vibrators embedded in a coat or pack worn tightly pressing
against the skin of their back and shoulders. Information about
the visible environment picked up by the camera would be ampli-
fied and fed into the nervous system by corresponding patterns of
gentle tactile stimulation of the skin on the back by the vibrators.
(Thus, e.g., a side-to-side rotation of one's head-with-camera past
a vertical bar would generate a corresponding bar-shaped wave of
tactile stimulation across one's back, etc.) The hypothesis appears
to imply that, e.g., a previously sighted, but now blind, person who
learned to guide his movements and behavior by means of such a
device no longer would experience the vibrations on his back as
tactile stimulations, but instead would begin literally again to *see*
his environment (that is, have and agree that he has visual experience just as he did previously when he had sight). For—with
appropriate allowances for limits of resolution, etc., imposed by
technical constraints plus the fact that a wearer must move his
head rather than eyeballs to scan a scene—an adapted, blindfolded subject employing a "tactile vision substitution system"
(TVSS) of the sort described would constitute a possible "permutation" of the original sighted subject satisfying the same FSTs
(almost), and therefore, by the hypothesis, could be in exactly the
same sensory states as previously when using his natural eyes.
Thus, instead of taking his seeing-eye dog when going for a walk,
a blind person could simply strap on his high-resolution portable
"seeing-eye coat" (with camera in hood) and thereby actually
view the surroundings through which he walked. Incredible as it

seems on traditional theories, this prediction appears partially confirmed by recent research in visual prosthesis.[42] Bach-y-Rita describes his apparatus:

> The TVSS in operation at present includes 400 solenoid stimulators arranged in a 20 × 20 array built into the back of a dental chair. The stimulators, spaced 12 mm apart, have 1 mm diameter Teflon tips which vibrate against the skin of the back. Their on-off activity is triggered by the patterns of light and dark viewed by a television camera, and can be monitored visually on an oscilloscope as a two-dimensional pictorial display. In most of our experiments to date the subject has manipulated the TV camera mounted on a tripod.
>
> More than thirty blind subjects have been trained to use the TVSS. Of these, eight (six congenitally blind) have received 40 or more hours (40–200) of training.
>
> After being introduced to the mechanics of operating the apparatus, subjects are trained to discriminate vertical, horizontal, diagonal and curved lines. They then learn to recognize combinations of lines (circles, squares and triangles) and solid geometric forms. After approximately one hour of such training, they are introduced to a "vocabulary" of twenty-five common objects: a telephone, chair, cup, toy horse and others. With repeated presentations, the latency or time-to-recognition of these objects falls markedly; in the process, the students discover visual concepts such as perspective, shadows, shape distortion as a function of viewpoint, and apparent change in size as a function of distance. When more than one object is presented at a time, the subjects learn to discriminate overlapping objects, and to describe the positional relationship of three and four objects in one field. The visual analysis technique and concepts thus developed are then used in letter recognition, in the perception of moving stimuli and in the exploration of other persons standing before the camera. Our subjects learn to discriminate between individuals, to decide where they are in the room, to describe their posture, movements, and individual char-

42. Paul Bach-y-Rita, "Sensory Plasticity: Applications to a Vision Substitution System," *Acta Neurologica Scandinavica*, 43 (1967), 417–426; Paul Bach-y-Rita, C. C. Collins, F. Saunders, B. White, and L. Scadden, "Vision Substitution by Tactile Image Projection," *Nature*, 221 (1969), 963–964; Paul Bach-y-Rita, C. C. Collins, B. White, F. Saunders, L. Scadden, and R. Blomberg, "A Tactile Vision Substitution System," *American Journal of Optometry*, 46 (1969), 109–111; Paul Bach-y-Rita, "Neurophysiological Basis of a Tactile Vision Substitution System," *IEEE Transactions on Man-Machine Systems*, MMS-11 (1970), 108–110.

acteristics such as height, hair length, presence or absence of glasses and so on.[43]

Despite what its developer describes as the "primitive" nature of this TVSS, the predictions of the hypothesis appear confirmed:

> Our subjects spontaneously report the external localization of stimuli, in that sensory information seems to come from in front of the camera, rather than from the vibrotactors on their back.[44]

If the concept of receptor specificity were interpreted strictly, it would be expected that stimulation from the tactors would produce cutaneous sensations such as touch. However, after several hours of training, the sensation produced during a perceptual task is not cutaneous: the cutaneous receptors are mediating tele-receptor pattern information and in that sense the sensation is comparable to a visual sensation. The blind subject, using the TVSS to explore such objects as a telephone or a stuffed animal, perceives what a sighted subject sees when looking at the same objects on the oscilloscope monitor. This includes depth information, obtained by "monocular" cues such as occlusion and elevation in the visual field when perceiving spatially distributed arrangements of objects.[45]

"It felt as if I was seeing things," proclaimed one partially converted former skeptic (a normally sighted M.D.) after only a half-hour's practice with Bach-y-Rita's early TVSS prototype. In the present stage of development of this device, of course, these initial reports can be considered little more than anecdotal evidence. Extensive further research and development obviously is required before it can be determined conclusively whether the prediction entailed by the hypothesis is confirmed or disconfirmed by these experiments. But these early reports do encourage favorable expectations.

43. Paul Bach-y-Rita, "Sensory Substitution and Limb Prosthesis," in *Advances in External Control of Human Extremities*, Proceedings of the Third International Symposium on External Control of Human Extremities, Dubrovnik, August 1969, ed. M. M. Gavrilović and A. Bennett Wilson, Jr. (Belgrade: Yugoslav Committee for Electronics and Automation, 1970), pp. 10–11.

44. *Ibid.*, p. 11.

45. Paul Bach-y-Rita, "A Tactile Vision Substitution System Based on Sensory Plasticity," in *Visual Prosthesis: The Interdisciplinary Dialogue*, Proceedings of the Second Conference on Visual Prosthesis, ed. T. D. Sterling, E. A. Bering, Jr., S. V. Pollack, and H. G. Vaughan, Jr. (New York: Academic Press, 1971), p. 287.

Regardless whether future experiments confirm or disconfirm the hypothesis, the derivation from it of these empirical predictions establishes independently a fact of considerable theoretical interest: the deduction establishes that (contrary to Wittgensteinian and positivistic metaphilosophical doctrines rejected in the Introduction to this book) a theory engineered in response to a "philosophic problem" *can* entail specific experimental scientific predictions. Indeed, the empirical falsifiability of the hypothesis demonstrates that it passes the test by which Karl Popper, for example, would demarcate "scientific" theories.[46]

Remark: If corroborated by further research and experimentation, the same results that confirm my hypothesis apparently would refute Putnam's attempted formulation of a functionalist hypothesis. Putnam's crucial axiom (which he states only for the special case of pain sensations) entails the following:[47]

> *(4) For every state table description of a certain kind possessed by an organism, M, there exists a subset of the sensory inputs such that an organism with that description is in pain when and only when some of its sensory inputs are in that subset.*

Generalizing the same principle to visual sensation(s) would entail the following:

> *(4 Visual) For every state table of a certain kind realized by M, there exists a subset of (sensory) inputs such that any organism realizing that state table has visual sensation(s) when and only when some of its (sensory) inputs are in that subset (or of that kind).*

And for cutaneous or tactile sensation:

> *(4 Tactual) For every state table of a certain kind realized by M, there exists a subset of (sensory) inputs such that any organism realizing that state table has tactual sensation(s) when and only when some of its (sensory) inputs are in that subset (or of that kind).*

---

46. "I . . . require of a scientific system . . . that its logical form shall be such that it can be singled out, by means of empirical tests, in a negative sense: it must be possible for an empirical scientific system to be refuted by experience," (Karl R. Popper, *The Logic of Scientific Discovery* [London: Hutchinson, 1959], pp. 40–41).

47. Hilary Putnam, "Psychological Predicates," in *Art, Mind, and Religion*, Sixth Oberlin Colloquium in Philosophy, 1965, ed. W. H. Capitan and D. D. Merrill (Pittsburgh: University of Pittsburgh Press, n.d.), p. 42; reprinted as "The Nature of Mental States," in *Materialism and the Mind-Body Problem*, ed. David M. Rosenthal (Englewood Cliffs, N.J.: Prentice-Hall, 1971), p. 155.

From Chapter 1 readers may recall that in Putnam's formulation the "inputs" (which he calls "sensory inputs") are interpreted to be events for which "the physical realization[s] of the sense organs [are] responsible," that is, presumably, specific causal effects of the operation of the various physical sense organs. Thus, in the case of visual sensation(s), the relevant "sensory inputs" might be, for example, certain neural events in the peripheral visual system, e.g., neuron firings in the optic nerve or in the primary visual projection areas of the "visual cortex" of the brain. For tactual sensation(s), the relevant "sensory inputs" might be, e.g., presumably, activated hair follicle receptors, stimulated free nerve endings in the skin, or the firings of certain fibers in the spinal cord. So interpreted, the generalization of Putnam's principles entails that a subject or organism, *M*, will have *visual* sensation(s) when and only when events of a certain kind occur in *M*'s peripheral visual system (e.g., firings in the optic tract), and that *M* will have *tactual* sensation(s) when and only when hair follicle receptors or free nerve endings in the skin are stimulated. This being so, the results predicted by my formulation of the functionalist hypothesis and apparently observed in the described experiments refute Putnam's hypothesis. For in these experiments, subjects apparently have visual sensation(s) when *no* "sensory inputs" of the indicated kind (e.g., neuron firings in the peripheral visual system) are present or exist; and they do not have cutaneous or tactual sensations although "inputs" of the indicated kind (activated hair follicle receptors and free nerve endings in the skin) are produced by the vibrotactors. Indeed, apparently there is *no* set of peripheral neural events whose existence or presence is a necessary and sufficient condition for the organism having tactual sensation(s); likewise for visual sensation(s). Thus it seems that Putnam's hypothesis is empirically falsified by experimental results of a sort that will (if substantiated) confirm the present hypothesis.

The foregoing argument furthermore establishes that the hypothesis formulated by Putnam (under a natural physicalistic interpretation, at least, and in the context of the assumed auxiliary hypotheses) is *logically incompatible* with the hypothesis of my model. For my hypothesis implies a prediction regarding fully adapted TVSS users which, if it is confirmed, refutes Putnam's hypothesis. That is, if my hypothesis is true, then fully adapted TVSS users will have visual sensory experience; and if fully adapted TVSS users have visual sensory experience, then Putnam's hypothesis is not true. Therefore, if my hypothesis is true, Putnam's hypothesis is false; and if Putnam's hypothesis is true, then my hypothhypothesis is false. Thus, far from being identical or even equivalent theories, the two theories are contrary to each other: both could be false, but if either of them is true, then the other is false.

Objection: The TVSS is pretty interesting on its own, but I doubt that the results cited have much to do with your hypothesis. My reason for thinking so is as follows. As I understand it, your claim is that if organisms satisfied the same FSTs, they had the same subjective experience. Now the blind subjects using TVSSs don't satisfy the same FSTs as sighted subjects or even that portion of the FST relevant to viewing the monitor. So it isn't obvious that your theory makes any prediction about the experience of these subjects.[48]

Reply: On the contrary, the conclusion that fully adapted subjects using a TVSS would satisfy the same FST as sighted subjects follows directly from the basic definition of a functional state table (FST) and what it is for a system to "satisfy" or realize an FST. An FST is an abstract "input-output" characterization that delineates or individuates "states" of a system exclusively in terms of the system's input-output characteristics. Suppose that system A "satisfies" or realizes FST F_1. Suppose that another system, B, would (counterfactually) respond to every possible different sequence of the "inputs" listed in F_1 by producing the same sequence of "outputs" mentioned in F_1 as would system A. Then B also realizes or satisfies F_1. This is implied by the definition of an FST. Two systems having identical overall input-output characteristics satisfy the same FST.

(These conditions are expressible more rigorously so as explicitly to take into account the fact that the string of outputs a certain system will produce in response to a given string of inputs depends on its F-state when it receives the initial input. Thus, more precisely: Suppose system A realizes FST F_1 and system B realizes FST F_2. If corresponding to *each* state, S_i^A, in F_1 there exists a state, S_j^B, in F_2 such that a realization of F_1 started in S_i^A would respond to any possible sequence of inputs from F_1 by producing a string of outputs of the same kind as would a realization of F_2 started in S_j^B, and vice versa, then systems A and B realize the same FST. For purposes of brevity, I will assume the existence of corresponding states to be understood in the following discussion.)

One premise, then, of the deduction is: If system B would respond to all the same possible sequence of inputs (mentioned in FST F_k) by producing the same sequences of outputs (of kinds mentioned in F_k) as would system A, which realizes F_k, then system B also "satisfies" or realizes F_k.

48. This objection is due to Charles E. Marks (personal correspondence).

Second, as has been emphasized repeatedly, the claim in question is made in relation to FSTs that take as "inputs" *external physical objects or events in the organism's environment* and show as "outputs" motor movements or behaviors by the organism. (This, of course, is one of the respects in which my hypothesis differs from that of Putnam, who takes the "inputs" to be events inside the organism.)

Suppose that F_α is an FST of this sort. From this supposition plus the premises above, it logically follows that if subject A satisfies F_α and subject B'would respond to all the same possible sequences of external physical objects or events (listed in F_α) by producing the same sequences of bodily movements or behaviors (listed in F_α) as A, them system B also satisfies the same FST, F_α.

But a (hypothetical) fully adapted subject using an operating TVSS would respond to all the same sequences of external environments by producing the same output movements or behaviors as, say, he previously produced or would have produced when using his natural eyes. For example, asked to read an illuminated eye chart (the "input"), he will reel off the same sequence of letters ("output") as the naturally sighted subject. If in the mood to do so, he can point to and track distant moving visible objects with his finger. When a ball is hit into the air, he can run to the appropriate place and catch it as previously when normally sighted. In driving a car, he would respond to various possible external traffic circumstances (input) by performing exactly the same sequences of physical movements or operations (output) as previously when naturally sighted. One even might assume that when attending films (including silent movies), the subject enjoys them as formerly, showing all the same emotional reactions to their dramatic content as before, recounting their plots afterward as well as anyone else, etc. And so on. (Obviously, we are not here talking about current wearers of presently existing TVSSs, but about hypothesized ideal cases. Also, of course, either we are imagining a TVSS that additionally operates so as to enable color discriminations, or else we are expressly excluding color-discriminatory behavior and the awareness of colors from the present theoretical derivation. Different responses before and after to questions like 'When did you first use a TVSS?' also here are ignored as presumably irrelevant to the subject's sensory state.) By definition, then, a formerly sighted now *fully adapted* "blind subject using a TVSS" would respond to all the same possible sequences of external physical environments by producing the same sequences of behavior (i.e., the same sequences of outputs) as previously when naturally sighted.

Conjoining this fact with the previous conclusion (that two systems that would respond to similar possible sequences of environments by producing similar sequences of behaviors satisfy the same FST) logically entails that fully adapted blind subjects using a TVSS would satisfy the same (or almost the same) FST as, e.g., before when using their natural eyes. Note that it is the *adapted-subject-cum-TVSS*, i.e., the total compound system consisting of organism plus machine, that responds to the same inputs (external environments) by producing the same outputs (behavior) as a sighted subject, and it is *this* system (and *not* just the adapted subject alone, considered as an isolated system, minus his "artificial eye") that satisfies (approximately) the same FST as the normally sighted subject. An adapted subject alone, considered in isolation, minus his TVSS, does not satisfy the same FST. It is only the *compound* entity consisting of adapted subject *plus* TVSS that the theory predicts will "see."

Thus the conclusion is reached that a fully adapted blind subject using a (perfect) TVSS *would* satisfy the same FST as a sighted subject. For clarity and rigor, this argument is formalized in Figure 11.[49] Notice that this derivation requires for premises only definitions or "analytic" statements (which shows that the point simply follows from the definitions of the concepts involved). From the conclusion that a fully adapted blind subject using a TVSS would satisfy the same FST as a naturally sighted subject, it further follows, by my hypothesis, that both subjects will have similar subjective experiences, the predicted experimental result.

[An experimental situation approximating return to the same original FST is idealized, of course, by the foregoing analysis. Instead of explaining the predicted phenomenon by reference to this idealization, one could reason alternatively, "Because the fully adapted TVSS user returns to almost the same FST as originally, if the hypothesis is true, he should again have almost the same sensory experience as originally." Likewise in reference to experiments with inverting spectacles, one can reason, "Adapted wearers of inverting spectacles return to approximately the same

49. The obvious (I hope!) meaning of the lines, arrows, and other notation in this diagram is explained explicitly in the author's basic textbook, *Practical Reasoning in Natural Language* (Englewood Cliffs, N.J.: Prentice-Hall, 1977).

PROOF

(By definition): For any FST, say F_i, if system A satisfies F_i and system B would respond to all the same possible sequences of inputs (listed in F_i) by producing the same sequences of outputs (listed in F_i) as system A, then system B also satisfies F_i.

+

(By stipulation of the intended interpretation of the stated axioms or by "definition"): For Thomas's postulated FSTs, external physical environments are the "inputs" and physical motor behaviors are the "outputs."

(deductively valid)

(By definition or analytic judgment explicating the meaning of a "fully adapted" user of a TVSS): If a naturally blind subject using a TVSS is fully adapted (let us call him "Jones-afterward" for short), then he would respond to all the same possible sequences of external physical environments by producing the same sequences of physical motor behaviors as previously when sighted (i.e., the same as "Jones-before").

For any FST, say F_α, of the kind postulated by Thomas, if system A satisfies F_α and system B would respond to all the same possible sequences of external physical environments (listed in F_α) by producing the same sequences of physical motor behaviors (listed in F_α) as A, then B also satisfies F_α.

(deductively valid)

(deductively valid)

If "Jones-afterward" is a (naturally blind) fully adapted TVSS user, then he would respond to all the same possible sequences of external physical environments (listed in F_α) by producing the same sequences of physical motor behaviors (listed in F_α) as "Jones-before."

+

For any FST, say F_α, of the kind postulated by Thomas, if "Jones-before" satisfies F_α and "Jones-afterward" would respond to all the same possible sequences of external physical environments (listed in F_α) by producing the same sequences of physical motor behaviors (listed in F_α) as "Jones-before," then "Jones-afterward" also satisfies F_α.

(deductively valid)

If "Jones-afterward" is a (naturally blind) fully adapted TVSS user, and F_α is an FST of the kind postulated by Thomas, and F_α was satisfied by "Jones-before," then "Jones-afterward" also satisfies F_α.

It is *not* the case that "blind subjects using TVSS's don't satisfy the same FSTs as sighted subjects."

Figure 11.

FST as before donning the glasses; therefore, if Principle 4 is true, it is reasonable to expect them to return to approximately the same psychological states, with approximately the same sensory experience, as before."]

4. Implications for Psycholinguistics

The present theory has important implications for psycholinguistics. This section discusses its consequences for (1) the recent claim that certain observed facts of linguistic behavior necessitate the positing of special "mental" operations; (2) the problem of finding the proper theoretical framework for the semantic theory of a natural language; and (3) Quine's thesis of indeterminacy of translation.

1) Jerry A. Fodor has claimed that certain observed facts of linguistic behavior cannot be understood behavioristically but instead necessitate the positing of special "mental" operations. These facts are as follows. In actual experiments, when subjects were presented with acoustic signals expressing utterances in their native language and asked to indicate where they "heard pauses," it was discovered that they were more likely to report pauses "at the syntactic boundary between words than at those points at which acoustic pauses occur within words."[50] For example,

> Almost everyone who speaks English will locate a pause in the juncture of the phrase 'Bob#Lees' [the symbol '#' here shows the place of the pause] though one can certify by spectographic analysis (or for many speakers, just by carefully attending to repetitions of the phrase) that the acoustic pattern is closer to 'Bo#bLees'—that is, that the point of greatest acoustic energy drop is before the second 'b'.[51]

This and similar experiments seem to show that there is no simple direct correlation between drops in acoustic energy ("acoustic pauses") in the spoken utterance and the pauses located by the subject. Moreover, the location of pauses in more complex utterances, such as sentences, has been observed to correspond to the major grammatical breaks more nearly than it does to actual drops in the acoustic energy in the utterance. For example, in

---

50. Jerry A. Fodor, *Psychological Explanation* (New York: Random House, 1968), p. 81. The experiments and their results, informally described in that work, are presented in detail in Jerry A. Fodor and T. Bever, "The Psychological Reality of Linguistic Segments," *Journal of Verbal Learning and Verbal Behavior*, 4 (1965), 414–420; and M. Garrett, T. Bever, and Jerry Fodor, "The Active Use of Grammar in Speech Perception," *Journal of Perception and Psychophysics*, 1 (1966), 30–32.

51. Fodor, *Psychological Explanation*, p. 82.

the case of the simple sentence

((The) (man)) ((hit) ((the) (colorful) (ball)))[52]

"most speakers tend to locate the longest pause on one or the other side of 'hit' . . . although, in acoustic fact, normal utterances of this sentence contain no major energy drop at all."[53] This observation supports the conclusion that the subject "apparently locates pauses largely by reference to the constituent structure of the sentences in which they are heard."[54]

These data, Fodor says, raise for psycholinguistics the problem: "How is the constituent structure of a sentence recognized by the person who hears it?" He remarks:

> The general outlines of the answer to this question are now fairly clear. The constituent structure of a sentence is automatically specified by the rules of certain sorts of grammars. Such grammars also have a number of other properties that are clearly related to the capacities actually exhibited by speakers of natural languages: they afford a recursive characterization of the set of grammatical sequences of morphemes, they provide analyses of certain types of structural ambiguity that are exhibited by some sentences of all natural languages, they predict the obligatory stress patterns exhibited in spoken sentences, and so on.[55]

Fodor is here, of course, referring to "grammars" of the kind developed by Noam Chomsky and others.[56] He continues:

> The inference would appear to be that the data-processing that is involved in the perception (or, for that matter, in the production) of a sentence in one's own language involves the appli-

---

52. The parentheses in the quoted example indicate its grammatical parsing or, as it is also called, its "constituent structure."
53. Fodor, *Psychological Explanation*, p. 82.
54. *Ibid.*, pp. 82–83.
55. *Ibid.*
56. The interested reader may consult Noam Chomsky, *Syntactic Structures* (The Hague: Mouton, 1957); also "On the Notion 'Rule of Grammar'" (1961), re- reprinted in *The Structure of Language*, ed. Jerry A. Fodor and Jerrold J. Katz (Englewood Cliffs, N.J.: Prentice-Hall, 1965), pp. 119–136; also Chomsky, *Aspects of the Theory of Syntax* (Cambridge, Mass.: The M.I.T. Press, 1965); also Jerrold J. Katz and Paul M. Postal, *An Integrated Theory of Linguistic Descriptions*, Research Monograph No. 26 (Cambridge, Mass.: The M.I.T. Press, 1964). Chomsky also maintains that "behaviorism" can provide no valuable insight into any significant linguistic process; see Chomsky, "Review of Skinner's *Verbal Behavior*," *Language*, 35 (1959), 26–58.

cation of the sort of rules that such grammars formulate. In particular, understanding a sentence in one's native language involves using rules to assign the appropriate constituent analysis and it is that assignment, in turn, that dictates the perceived pausal segmentation the sentence bears. This hypothesis accounts for the fact that different speakers agree on the location of pauses in the sentence of their language, as well as for the fact that the ability to apprehend such pauses is confined to sentences uttered in a language one understands. For in the former case all speakers of a language presumably employ the same constituent structure rules and in the latter case learning the constituent structure rules for a language is a part of learning the language.[57]

Explaining the observed facts of overt linguistic behavior therefore requires postulating that a great deal of unconscious data processing takes place inside the subject.

Fodor argues that these facts have important implications for theory construction in psychology. They show, he says, that

> some patterns of explanation in psychology require the hypothesizing of psychological events and processes that may be arbitrarily remote from behavior. This contention, if correct, would appear to be incompatible with adopting any form of behav-

---

57. Fodor, *Psychological Explanation*, pp. 83–84. When Fodor says that the data processing "involves the application of" certain rules, he presumably means that the data-processing operations underlying the subject's speech comprehension and production *take place in accordance with* such rules. Fodor's way of speaking should not lead one to assume that somehow a speaker covertly consults an actual internal statement or other expression of the rule in the course of his operations. Wittgenstein first stressed the important difference between *acting in accordance with a rule* and *actually making reference to an expression of it*, and pointed out that the former can occur without the latter (*Blue Book*, p. 13). True, when one has the necessary training, consulting an expression of a rule sometimes may aid one in operating in accordance with it, but one need not always do this. In speech comprehension and production, the speaker operates *in accordance with* rules of the sort expressed in grammars, but this does not imply that in performing these operations he must, "consciously" or "unconsciously," make reference to internalized statements or expressions of these rules. Thus, in psycholinguistic contexts it perhaps would be preferable to say that the subject "embodies" or "realizes" these rules, rather than that he "applies," "obeys," "uses," or "refers to" them. This does not mean, of course, that it is wrong for linguists and psycholinguists to express their theories in terms of explicit statements of "grammatical rules." For what from one standpoint is a rule, from another is a description. The speaker's linguistic operations are "described" by such rules in the sense that they *accord* with them, but this does not mean that speakers of the language must make covert reference to some expression of the rule in order to carry out the operations they perform.

ioristic strictures upon the relation between observation language and theoretical terms in psychological theories.[58]

According to Fodor, "the psychological events and processes" that must be hypothesized to explain these linguistic abilities shown by speakers are "mental" operations of a certain sort:

> But now, what of the operations that are involved in applying such rules [of grammar]? . . . In the first place, it is clear that they are *unconscious* operations in the sense that they cannot be reported by subjects. . . . More to the point, it is clear that there are no behavioral *correlates* for such operations. . . . Behavior is produced when the sentence is understood, if it is produced at all; thus, individual mental operations are related to behavior only via the entire computational process of which they form a part. The justification for positing such operations in a psychological explanation can be, then, neither that subjects report their occurrence nor that some nonverbal behavioral index of their occurrence has been observed. Rather, we posit such operations simply because they are required for the construction of an adequate theory of speech perception.[59]

Fodor thus justifies rejecting behaviorism and accepting what he calls "mentalism" on the grounds of the necessity, from the psychologist's standpoint, of postulating unconscious mental operations.

At the same time, Fodor acknowledges that an objection might be raised to his claim that it is necessary to postulate *mental* events:

> It may be argued that there is no reason for thinking of the events that are postulated in psychological explanations of the sort we have been considering as mental events.[60]

But he cites two points in favor of calling them "mental":

> Unlike such unconscious processes as capillary contraction, the kinds of events that are necessary for the comprehension of language are clearly such that if they *were* conscious, one would not hesitate to call them intelligent performances; they would indeed be paradigms of the sort of processes that we describe as mental. The second point is that the alleged processes eventuate in unequivocally intelligent behavior.[61]

58. Fodor, *Psychological Explanation*, p. 86.
59. *Ibid.*, p. 84.
60. *Ibid.*, p. 86.
61. *Ibid.*, p. 87.

According to Fodor, "the fact that understanding a language is an intellectual achievement provides at least some reason for regarding as mental processes the data-process[ing] that it requires."[62] Objections also might be raised against saying that these alleged mental events are "unconscious":

> It is possible to maintain that to entertain the notion of an unconscious mental process is either to indulge in an incoherence or to implicitly suggest that we redefine "mental."[63]

Fodor explains that he calls these processes "unconscious" because "they cannot be reported by the subject."[64]

Fodor thus thinks that characterizing these linguistic abilities requires postulations incompatible with behaviorist strictures, meaning by 'behaviorism' any view according to which "for each mental predicate that can be employed in a psychological explanation, there is some description of behavior to which it bears a logical relation."[65] Since, as shown in Appendix II, my functionalist hypothesis entails that for each pure mental predicate, there exists some description of behavior whose satisfaction is a logically sufficient condition for that predicate's ascription, my hypothesis entails behaviorism in Fodor's sense. So if the posits necessary to characterize these linguistic abilities are incompatible with behaviorism, as Fodor claims, then they also must be incompatible with my functionalist hypothesis (which entails behaviorism). So Fodor's contention entails that my hypothesis is inconsistent with facts such as those he cites. That is, if Fodor's claim were true, linguistic phenomena such as those he cites could not be characterized consistently with the present theory. So now I wish to show that, contrary to Fodor, these facts can be described naturally and perspicuously by an account of the proposed form. This will be demonstrated directly by actually constructing such a description. Doing so will serve the further purpose of providing a paradigm for the analysis of more complex aspects of linguistic behavior.

A partial FST-description will now be formulated characterizing the competence exhibited in the simple "Bob Lees" experiment. Since the table below is only a simple illustration, the liberty has been taken of also including in it the probable results

62. *Ibid.*
63. *Ibid.*, p. 86.
64. *Ibid.*
65. *Ibid.*, p. 51.

of additional experiments with other different sound patterns. Entries in the input list are general terms designating sounds of various kinds. Here simple symbols like 'Ba', 'bLees', and 'Jones' have been used to indicate sounds of the sort produced by a normal English-speaking reader's pronouncing these symbols (a less imprecise analysis would strive to describe these sounds purely in terms of physical acoustics). Notice that the illustration also mixes microlevel with macrolevel inputs, outputs, and states.[66] That is, some of the inputs shown consist of only a syllable, while others are complete sentences, and all outputs shown are complete sentences. (It would be highly desirable to have an FST constructed at the microlevel throughout, but such an FST would constitute a complete theory of linguistic behavior which psychology does not presently possess.) Positions in the table involving changes of state leading to parts of the FST not shown in the illustration have been left blank. Table 4–7 partially characterizes the competence shown by speakers in the "Bob Lees" experiment.

	S_I	S_J	S_L	S_{Ba}	S_{Bc}	*States* S_{BL}	S_{Bl}	S_{BB}	S_{BJ}
'			$S_{Ba}(\Lambda)$		$S_{BB}(\Lambda)$				
ees'				$S_{Bl}(\Lambda)$	$S_{BL}(\Lambda)$				
nes'					$S_{BJ}(\Lambda)$				
here s the use ne in fol- ing?'	$S_J(\Lambda)$								
ty- li- ond ustic				$S_{Bc}\,\Lambda$					
- ond nce		$S_L(\Lambda)$	$S_L(\Lambda)$			S_x ("Between 'Bob' and 'Lees'")	S_y("No pause—the word is 'Bobblies'")	S_z ("Between the two 'Ba's'")	S_x ("Between 'Ba' and 'Jones'")

Table 4–7.

66. See Appendix I.

Let us follow the subject as he "unconsciously computes" a pause between 'Bob' and 'Lees' from the acoustic input 'Ba#bLees'. Suppose he starts in S_I. The experimenter says, 'Where does the pause come in the following?' and the subject passes into state S_J. After a pause of two seconds, the subject passes into S_L where he stays until the experimenter starts talking again. (If the experimenter said 'Ba#bLees' *immediately* after saying 'Where does the pause come in the following?' without the intervening two-second pause, this subject would pass into a state not shown in this [partial] FST with different subsequent behavior; the macrolevel mentalistic description of what happened would be that the subject interpreted the experimenter as saying, "Where does the pause come in the following, Bob Lees?", i.e., addressing him as if the experimenter thought the subject's name was 'Bob Lees'.) As the experimenter utters 'Ba#bLees', the subject passes through a series of states. With the sound 'Ba', he passes into microstate S_{Ba}, with the sixty-millisecond pause he passes into S_{Bc}, and with 'bLees' he passes into S_{BL}. After a two-second silence, he says 'Between "Bob" and "Lees".'[67] Thus, from the input 'Ba#bLees' he arrives at 'Bob Lees'. Different inputs would have elicited different responses. For example, given 'Ba' followed by 'bLees' without the sixty-millisecond acoustic pause, he would identify the input as 'Bobblies' (pronounced as one word sounding somewhat like the name of a new breakfast cereal). Or if given 'Ba#Jones', he would report that the pause comes between 'Ba' and 'Jones'. A realization of this FST, then will report a pause between 'Bob' and Lees' in the sound 'Ba # bLees', but will respond to 'BabLees' as 'Bobblies' and 'Ba#Jones' as 'Ba Jones'. In *these* operations, then, a realization of this FST exhibits the linguistic competence shown by speakers in the "Bob Lees" experiment.

This construction illustrates how linguistic behavior of the sort Fodor describes is characterizable within the present theoretical framework. The partial FST in the example obviously does not characterize every aspect of these phenomena (nor was it intended to do so), but it does show the general form of such a characterization, requiring for completion only that additional facts be incorporated in the manner it illustrates. To develop the

67. This output expresses the subject's report of the location of the pause.

characterization would require, for one thing, filling in the rest of the microsteps underlying the transitions from the inputs to the outputs. That is, the input question, 'Where does the pause come in the following?' should be broken down into a sequence of parts and an account given of how this sequence gets the system into state S_J. Likewise, one would like to see in microdetail, including all the processes involved in constructing the output utterance, how the system gets from state S_{Bc} to outputting the sentence "Between 'Bob' and Lees'." And one would want to see the FST filled in to show how the system would perform similar operations for all other input sequences for which it can do this. Although this is clearly a prodigious undertaking, no difficulty opposes doing it within the present framework. The FST in the illustration shows only a small stretch of the microlevel data processing underlying the ability Fodor describes, but no reason exists to think that the remainder of the FST cannot be similarly filled in.

Such an FST, when completed, would provide a full description of these linguistic abilities, not only characterizing the facts in detail, but also yielding predictions extending beyond the original behavioral data. For example, suppose a formerly normal speaker develops a disability in producing outputs X, Y, and Z, and that these outputs have in common the fact that passage through F-state S_m is requisite to their production. A plausible hypothesis then would be that something has gone wrong in him either preventing his passage into this state or his passage out of it in his former way. This hypothesis might be tested further by applying other untried inputs and observing the outputs. Indeed, if the concrete mechanisms underlying his FST were known, one could, in principle, directly intervene in the subject's neural machinery to correct his difficulty. So an account of the proposed form is not a mere restatement of the data, but a full and complete characterization of the phenomenon, including underlying complex events involved. The only aspects of the speaker's competence left uncharacterized by an FST-description of this sort would be its genesis (i.e., how the speaker came to have this FST) and its neuropsychology (i.e., by what concrete mechanisms these operations are performed).

A characterization of this form not only fits nicely with linguistic theory and leads to specific predictions, it also accords well with some of the psycholinguist's more general expectations. Since the transitions from state to state within the system constitute computational operations, the account shows, as Fodor demands, "the operations involved in applying" the rules of grammar.[68] Moreover, as may be confirmed by noting the presence of the null output ('Λ') at many of these stages, the FST shows many operations for which "there are no behavioral correlates."[69] Indeed, the descriptions of the postulated states are connected to the descriptions of outward behavior (the inputs and outputs) only by the FST-description that characterizes the overall functioning of the system. So the account shows, as Fodor had speculated, that the "individual mental operations are related to behavior only via the entire computational process of which they form a part."[70] It shows, furthermore, exactly *how* the postulated states and processes are related to overt behavior, i.e., it shows the *precise relationship* between these states and processes and the overt behavior.

2) Also characterizable within the present theoretical framework are the *semantic* aspects of linguistic competence. In fact, the hypothesis solves a hoary theoretical puzzle by showing how a natural language's so-called "meaning rules" can be expressed in symbols themselves possessing conventional linguistic meaning without circularity, triviality, or reference to such occult entities as "meanings" or "intensions." For my theory entails that *a complete semantic representation of a natural language is given by an FST-description of a normal speaker of it*. This corollary derives as follows. Such descriptions as 'comprehends the meaning of English', 'understands French', 'knows the word's meaning', etc., are mentalistic, so they or their mentalistic components, according to the hypothesis, are functionally determined. More precisely, the existence is entailed of FSTs whose realizations, ipso facto, speak and comprehend the language (as well as possessing all other mentalistic attributes associated with this ability, such as "knowing what the words mean," "under-

---

68. Notice that although a realization of this FST acts in accordance with certain rules, the FST does not represent him as making reference to any expression of these rules. He simply receives the acoustical signal, passes through a series of states, and outputs the correct answer. No reference to a statement of the rule (as it might be, "Ba#bLees → Bob#Lees") is required. The rules, insofar as they are "internalized" in the subject, are reflected in his FST.

69. Fodor, *Psychological Explanation*, p. 84.

70. *Ibid.*

standing what was just said," etc.).[71] Everything requisite or necessary to understanding the language therefore must be incorporated in such FSTs. Since "a semantic theory of a natural language has as its goal the construction of a system of rules which represent what a fluent speaker knows about the semantic structure of his language that permits him to understand its sentences,"[72] such FSTs achieve the goal of a semantic theory. That is, if an FST is constructible such that a system need only realize it to possess all aspects of linguistic competence, then it (or some part of it) must itself comprise an expression or representation of all the contents and rules of that language (including semantic rules)—and my hypothesis entails the existence of such FSTs; hence, the hypothesis entails that the "meaning rules" or "semantics" of a natural language can be completely specified (and the goal of semantic theory accomplished) by FST descriptions of its speakers. Or varying this corollary's statement with the terms of Wittgenstein's metaphor or model: any language game's complete rules are fully represented by an FST-description of its players.

Such an FST's realizations can produce, comprehend, and respond appropriately to utterances in the given language. Listing the language's words, phonemes, or morphemes along with other possible stimulus inputs, the FST will show how, depending on an auditor's functional state at the time he receives them, different possible strings of these inputs would affect him, perhaps changing his mental state and eliciting relevant motor responses, and how, depending again on his functional state (perhaps when he has certain intentions or purposes), a realization may form and produce output-utterance sequences expressing meaningful statements suitably constructed to activate appropriate responses in other realizations of similar FSTs. Such FSTs also, of course, will characterize many of a speaker's nonlinguistic abilities; they will show his perceptual sensitivities, his motor skills, emotional susceptibilities, reasoning capabilities, factual beliefs, etc., as well as his linguistic competence. So from such an FST, semantic theory must abstract the features specifically constitutive of a realization's semantic competence. But although the postulated FSTs may in this respect contain too much information, it remains

71. See Chapter 3, Section 4.
72. Jerrold J. Katz, "Analyticity and Contradiction in Natural Language," in *The Structure of Language*, Fodor and Katz, eds., pp. 519–520.

true that if the hypothesis is correct, an FST-framework is adequate for the expression or formulation of a semantic theory, i.e., semantic representations can have the formal structure of an FST.

With its rejection of private-inner-object psychological models, my hypothesis naturally suggests a paradigm of language's role in communication quite different from that presupposed in traditional or classical efforts to construct a semantic theory. Jerrold J. Katz, for example, like John Locke,[73] conceives of linguistic communication as a process wherein unknown "mechanisms operate to encode and decode verbal messages"[74] that express or report speakers' inner mental contents, thoughts, or meanings:

> [Linguistic communication] is a process that involves the transmission of one person's thoughts to another by means of disturbances in the air which the first person creates for this purpose. Somehow the speaker encodes his inner thoughts in the form of external, observable acoustic events, and the hearer, perceiving these sounds, decodes them, thereby obtaining for himself his own inner representation of the speaker's thoughts. It is in this way that we use language to obtain knowledge of the contents of another's mind.[75]

Since my functionalist hypothesis rejects private-inner-object psychological models, of course, it must reject any such account of linguistic communication. Instead, it suggests the more Wittgensteinian paradigm of a group of FSTs[76] talking to one another, each affecting the others' functional states, behavior, and responses to subsequent stimuli by the production of special outputs that serve as inputs to others. (The difficult special case of utterances that do report the speaker's own mental state ["inner thoughts"] already has been treated at length in the account in Chapter 1 of first-person mental self-description.)

These fundamentally different underlying models of linguistic communication lead to different judgments about how semantic representations of natural language should be structured formally. While my hypothesis supports trying to construct a semantic theory by relating sentences to external stimulus situations, behavioral outputs, and abstract functional states, Katz would

---

73. John Locke, *Essay Concerning Human Understanding* (1690), Book III.
74. Jerrold J. Katz, "Mentalism in Linguistics," *Language*, 40 (1964), 128.
75. Jerrold J. Katz, *Semantic Theory* (New York: Harper & Row, 1972), p. 24.
76. Or, more precisely, their realizations.

build semantic theory by trying to relate these same linguistic objects to the meanings (or "inner thoughts") he supposes them to express. So naturally Katz's "main concern is with the discovery of hypotheses about the mental capacities that underlie the complex chain of operations by which structures expressing the meaning of a sentence are related to its physical exemplifications"[77] (that is, explaining the encoding of an "inner thought" into a symbolic linguistic expression). Katz's assumption that a theoretical account of the essential structure of natural languages "must begin by explicating the principles of encoding and decoding by which speakers of a natural language find the appropriate words for expressing their thoughts and find out what thoughts are expressed by the words they hear"[78] is directly reflected in the formal framework he proposes for semantic theory: a *dictionary* containing an entry giving "senses" for each lexical item in the language, a *grammar* providing a characterization of the syntactic structure of each sentence considered, and a set of *projection rules* using information from the dictionary and grammar to map each sentence of the language onto formal objects called its "semantic interpretations,"[79] entities supposedly representing or somehow corresponding to the meaning(s) of each sentence as determined compositionally from the senses of its constituent lexical items and the grammatical relations between its syntactic components.[80]

The semantic interpretations produced by a semantic theory constitute the theory's description of the semantic structure of a language. Since a speaker's knowledge of semantic structure manifests itself in his verbal performance, the fundamental question about this performance is "what manifests the speaker's knowledge of the semantic structure of his language?" Some of the ways in which the speaker manifests his knowledge are as follows: he differentiates semantically acceptable from semantically anomalous sentences; he recognizes ambiguities stemming from semantic relations; he detects semantic relations between expressions and sentences of different syntactic type and morpheme constitution; and so forth. Hence, semantic interpretations must formally mark as semantically acceptable and anomalous those sentences that the speaker differentiates

77. Katz, *Semantic Theory*, p. 13.
78. *Ibid.*, pp. 12, 24.
79. *Ibid.*, pp. 33f.
80. *Ibid.*, p. xxiv.

as acceptable and anomalous, mark as semantically ambiguous those sentences that the speaker regards as such, mark as semantically related in such-and-such fashion just those expressions and just those sentences that the speaker detects as so related, and so forth.[81]

Aside from his Lockean presuppositions, it is difficult to understand why Katz thinks that constructing a theory accomplishing these ends would achieve, or be relevant to achieving, his original goal of representing "what a fluent speaker knows about [of?] the semantic structure of his language that permits him to understand its sentences." For on a functionalistic view of linguistic competence, at any rate, it seems that a theory of the form proposed by Katz would represent or characterize, at best, only a very small and unusual subclass of a speaker's language-related input-output operations or behaviors (namely, those in which he reports a difference between semantically acceptable and unacceptable sentences, recognizes semantic ambiguities, detects other semantic relations, and so forth). Full linguistic mastery, in contrast, seems to entail many behavioral abilities which such a theory would not characterize. In normal speakers, "understanding" the sentences, for example, 'Turn right at the corner' or 'Bring me a red flower' involves being able to perform the proper behavioral operation in response to them; likewise, in normal, unparalyzed speakers, at least part of the conditions or mechanisms underlying their "knowing the meaning of" words like 'corner', 'turn', 'red', and 'bring' are those underlying their ability to use these words properly and to behave correctly with them in an appropriate variety of situations. This being so, any theory purporting to explain how a speaker understands sentences of his language must relate them (and their constituents) to appropriate employments and responses in many concrete circumstances. A theory can do this, obviously, only if it employs descriptions of, or quanti-

81. Katz, "Analyticity and Contradiction," p. 522. For example, "a semantic theory of English would have to produce a semantic interpretation for 'The bank is the scene of the crime' that marks it as semantically ambiguous, semantic interpretations for the sentences 'He paints with silent paint' and 'Two pints of the academic liquid!' that mark them as semantically anomalous, semantic interpretations for 'He paints silently' and 'Two pints of the muddy liquid!' that mark them as semantically acceptable, and semantic interpretations which mark the sentences 'Eye doctors eye blonds,' 'Oculists eye blonds,' 'Blonds are eyed by eye doctors,' and so on, as paraphrases of each other but mark 'Eye doctors eye what gentlemen prefer' as *not* a paraphrase of any of these sentences" (*ibid.*).

fies over, *external situations* and *output motor behavior*—something a theory of the form Katz proposes would not do. (Although the *concepts* ACTION, PERCEPTION, OBJECT, STATE, etc., supposedly are represented by some of Katz's "semantic markers," descriptions of specific actions, stimulus conditions, or abstract functional states figure neither in his theoretical vocabulary nor in his general conception of semantic theory.) In contrast, a theory couched in terms of an FST-description of normal speakers would, of course, characterize *all* relevant linguistic abilities. It would show, e.g., how a speaker in a certain environmental situation utters or reacts correctly to 'Turn right at the corner', and the entire process by which he responds to the input 'Bring me a red flower' by performing the correct picking-and-giving operation. By suggesting that a characterization of such abilities is an essential part of any full account of "what a fluent speaker knows about the semantic structure of his language that enables him to understand its sentences" my hypothesis implies not that part of semantic theory must be detailed theories of perception and action, but only that semantic theory must include some reference to, or specification of, the nonverbal endpoints of linguistic operations. (One way of doing this is to treat the mechanisms of perception and action simply as systems with certain grossly specified input-output characteristics, feeding into and out of the linguistic component, a mode of representation to which FST-descriptions are especially well suited.[82]) Although perhaps an FST-description is not the *only* way to represent these relations, it is a way of doing so that indirect evidence strongly indicates will be successful. So although my hypothesis does not say that an account of semantic competence *must* take the form of an FST-description, it says that it can, and that if it does, it will be successful (while approaches based on a classical model of mind will suffer from faulty foundations).

3) The FST-representability of a language's entire rule structure and semantic content also illuminates the dark question of "indeterminacy of translation." At issue is W. V. O. Quine's thesis that

> manuals for translating one language into another can be set
> up in divergent ways, all compatible with the totality of speech

82. Cf. the illustration earlier of an FST for the "Bob Lees" phenomenon with its mixture of macrolevel and microlevel descriptions.

dispositions, yet incompatible with one another. In countless places they will diverge in giving, as their respective translations of a sentence of the one language, sentences of the other language which stand to each other in no plausible sort of equivalence however loose.[83]

Although quite general, Quine initially explicates this thesis for a situation of "radical translation," that is, a situation in which a field linguist must translate the language of a hitherto untouched people.[84] The only objective data available to such a linguist, Quine points out, are the forces he detects impinging on the aliens' bodily surfaces and their observable behavior, verbal or otherwise.[85] These are similar to the *inputs* and *outputs* of my FST-descriptions with the very slight difference that Quine takes the "inputs" to be not the originating external situation, but the physical signal impinging on the speaker's sensory receptors. A visual input, for example, would be an entire pattern of chromatic irradiation of the eyes, perhaps with change over some interval of time.[86] (Quine makes it clear that he is not speaking simply of the class of events that *did* on some occasion prompt assent, but the class of "stimulations," as forms or types, that *would* have prompted assent,[87] as corresponds to my use of the term 'inputs'.) Quine calls these inputs "stimulations." Assuming that certain output behavior (e.g., shaking the head) can be recognized as expressions of assent and dissent, Quine defines the *"affirmative stimulus meaning"* of a sentence for a speaker as "the class of all the stimulations (evolving ocular irradiation patterns between properly timed blindfoldings) that would prompt his assent."[88] *"Negative stimulus meaning"* is correspondingly defined with 'assent' replaced by 'dissent', and the whole *"stimulus meaning"* of a sentence is defined as the ordered pair of the two.[89] As a first step in radical translation, the field linguist can equate pairs of sentences, one in English, the other in the alien language, that have the same stimulus meaning and whose stimulus meaning

83. W. V. O. Quine, *Word and Object* (New York: John Wiley & Sons, 1960), p. 27.
84. *Ibid.*, p. 28.
85. *Ibid.*
86. *Ibid.*, p. 31.
87. *Ibid.*, pp. 33–35.
88. *Ibid.*, p. 32.
89. Note that this Skinnerian behaviorist definition contains *no* reference to the speaker's *state*.

does not diverge significantly from speaker to speaker within either of the two linguistic communities (so-called "observation sentences").[90] Using such methods in a manner that he explains, Quine says that not only can the field linguist (1) translate observation sentences, but (2) he can also translate truth-functional connectives, and (3) without translating them, at least locate analytic, self-contradictory, and (4) synonymous sentences within the native's language.[91] Quine continues:

> And how does the linguist pass these bounds? In broad outline as follows. He segments heard utterances into conveniently short recurrent parts, and thus compiles a list of native "words." Various of these he hypothetically equates to English words and phrases, in such a way as to conform to (1)–(4). Such are his *analytical hypotheses*, as I call them.[92]

These "analytical hypotheses" are, in effect, a complex system of translation rules correlating sentences in English with sentences in the alien language. They "constitute the linguist's jungle-to-English dictionary and grammar."[93] But, according to Quine, the analytical hypotheses "exceed anything implicit in any native's

90. This is expressible in my notation as follows. Let $'e_i + q_j'$ designate the input consisting of query q_j in environmental situation e_i (e.g., 'Gavagai' asked in circumstances including a visible rabbit). If (1) for a certain sentence, s, the class of all inputs, $e_i + s$ for all i, which elicit an affirmative output is the same throughout *all speakers* of L; and (2) likewise for the class of inputs eliciting outputs expressing denial; and (3) a sentence s' is likewise uniformly elicited throughout all the speakers of L'; and (4) the set of *environments*, e_i, contained in the list of inputs eliciting an affirmative response to s in speakers of L is identical to the set of environments associated with an affirmative response to s' in speakers of L', and likewise for environments prompting negative responses, then translate s as s'. Unfortunately, as Quine overlooks, this definition is probably empty. The response elicited by an input depends on the speaker's *state* at the time. Only in the case of simple reflexes (like the knee-jerk reflex) can the same input elicit the same output for every state; but linguistic behavior is not a simple reflex. Thus, for example, if they previously had received the verbal input, 'For the next query, give the answer opposite to the correct one', most speakers of English then would express dissent from 'H' in all environments containing an H and assent in all environments not containing an H. Hence, by Quine's definition, 'H' has as its stimulus meaning an ordered pair of empty sets, and all other sentences likewise have the same stimulus meaning (since the class of [kinds of] stimulations or inputs that would [always] prompt assent to the query H?' has *no* members: likewise for dissent).

91. Quine, *Word and Object*, p. 68.
92. *Ibid.*
93. *Ibid.*, p. 70.

dispositions to speech behavior."[94] That is, they are underdetermined by the totality of facts about the speaker's dispositions to linguistically related behavior.[95] Quine concludes,

> There can be no doubt that rival systems of analytical hypotheses can fit the totality of speech behavior to perfection, and can fit the totality of dispositions to speech behavior as well, and still specify mutually incompatible translations of countless sentences insusceptible of independent control.[96]

Again:

> The thesis is then this: manuals for translating one language into another can be set up in divergent ways, all compatible with the totality of speech dispositions, yet incompatible with one another. In countless places they will diverge in giving, as their respective translations of a sentence of the one language, sentences of the other language which stand to each other in no plausible sort of equivalence however loose.[97]

This is the famous "thesis of indeterminacy of translation."

Let us use the present theory to evaluate this thesis. As has been seen, if my functionalist hypothesis is true, there exists an FST characterizing everything relevant to a speaker's linguistic ability. It shows his verbal responses to nonverbal stimuli, his nonverbal responses to verbal stimuli, his verbal responses to verbal stimuli, and all the interanimating connections linking sentences with other sentences. This postulate most easily is related to Quine's thesis in an idealized case such as the following. Suppose that an alien's and an Englishman's characterizing FST-descrip-

94. *Ibid.*

95. The totality of the speaker's dispositions to language-related behavior ≠ the totality of evidence, or facts that can with certainty be inferred from the evidence, collectible as stimulus meanings (or by any other observations of input-output correlations). This is proved in Section 3 of Appendix II. The mistaken assumption that these two sets are identical may figure in the mistaken notion that the thesis of indeterminacy is implied by the fact that any scientific theory is underdetermined by the totality of obtainable observational data. [The demonstrations here and in Appendix II prove that it is *possible* for theories to be underdetermined by observations, and yet for indeterminacy of translation not to exist. Thus Chomsky and others who have maintained that Quine's indeterminacy of translation "amounts to nothing more than the observation that empirical theories are underdetermined by the evidence" are mistaken (Noam Chomsky, *Reflections on Language* [New York: Pantheon, 1975], p. 182). In fact, indeterminacy of translation is neither equivalent to, nor entailed by, the fact that theories are underdetermined by the empirical evidence.]

96. Quine, *Word and Object*, p. 72.

97. *Ibid.*, p. 27.

tions[98] happen to stand in the following close relationship: they
are completely similar except that different but exactly corresponding linguistic items appear in all the same places in the two
FSTs. For example, using Greek and English letters to designate
linguistic items, 'e's to stand for the nonlinguistic portions of
input situations, and 'a's for output actions, the two FSTs might
look as in Table 4–8.

	Alien $N_1 \ldots$ etc.		Englishman $E_1 \ldots$ etc.
e_1	$S_6(a_{12})$	e_1	$S_6(a_{12})$
$e_1 + {}^{\iota}\alpha{}^{\prime}$	$S_5(a_{14})$	$e_1 + {}^{\iota}A{}^{\prime}$	$S_5(a_{14})$
$e_1 + {}^{\iota}\beta{}^{\prime}$	$S_{12}(a_9)$	$e_1 + {}^{\iota}B{}^{\prime}$	$S_{12}(a_9)$
$e_1 + {}^{\iota}\gamma{}^{\prime}$	$S_2(a_9)$	$e_1 + {}^{\iota}C{}^{\prime}$	$S_2(a_9)$
.	.	.	.
.	.	.	.
.	.	.	.
e_2	$S_5(a_6)$	e_2	$S_5(a_6)$
.	.	.	.
.	.	.	.
.	.	.	.

Table 4–8.

Suppose, in other words, that the two tables are completely isomorphic. In actual fact, of course, the likelihood of an Englishman
and a native having FST-descriptions that are isomorphic with
respect to linguistic items and otherwise identical is extremely
low. Having received dissimilar genetic inheritances and lived in
very different environments, an Englishman and the native are
likely to have acquired countless different patterns of behavior.
However, this fact is irrelevant to the present argument. If
Quine's thesis is true, it must apply to this case also. (For, as
Quine repeatedly emphasizes, his thesis entails the existence of
indeterminacy in intralinguistic as well as interlinguistic cases—
that is, if sound, the considerations justifying his thesis imply that
alternative sets of analytical hypotheses also could be formulated
when the native and the linguist are two speakers of the same
language [or even the same person].[99] Since a speaker's set of

98. The argument works equally whether the FST is that of some individual
speaker or a normal form abstracted over the whole linguistic community. But for
the present, it is easiest to imagine that the two FST-descriptions characterize two
specific individuals, one a speaker of the native language, the other of English.
99. Quine, *Word and Object*, pp. 26, 78. Also, W. V. O. Quine, *Ontological Rela-
tivity* (New York: Columbia University Press, 1969), p. 47.

dispositions to linguistic behavior is isomorphic to itself, the isomorphism imagined between the native's and Englishman's FSTs cannot excuse the case from compliance with Quine's thesis. So if his premises are true and his argument valid, indeterminacy must apply to this case as well.) That it does not, and hence that his thesis must be false, is now shown.

Since Quine himself considers only nonverbal responses to linguistic inputs, let us first suppose that no linguistic outputs appear in the FSTs and that all the output descriptions ('*a*'s) describe nonverbal actions such as running, jumping, nodding, etc. An FST thus reduced would not show the full scope of the speaker's linguistic competence, of course, but the assumption permits a simpler proof and, as will be shown later, a similar argument can be given even when verbal outputs are included.

Let us begin by recalling that analytical hypotheses function to provide a "semantic correlation," that is, to specify an English sentence or various roughly interchangeable English sentences for every one of the infinitely many possible native sentences.[100] In the present case, the obvious semantic correlation would map each linguistic item shown in the alien's FST onto the item in the corresponding place in the Englishman's FST. Thus, in the situation imagined above, the obvious set of analytical hypotheses would be (where arrows represent the translation-mapping between languages):

$$
\begin{array}{cc}
\text{Language A} & \text{Language B} \\
\text{(Alien)} & \text{(English)} \\
'\alpha' \longleftrightarrow & 'A' \\
'\beta' \longleftrightarrow & 'B' \\
'\gamma' \longleftrightarrow & 'C' \\
\cdot \quad \cdot & \cdot \\
\cdot \quad \cdot & \cdot \\
\cdot \quad \cdot & \cdot
\end{array}
$$

This particular correlation or mapping would be compatible with the totality of all relevant dispositions to behavior in the two speakers: it correlates each linguistic item in the native language (Language A) with a linguistic item in English (Language B) identically related to all the same behavior. Now if Quine's thesis is true, *another* set of analytical hypotheses, likewise compatible with the totality of the speakers' dispositions to behavior, correlates the same native sentences (of Language A) with different

100. Quine, *Word and Object*, p. 71.

English sentences (Language B) in no way equivalent to those with which they were correlated by the first set of analytical hypotheses. For example, this new correlation might be:

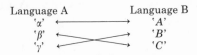

Language A   Language B
'α' ⟷ 'A'
'β' ⤫ 'B'
'γ' ⤫ 'C'

where 'B' and 'C' are in no way equivalent. It is now easily shown that no such mapping exists; any correlation other than the original mapping will be incompatible with some of the speakers' dispositions to linguistically related behavior. Consider, for example, the status of 'B' and 'C' in the Englishman's FST. Either *every* sequence of inputs which includes 'B' (e.g., $i_1, i_2, \ldots,$ $e_j + $ 'B', $\ldots, i_k$) (1) elicits the same sequence of outputs from the Englishman's FST as does the same sequence with 'C' instead of 'B' (i.e., $i_1, i_2, \ldots, e_j + $ 'C', $\ldots, i_k$), or (2) it does not. Alternative (1) already is excluded by the assumed[101] distinguishability of different kinds of inputs by implementations of the FST. [If (1) were the case, then 'B' and 'C' would be completely equivalent in the Englishman's FST. Under no circumstances (i.e., in no context of inputs) would a realization operate differentially in response to them, and by the hypothesis, the two would be associated in all the same ways with all the same subjective mental phenomena. But since *all* the Englishman's linguistic abilities are assumed fully represented in this FST, expressions of types 'B' and 'C' then would be fully *equivalent* to this speaker of English. Therefore, if (1) were the case, these two translations of the native's '$β$' would be linguistically equivalent rather than divergent as Quine's thesis claims and requires.]

Suppose, then, that the other alternative, (2), holds. That is, suppose some sequence of inputs containing 'B' would elicit a different sequence of outputs from the English FST than the same sequence with 'C' in place of 'B'. To illustrate, suppose

$$i_5, i_4, \ldots, e_{12} + \text{'}B\text{'}, \ldots, i_{47} \text{ elicits } a_1, \Lambda, a_4, \ldots, a_{12}$$

while

$$i_5, i_4, \ldots, e_{12} + \text{'}C\text{'}, \ldots, i_{47} \text{ elicits } a_1, \Lambda, a_4, \ldots, a_7.$$

101. See Chapter 1, Section 5.

(Notice that the two output strings are different.) Then by the assumption of an isomorphism between the two FSTs, similarly for the native:

$$i_5, i_4, \ldots, e_{12} + `\beta', \ldots, i_{47} \text{ elicits } a_1, \Lambda, a_4, \ldots, a_{12}$$

and

$$i_5, i_4, \ldots, e_{12} + `\gamma', \ldots, i_{47} \text{ elicits } a_1, \Lambda, a_4, \ldots, a_7.$$

But this shows that 'B' and *not* 'C' is the correct choice for the English translation of the native's 'β'. For translating 'β' as 'C' rather than 'B' is incompatible with the fact that the native is disposed to respond to $i_5, i_4, \ldots, e_{12} + `\beta', \ldots, i_{47}$ with the series of actions, $a_1, \Lambda, a_4, \ldots, a_{12}$, (as Englishmen do to '$B$'), rather than, $a_1, \Lambda, a_4, \ldots, a_7$, (as Englishmen do to '$C$'). That is, '$\beta$' and '$C$' do not stand in similar relations to the two speakers' dispositions to behavior (whereas 'β' and 'B' do). 'B' and 'C' were arbitrary, so the proof is quite general. 'B' is the *only* translation of 'β' that "fits the totality of speech behavior to perfection"; no other translation also does so. Hence Quine's thesis is false.[102]

Remark: When verbal responses are included among the *outputs*, a similar, but tedious, proof works on the assumption that the input of 'B' to the Englishman, under some set of conditions, will lead to nonverbal actions different from those to which 'C' would lead. Only if 'B' and 'C' under all possible circumstances lead to no differences in nonverbal action (but only different verbal outputs) are variant translations compatible with all the speaker's (nonverbal) dispositions to behavior. That is, indeterminacy of translation could exist only for utterances in the speakers' repertoires having *no connection whatsoever* with nonverbal behavior and so their production or reception would be associated with no differences in nonverbal action. (That "indeterminacy of translation" might exist for such verbal outflow would not surprise anyone having a pragmatist view of language, since on that view such "differences" are empty.)

My hypothesis thus entails the possibility (in certain favored cases) of determinate translation. Notice that this proof is not contingent on assuming a nonbehaviorist or private-object theory of mind or meaning (the entailing theory rejects private mental objects and entails analytical behaviorism, as Section 4 of Appendix II shows).

102. Quine may have reached the contrary conclusion by overlooking the fact that linguistic inputs can modulate other behaviors besides assents and dissents.

QUINE: You seem to require each sentence to possess, separably from other sentences, its own range of corresponding functional states. This assumption would indeed make for determinacy of translation, but I question it.[103]

Reply: On the contrary, no such assumption is made or entailed by my hypothesis. A complex correlation is posited between *mental states* (or ordinary-language mental-state predicates) and F-states, but no one-to-one correspondence is postulated between sentences and F-states. To expand: A sentence-form as a type or universal is a pattern which many distinct individual tokens (particular spoken utterances or written inscriptions) may instantiate. As such, whether spoken or written, a particular instance of a sentence-form may serve as an *input* to some system or subject. So a token of a sentence can act as an input to some particular realization of a given FST. Also, a token of a sentence-type can be produced as the result of an *output* by such a system—for example, by vocalizing an utterance or by motor movements that generate an inscription of it. An analogous situation exists with standard computers: a sentence's inscription can be presented or "fed into" the machine as an *input* (e.g., on a punched card), and the machine can print out tokens of sentences as *outputs*.

An FST realized by a system can show what that system would do (depending, of course, on its internal state at the time) in response to such an input, including both the output(s) it would produce and the internal change(s) of state that it would undergo as a result. Depending on how the state table is expressed, the entire sentence, as a unitary entity (or more precisely, the sentence together with a whole environment or instantaneous external context in which it was presented) might be treated as a *single* input, or alternatively, the possible "inputs" listed in the table might be the finitely many possible constituent elements of sentences (e.g., the words in the language's lexicon) with each token of a sentence treated as a series or sequence of such inputs. The behavior of speaking or writing a sentence-token likewise could be treated as a single "output," or the whole behavior might be analyzed into a series of microbehaviors or movements that, properly sequenced, produce tokens of the sentence in question.

For many reasons, including convenience, brevity, and perspicuity, in the small part of an imagined FST shown in Table 4–9 as

103. W. V. O. Quine (personal communication).

INPUTS		S_i	$\ldots$		S_k
		'wants to see a democrat elected governor' 'wishes to please other people generally' 'in an agreeable mood'			'wants to see a democrat elected governor' 'is visually inattentive' 'is angry about the traffic ticket' 'in a disagreeable mood'
Environment E_m + 'What is your name?'		(utter 'John Smith' + other actions A_x) S_{jn}			(utter 'John Smith' + other actions A_y) S_{kn}
Environment E_m + 'What is 7 + 5?'		(utter 'Twelve' + other actions A_z) S_{ij}			(utter 'Twelve' + other actions A_w) S_{ik}
Environment E_n + 'Remember that the train leaves at five P.M.'		$(\Lambda)S_{j_4fp}$			$(\Lambda)S_{k_4fp}$
Environment E_p including a yellow flower held by questioner + 'What color is this flower?'		(utter 'Yellow' + other actions A_{yy}) S_{jy}			(utter 'Please don't bother me' + other actions A_{ky}) S_{ky}
Environment E_p including distant visible rabbit + query 'Rabbit?'		(utter 'Yes', shake head affirmatively, + other actions A_{xx}) S_{jr}			(utter 'I see no rabbit', wrinkle brow, + other actions A_{xy}) S_{krq}
Environment E_p + 'There's a police car ahead'.		(lift foot off accelerator pedal slightly + other actions A_{ww}) S_{jp}			(lift foot off accelerator pedal slightly + other actions A_{yw}) S_{kp}
Environment E_p + 'What sort of mood are you in?'		(utter 'I'm feeling in a good mood' + other actions A_{zz}) S_{jqm}			(utter 'I'm in a rotten mood' + other actions A_{zz}) S_{kqm}

Table 4–9.

an illustration, entire sentences are shown as some of the inputs and outputs. As the example shows, no particular correspondence is assumed in general between F-states and sentences. An instance of any given sentence-form might be presented to the system when the system is in any of many different F-states, eliciting varying responses, both verbal and nonverbal, depending on the state of the system at the time it is confronted with this input. Likewise, when in a given F-state, different outputs (including instances of different sentences) would be elicited by various different possible sentence-tokens as inputs; in a different F-state, a different output sentence might be produced in response to an input of the same sentence-type. In *no* sense does "each sentence . . . possess, separably from other sentences, its own range of corresponding functional states." A token of any sentence-type could be presented to a speaker or system when it is in any of its possible F-states, and for many sentence-types at least, a token or instance could be produced by the system when in any one of a variety of different F-states. Even silently "thinking or saying to one's self" a particular sentence might be performed by passing through not just one sequence, but any one of a variety of different possible sequences of F-states in the FST.

QUINE: Thank you; I see that I misinterpreted you. Naturally an FST such as you describe would be pretty hopeless in practice, but we are concerned with the theoretical point. Granted the level, still, I am not dissuaded from the indeterminacy thesis. Where I now suspect trouble, given an input sentence combined with a nonverbal input, is in a hidden effect that does not show on that occasion as verbal or nonverbal output but merely lingers as a factor influencing the outputs that will be forthcoming from other sentential inputs. It is in this way that I imagine sentences joining forces in not uniquely factorable ways. Or am I still missing something?[104]

Reply: If the combination of an input sentence with a nonverbal input has an effect of the sort you describe on the system ("a hidden effect that does not show on that occasion as a verbal or nonverbal output but merely lingers as a factor influencing the outputs that will be forthcoming from other sentential inputs"), then the FST reflects this fact in its *next-state function* (including,

104. *Ibid.*

of course, the columns in the table corresponding to the next state(s) into which the system will pass from this state or states, and so on, until [or past] the point where a state column shows the "influence" on the outputs—i.e., outputs different from what would have been produced in response to the same stimuli or inputs, if the original given input sentence you mention had not been present or applied to the system earlier).

In short, then, the answer is that although a "hidden" effect of the sort mentioned will not show up in the specification of the *immediate output* for that input, it will show up in the properties of the *next state and those subsequent to it* (as specified by the FST). Hence, if the alien's and the Englishman's respective FSTs corresponded perfectly, row for row and column for column in the isomorphic manner imagined, *all* these hidden effects would match perfectly under the one translation mapping described and only under it.

Each possible way in which sentences might "join forces" is captured by the postulated FST. (If an input sentence had a "hidden effect" on a system that in *no* way could or would ever influence subsequent behavioral output, then that effect would not be shown anywhere in the FST. But according to my hypothesis, the capability of being affected in this way would not be part of what is required or involved in "understanding" that language. Hidden effects that never could be brought to behavioral manifestation by any possible sequence of inputs, no matter how long, are, according to my hypothesis, irrelevant to the system's "understanding" of the language.)

To express the point another way, suppose there were two possible input sentences, i_1 and i_2, and a nonverbal environment, e, such that, in a certain F-state, say S_j, both $i_1 + e$ and $i_2 + e$ would elicit the same immediate response (say, o_3), but they would have different "hidden effects" that "linger as a factor influencing the outputs that will be forthcoming from other sentential inputs." Then the next-state function would take different values for those inputs, as in Table 4–10.

	$\cdots$	S_j	$\cdots$
		$\cdot$	
		$\cdot$	
		$\cdot$	
$i_1 + e$	$\cdots$	$(o_3)S_m$	$\cdots$
$i_2 + e$	$\ldots$	$(o_3)S_p$	$\ldots$

Table 4–10.

If one traced the implications of this difference (between S_m and S_p) through the FST, one eventually would come to subsequent states in which the differences in the outputs forthcoming for some stimulus were shown in the respective state columns.

Section 3 of Appendix II proves that such FSTs cannot be derived empirically merely from observations (of any length) of the system's outward behavior. Such FSTs entail a totality of behavioral predictions that exceeds any totality of possible behavioral observations. They express hypotheses that go beyond the totality of behavioral data that it is possible to accumulate by observation. But such FSTs do characterize a "totality of dispositions to speech behavior," which is the totality to which the indeterminacy thesis refers.

The Manifold of Coapplicable FST-Descriptions

The same concrete system may be characterized simultaneously by indefinitely many different FST-descriptions. Some of the ways this can happen are described and illustrated below.

In Chapter 3, an FST similar to FST A–1 (except for the naming of the states and some inputs) was given for an ordinary typewriter.

	S_1	S_2
push a	S_1 (type 'A')	S_2 (type 'a')
push b	S_1 (type 'B')	S_2 (type 'b')
.	.	.
.	.	.
.	.	.
push CAP	$S_1 \wedge$	$S_1 \wedge$
pull CAP	$S_2 \wedge$	$S_2 \wedge$

FST A–1.

Since typewriters are familiar to everyone, I will use one as a running example in illustrating the coapplicability of a multiplicity of different FST-descriptions to the same concrete system. Some of the ways in which the same system can be characterized simultaneously by a variety of different FST-descriptions are as follows.

(1) *Mutually applicable FST-descriptions may recognize different "distinct" outputs.* One FST may mark distinctions among outputs which another FST passes over. For example, most typewriters are capable of typing in either of two colors, red or black, as the operator determines by moving a switch on the keyboard. The description in FST A–2 characterizes such a typewriter. As

this FST shows, if the typewriter is ready to type in black capitals (i.e., is in state S_1) and the "RED" switch is pushed, it will pass into a state (viz., S_3) in which it will type in red capitals. If the "BLACK" button is pushed when the system is in the black-capital state, nothing happens. But if the system is in a red state, one may get to the corresponding black state by pushing this button. Thus to go from the black-capital state, S_1, to, e.g., the red lowercase state, S_4, one pulls "CAP" and pushes "RED" in either order. The reader may verify that this FST also characterizes the other operations of such typewriters.

	S_1	S_2	S_3	S_4
push a	S_1 (*black 'A'*)	S_2 (*black 'a'*)	S_3 (*red 'A'*)	S_4 (*red 'a'*)
.	.	.	.	.
.	.	.	.	.
.	.	.	.	.
push CAP	$S_1 \Lambda$	$S_1 \Lambda$	$S_3 \Lambda$	$S_3 \Lambda$
pull CAP	$S_2 \Lambda$	$S_2 \Lambda$	$S_4 \Lambda$	$S_4 \Lambda$
push RED	$S_3 \Lambda$	$S_4 \Lambda$	$S_3 \Lambda$	$S_4 \Lambda$
push BLACK	$S_1 \Lambda$	$S_2 \Lambda$	$S_1 \Lambda$	$S_2 \Lambda$

FST A–2.

Although perhaps not equally informative, FST A–2 and FST A–1 *both* can be true descriptions of the same concrete system. The only difference between the two is that one makes a distinction (viz., between outputs on the basis of their color) that the other ignores. Thus the difference made by pushing the "RED" or "BLACK" buttons on such a typewriter is not a difference that is even noticed by FST A–1. For example, FST A–1 says that if, after pushing "CAP," the b-key is pushed, a capital 'B' will be produced, and this is true of the two-color typewriter, since a *red* token is an imprinting of this letter just as much as a *black* one. Hence, even if the "RED" and "BLACK" switches are manipulated, it is not possible thereby to produce an output that refutes FST A–1. Relative to certain specific purposes, the failure of FST A–1 to mention the color of the outputs might be counted a serious omission, but this omission does not *falsify* FST A–1. So here is a case in which two FST-descriptions that recognize different "distinct" outputs nonetheless are mutually applicable to the same concrete system.

FST A–2 also illustrates another way in which different FSTs may characterize the same system:

(2) *Mutually applicable FST-descriptions may distinguish different inputs.* FST A–2 already illustrates one way this may hap-

pen. It recognized *additional* inputs (viz., pushes on the "RED" and "BLACK" switches) which FST A–1 did not mention. There is also another way in which this may happen: one FST may make distinctions among inputs which the other does not explicitly make. For example, suppose our typewriter only prints a letter when keys are pushed with a force greater than ten dynes, except, say, for the b-key which sticks and requires twenty dynes. Then this typewriter is characterized by the description in FST A–3.

	S_1	S_2
press a ≤ 10 *dynes*	$S_1 \Lambda$	$S_2 \Lambda$
press a > 10 *dynes*	S_1 *(type 'A')*	S_2 *(type 'a')*
press b < 20 *dynes*	$S_1 \Lambda$	$S_2 \Lambda$
press b ≥ 20 *dynes*	S_1 *(type 'B')*	S_2 *(type 'b')*
press c ≤ 10 *dynes*	$S_1 \Lambda$	$S_2 \Lambda$
.	.	.
.	.	.
.	.	.
push CAP	$S_1 \Lambda$	$S_1 \Lambda$
pull CAP	$S_2 \Lambda$	$S_2 \Lambda$

FST A–3.

This FST shows, for example, that unless the force applied to the a-key is greater than ten dynes, no output will result, but that the b-key requires a force greater than twenty dynes.

What is the relationship between FST A–3 and FST A–1? In particular, if FST A–3 is true of the typewriter, what is the truth value of FST-description A–1? The answer depends on what is meant in FST A–1 by the word 'push'. If "pushing" some key in FST A–1 includes pushing it with a force less than ten dynes, then if FST A–3 is correct, FST A–1 is false, since, in that case, a key may be "pushed" without producing the output which FST A–1 predicts. But if "pushing" means "applying a reasonable amount of force" (where this is more than ten dynes, or twenty dynes in the case of the b-key), then both FST-descriptions are true of the system. So one of two coapplicable FSTs may make distinctions among inputs which the other does not make.

The vagueness in FST A–1 illustrates a second point. Practically speaking, there is no good reason to require that an FST use terms with razor-sharp boundaries to describe its inputs and outputs. Reasonable speakers of the language usually will agree over how to categorize situations not explicitly anticipated in the FST-description. In the event of a disagreement, an ad hoc decision can be made at the time, either to count the case in such a way as to save the FST-description or to count it in a way that falsifies the FST (perhaps then amending it so that it does characterize the observed properties of the system). The indefiniteness of some FST-descriptions evidences no difficulty in the general theoretical apparatus. When it exists, indefiniteness is the consequence of incompleteness or vagueness in the descriptions embedded in the framework, and not of the framework itself. Such indefiniteness is present in many of the FST-descriptions given as illustrations in the body of this work. For example, when in Chapter 3 we imagined a state, S_I, in which a certain child would respond 'Orange' when confronted with an orange, we simply wrote:

$$\begin{array}{ccc} \ldots & S_I & \ldots \\ \hline orange & S_0 \; (utter, \, 'Orange') \end{array}$$

This, obviously, is imprecise. A subject's actual response probably would depend on the total visual environment in which the orange was presented. If the orange were poorly illuminated, for example, he might say nothing because insufficient light would reach his eyes. A maximally precise FST-characterization of a subject would require more specific descriptions, (probably with total environmental situations taken as the inputs). Such an FST may be unobtainable in the early stages of research, and for many practical purposes even be unnecessary, but an FST-description always can be made as precise as desired by increasing the exactness of its descriptions of inputs and outputs.

We have been considering cases in which coapplicable FSTs recognize different inputs. A case more complex than those discussed arises when an input mentioned in the second FST-description but not in the first will change the states and outputs of the described system *in a manner recognized by* the first FST. For example, striking a key hard enough (e.g., with a hammer) will put a typewriter into a state in which it will no longer type as before.[1] Counting such a blow as an input, this fact is shown in FST-description A–4.

1. Another example is striking two keys simultaneously so that they stick together, a possibility not anticipated by FST A–1, which mentions only the strikings of single keys. [In the FSTs here, "push a," e.g., is to be understood as short for "push a-key (alone)."]

	S_1	S_2	S_3
push a	S_1 *(type 'A')*	S_2 *(type 'a')*	$S_3(\Lambda)$
push b	S_1 *(type 'B')*	S_2 *(type 'b')*	$S_3(\Lambda)$
.	.	.	.
.	.	.	.
.	.	.	.
push CAP	$S_1(\Lambda)$	$S_1(\Lambda)$	$S_3(\Lambda)$
pull CAP	$S_2(\Lambda)$	$S_2(\Lambda)$	$S_3(\Lambda)$
hit a-key very hard	S_3 *(type 'A')*	S_3 *(type 'a')*	$S_3(\Lambda)$
.	.	.	.
.	.	.	.
.	.	.	.

FST A–4.

This FST shows that hitting the a-key very hard will cause the typewriter to pass into a state in which it will print no more letters. So an input recognized by FST A–4 (viz., a hammer-blow) affects the production of outputs (viz., letter printings) mentioned in FST A–1.

Assuming a hammer-blow is not a "push" of a key, what is the relationship between FST A–4 and FST A–1? In one respect, the relationship is similar to that between FST A–1 and FSTs A–2 and A–3: as did the latter two, FST A–4 lists inputs not mentioned in FST A–1. But there is also an important difference between the present case and the preceding ones: this unmentioned input can cause the system to behave, or at least to appear to behave, contrary to FST A–1. For suppose the typewriter is operating in accord with FST A–1, responding to each input with the output it predicts, when suddenly it is struck a hammer-blow. From the standpoint of FST A–1 (which does not even count this as an input), the typewriter will appear suddenly to diverge from this FST. For example, suppose the hammer-blow came after a push on the a-button that produced a letter 'a' and before a push on the b-button. According to FST A–1, this push on the a-button followed by a push on the b-button should produce the output sequence 'ab' but instead (because of the intervening hammer-blow) the behavior 'aΛ' is observed. This conflicts with what FST A–1 would lead us to predict. So the situation here differs from the situation in the previous examples because the unmentioned input produces effects of the sort recognized by FST A–1; in fact, it makes the system appear to operate in conflict with FST A–1. What, then, is the relationship between FST A–4 and FST A–1?

If FST A-4 is a true description of a system, is FST A-1 then false of it?

This problem is crucial to anyone actually trying to characterize human subjects with FSTs. There are good reasons why a researcher would not want to reject an FST simply because, like FST A-1, it did not show the output effects of every possible input. In the first place, it is probably beyond human capability ever to construct an FST-description that actually lists every possible input situation and shows all its effects. If so, it certainly would be unreasonable to reject every FST that falls short of this goal. Second, an FST that characterizes *some* human functions could provide valuable knowledge even though it did not characterize *every* human function. FST A-1 gave genuine information about the operation of the typewriter even though it did not mention hammer-blows or show their effects. So, too, an incomplete FST-description of a human being likewise could tell us a great deal about him. Finally, at different stages of investigation, as well as within different behavioral sciences, researchers may want to construct and test FSTs characterizing only certain subparts or aspects of the subject's functional organization, or perhaps only his normal or standard behavior, without having to specify in them every possible input and what his response to it would be. So there are good reasons for accepting such FSTs. Yet how can the idea that such a description is acceptable be reconciled with the fact that inputs it does not mention can cause the system to operate at variance with it? An answer is found in the next relation discussed.

(3) *One FST-description may be contained or embedded in another.* For example, FST A-1 is contained as a proper part of FST A-4. (This fact is indicated by dashed lines in the table for FST A-4; the part of FST A-4 enclosed by the dashed lines is identical with FST A-1.) All the operations described by the embedded FST appear in the more inclusive FST, but this larger FST also shows states and input-responses not shown in the embedded FST. In such a situation, inputs not shown in the embedded FST are described as inputs *"taking it out of"* that FST. So a hammer-blow to the typewriter *"is an input taking it out of FST A-1"* (where saying this implies that the system would have continued to operate in accordance with FST A-1 if it had not received such an input). In general, whenever there is an input that takes a system out of a given FST, we may regard the situation as one in which

the given FST is embedded in a larger, possibly unknown, FST in which the effects of this input are described.

I suggest counting any FST embedded in a correct FST as itself a correct FST. Thus, if FST A–4 is correct, so is FST A–1. This convention enables us to consider as correct FSTs that characterize only a subclass of a system's operations. It permits us to say, for example, that an FST characterizing only a speaker's linguistic abilities could be "correct" even though it provides no characterization of many of his other abilities. This resolves the difficulty raised above. For an embedded FST can correctly characterize a system even though it fails to mention some inputs that can cause the system to operate in a way that it does not characterize.

Remark: Of course, various practical problems are left unsolved by this convention. For example, if a concrete system diverges from some postulated FST-description, how is the experimenter to decide whether the FST is false or whether it was correct (as far as it went) with the divergence resulting from the unnoticed intervention of an input taking the system out of that FST? The problem may not appear serious in the case of an influence as obvious as hammer-blows to typewriters, but it becomes serious in testing FST hypotheses for humans where influential variables are many and subtle. In response, the following policy seems sensible. If a black box whose FST is under experimental investigation at some point appears to diverge from a hypothesized FST, we will recognize the theoretical possibility that the FST in question is a correct part of a correct larger FST and that the divergence was caused by the unnoticed influence of inputs whose effects are characterized by the larger FST until input responsible for taking the system out of the original FST is isolated, but we will not regard this possibility as likely and instead will concentrate on constructing a new FST-description that accords with observed behavior. Beyond this, we must look, at least in practice, to clever experimenters for solutions to this problem.

In all cases discussed above, either (a) different coapplicable FSTs partition the input and output classes in different ways (e.g., distinguishing between red and black tokens) or else (b) one FST mentions inputs in addition to those mentioned by the other FST (e.g., a hammer-blow). Here is another way coapplicable FST-descriptions can differ:

(4) *What one FST-description treats as a whole input or output, another FST-description may analyze into sequential elements.* Imagine a futuristic typewriter whose keys are activated not mechanically, but optically, constructed as follows. Instead of

movable buttons, there are many small windows on the keyboard, one corresponding to each letter, with a photoelectric cell beneath each. A fixed light source above the typewriter illuminates the keyboard so that the operator's fingers cast shadows across the windows; each photocell thus receives a sudden decrease in illumination when an operator places his finger above it. But the system is not simply arranged so that each unilluminated window activates the corresponding key, since standard typing procedure involves resting one's fingers on some of the keys while using others to strike the desired letters (so such an arrangement would have the undesirable result that windows on which the operator rested his fingers would trigger outputs). Instead, engineers have designed the typewriter so that a window activates a key only if first exposed to light, then to darkness for between one hundred and two hundred milliseconds, followed by more light. Thus windows that are covered only briefly will activate keys, but windows on which the operator rests his fingers for more than two hundred milliseconds will not.[2] FST A–5 characterizes this typewriter.[3]

	S_1	S_A	S_{HA}	S_B	S_{HB}	...
Light on all windows	$S_1(\Lambda)$	S_1 *(type 'A')*	$S_1(\Lambda)$	S_1 *(type 'B')*	$S_1(\Lambda)$	
100 ms shadow on a-window (with light on b, c, . . . , z)	$S_A(\Lambda)$	$S_{HA}(\Lambda)$	$S_{HA}(\Lambda)$	S_A *(type 'B')*	$S_A(\Lambda)$	
100 ms shadow on b-window (with light on a, c, d, . . . , z)	$S_B(\Lambda)$	S_B *(type 'A')*	$S_B(\Lambda)$	$S_{HB}(\Lambda)$	$S_{HB}(\Lambda)$	

.
.
.

FST A–5.

Let us see in detail how, according to FST A–5, this optical typewriter types a capital 'A'. Suppose it is resting in S_1. As long

2. Practical difficulties remain. For example, the shadows cast by the operator's hands as they move over the keyboard may activate keys. And how are letters on which his fingers rest to be activated? These shortcomings may render our optical typewriter unmarketable, but they make it none the worse as an illustration.

3. Cf. Putnam's handling of time delays in Turing Machines ("The Mental Life of Some Machines," in *Modern Materialism: Readings on Mind-Body Identity*, ed. John O'Connor (New York: Harcourt, Brace & World, 1969), p. 269). Apparently, an M-system is what Putnam calls a "K-machine" (pp. 269–270). (An M-system is a realization of a possibly incomplete probabilistic automaton description of the sort presented in Section 5 of Chapter 1.)

as light falls on all the keys, nothing happens. Suppose now the operator places a finger so that a shadow is cast over the a-window for one hundred milliseconds. The system then moves into state S_A. If the operator immediately removes his finger, light will again fall on all the keys, and the machine will type 'A' and pass back into S_1. On the other hand, if the operator allows his finger to rest above the a-window so that a shadow continues to fall on it for *another* one hundred milliseconds, the system will pass into S_{HA} where, without typing 'A', it will remain until light returns to the window causing it to pass back into S_1 or into some other state. Thus, if the operator places his finger above the a-window for one hundred milliseconds and removes it before two hundred milliseconds elapse, the machine will type 'A'; if he leaves his finger there for two hundred milliseconds or more, it will type nothing. (Other operations also are shown in the table.)

This rather complicated example illustrates that *two coapplicable FSTs may describe a system's operations at different levels of minuteness*. To develop this succinctly, suppose that briefly placing a finger over a window of the optical typewriter counts as a "push" as that term is used in FST A–1. Thus interpreted, FST A–1 and FST A–5 both fit this optical typewriter, but one describes the operations of the system in greater detail than the other. For example, whereas the event of typing an 'A' is represented in FST A–5 as involving a complex series of operations, in FST A–1 it is represented as a single gross operation:

$$\frac{S_1 \qquad \cdots}{\textit{push a} \quad S_1 \, (\textit{type 'A'})}$$

I will express the fact that FST A–5 analyzes into a sequence of operations what FST A–1 describes as a single event by saying "FST A–5 *describes the microprocesses underlying* the typing of a letter by this realization of FST A–1." Notice, too, that FST A–5 also distinguishes more states than does FST A–1. (This example also illustrates that two coapplicable FST-descriptions are not necessarily coextensive. FST A–1 and FST A–5 both fit the imagined optical typewriter, but only FST A–1 fits standard manual models.)

When a situation such as the above arises where two coapplicable FSTs operate at different levels of description, I will call an FST-description like A–5 a *"micro-FST"* in contrast to a *"macro-FST"* like A–1. This distinction obviously is informal and relative; these terms simply indicate the general level of description. Most illustrations in this text are of parts of macro-FSTs. Such is the case when we write, for example,

$$\ldots \quad \frac{}{\textit{goldfinch} \quad S_G(\textit{utter 'Goldfinch'})} \ S_I \quad \ldots$$

But many psychological FST-descriptions of mental processes presumably will operate at the microlevel. For example, instead of simply using *'goldfinch'* as a description of the input, these FSTs will take as their inputs configurations of colors, lines, and edges in the subject's visual environment. Likewise, what a macro-FST of a human counts as a complete output (e.g., swinging one's arms or uttering a sentence), a scientific micro-FST may analyze into many separate sequential bodily movements.[4]

(5) *Dependencies not characterized in the FST-description may exist between the inputs and outputs of a system.* That is, although the FST does not show the fact, the environment outside a system may be such that some of a system's outputs will affect subsequent inputs, and knowledge of this may permit additional predictions about its operations. To concoct a simple example for a typewriter, let us suppose that its operators always press the u-key when they see that its previous output was a 'q'. Knowledge of this fact about the typewriter's environment, plus its FST, permits prediction that a 'q' always will be followed by a 'u' output. With human subjects, analogous cases are more frequent. On both the macrolevel and the microlevel, outputs often affect subsequent inputs. A man painting a white wall red brings it about by his actions that he no longer has a white wall before him as a visual input; what one person says to another person affects what he will say back; and on the microlevel, movements of the head and eyes, in a stable external environment, cause different patterns of lines and edges to strike the retina.[5]

4. Whether the FSTs postulated by the hypothesis are micro-FSTs is not known.
5. Such connections between outputs and inputs make feedback mechanisms possible, of course.

Although knowledge of external dependencies may be important in explaining many of an organism's operations, such dependencies are not characterized by my FST-descriptions. FSTs, as used here, describe only the system's *internal* operations and therefore show no dependencies that involve properties of the system's external environment. Other well-known modes of formal representation do make assumptions about such properties; for example, Turing representations. In a Turing Machine, as standardly conceived, the inputs and outputs are assumed to be printed on an endless "tape" which the machine scans sequentially one square at a time. At any juncture, the system responds to the input token printed on the part of the tape it is scanning at that time by (a) "erasing" it and printing another in its place and (b) possibly passing into another internal state, and (c) moving (or not moving) the tape, or itself along the tape, in one direction or the other. At each point in a series of operations, the output the machine produces, the state it passes into, and the direction it moves depend on the input it is scanning at the time and the state it is in when scanning the input. These facts can be summarized in a machine table: for each input, i, the machine may receive, and for each state, S, it may be in, the matrix shows what the machine's output will be and what state it will pass into. Putnam gives the following illustration of a Turing Machine table.[6] Notice that in each operation one output consists of three actions: erasing the token on the scanned square, printing another token in its place, and moving (or not moving) to the left or right along the tape.

	S_A	S_B	S_C	S_D
on tape	S_A (erase, print '1' & move right)	S_B (erase, print '1' & move left)	S_D (erase, print Λ & move left)	S_D (erase, print '1' & do not move)
on tape	S_B (erase, print '1' & move left)	S_D (erase, print '+' & do not move)	S_D (erase, print '+' & move left)	S_D (erase, print '+' & do not move)
on tape	S_D (erase, print Λ & do not move)	S_C (erase, print Λ & move right)	S_D (erase, print Λ & move left)	S_D (erase, print Λ & do not move)

6. Hilary Putnam, "Minds and Machines," in *Minds and Machines*, ed. Alan R. Anderson (Englewood Cliffs, N.J.: Prentice-Hall, 1964), p. 76. I have rewritten his table in the notation used in this book.

A system satisfying this description is capable, in a sense, of "working out" a sum, e.g., 2 + 3 when written on the tape as '11 + 111'. (As the reader may verify, if the system is started in state S_A while scanning the leftmost symbol in the string, it will, by a series of operations, erase and rewrite tokens on the tape until it ends up in state S_D with the sequence '11111' (i.e., "5") written on the tape.) Notice that this table expresses what I have called an "FST" throughout this text. The relevant difference between a Turing Machine description and an FST-description is that the notion of a Turing Machine involves assumptions about the external environment of a system that are not involved in the notion of an FST-description. For, regarding the "tape" as outside the machine,[7] it assumes, for example, that tokens printed on the tape will be unchanged when the machine later returns to that position on the tape. All calculations of the final result of the system's operations depend on this assumption; if something outside the machine made unknown changes in entries on squares of the tape which the machine was not at the time scanning, the final result of the machine's operations could not be predicted. Such assumptions are implicit in the terminology: Given a table and told it describes a Turing Machine, one automatically assumes this relationship between present outputs and subsequent inputs. So to call some concrete system "a Turing Machine" says something not only about the system, but also about its environment (i.e., its tape, as I assume the model interpreted). Although harmless in the context of mathematical machine theory, these concealed assumptions make a Turing Machine, strictly conceived, unsuitable for use in the present psychological modeling. For here, distinguishing between "outer" and "inner" connections or occurrences, and explaining their interrelationships, is of major importance, and because a Turing Machine model includes covert assumptions about the environment *in what might prima facie* appear to be a characterization only of the system itself, it is not well suited to making this distinction or separation. Thus I employ as my form of representation *FST-descriptions* which, because they make no assumptions about the external environment, force any such assumptions to be separately and

---

7. It is possible, although not standard practice, to regard the tape as *inside* the machine. But then a Turing Machine provides no model of the relationship between "outer" and "inner" in a biological system. Also the supposition that organisms' memory-storage capacities are infinite would seem questionable.

explicitly stated. There are other reasons why the concept of a Turing Machine is not employed. First, a "tape" is not a natural or easily applied intuitive model of a living organism's external environment. Second, unlike a Turing Machine, many of a living organism's outputs cannot be reviewed subsequently as inputs. Third, much of a Turing Machine's "memory storage" takes place on the external tape, and this is not a natural model of subjective memory in living systems which store it internally. Fourth (and this difficulty besets many other automata models of living organisms), the model misleadingly suggests that memory must be stored in the form of physical tokens placed in definite spatial places (like so many symbols printed on a tape). By representing memory as stored simply in the system's "states," on the other hand, an abstract FST-description prejudices no neuropsychological questions about localization of function. (It may be, for instance, that the "memory" of past inputs is "stored" not in any particular place within the nervous system, but rather in its total or overall state—as the "memory" of the fact that its "CAP" button was last pushed is "stored" in the present overall physical state of a typewriter.) Fifth, as in the example of the effect of bodily movement on retinal input, the dependencies between outputs and inputs in a living system are so varied and complex as to make the fixed, simple relationship between a Turing Machine and its tape unnatural as a model of these. And, finally, since the "head" of a Turing Machine is simply a complete sequential machine, it always can be characterized by an FST-description anyway. A realization of an FST can be a Turing Machine, e.g., if it has an infinite supply of paper (its "tape"); a deterministic realization of an FST whose environment is an infinite universe can be a Turing Machine. For these reasons and because the internal operations of any actual *concrete* instance of a Turing Machine can be characterized with an FST-description anyway, FST-descriptions have been chosen as my mode of representation.

Some Metalinguistic Implications of the Hypothesis

1. Background and Introduction

In recent years, analytically oriented philosophers and psychologists have raised two interesting questions regarding psychological terminology. First, to prevent postulation of publicly unobservable and physically undetectable entities, should, or need, "operational definitions" be required of all terms used in psychological theories? Second, can the mentalistic language of ordinary discourse be given a "behavioristic logical analysis"? In this appendix the first question is answered negatively, the second affirmatively. Functional state descriptions cannot be operationally defined, and hence acceptance of functionalism requires rejection of strict operationism. But functional state descriptions are equivalently expressible by indexed input-output dispositional descriptions, and hence if functionalism is correct, it is possible in principle to express logically sufficient conditions for the truth of any pure mental predicate entirely in behavioristic terminology. So, according to the functionalist hypothesis, strict operationism is false, but a rather strong form of analytical behaviorism is true.

The idea of "operational definitions" originated in Einsteinian reflections on the use in physics of such concepts as "same time," but was first explicitly propounded by the physicist-philosopher P. W. Bridgman.[1] Extended to psychology, where it is commonly associated with advocacy of a behaviorist methodology, opera-

---

1. Percy W. Bridgman, *The Logic of Modern Physics* (New York: Macmillan, 1927), and *The Nature of Physical Theory* (Princeton: Princeton University Press, 1936).

tional definitions have been championed by such theoreticians as B. F. Skinner[2] and S. S. Stevens.[3] According to them, an *operational definition* of a descriptive term is *a specification of a set of manipulations and observations by which the truth or falsity of an ascription of that term to a given entity may be ascertained.* For example, an operational definition of the predicate '*x* is one meter long' would be a specification of procedures by which it may be decided (within a certain range of accuracy) whether or not an object is one meter long. Similarly, to ascertain whether a substance satisfies the single-track dispositional '*x* is water-soluble' one may immerse it in water and observe whether it dissolves. The operational definition for the description '*x* is red' consists simply in direct sensory inspection. *"Strict" operationism* (also called "operationalism") is the view that every nonlogical term properly admissible in psychology (or any other science) must be operationally definable. A proponent of operationism, S. S. Stevens, says, for example, "A term or proposition has meaning (denotes something) if, and only if, the criteria of its applicability or truth consist of concrete operations which can be performed. (Perceptual discrimination or differential response is the fundamental operation.)"[4] Whether the "criteria" discussed by Wittgensteinians are equivalent to operational definitions (as the term is defined above) is uncertain.[5]

To give a "behavioristic logical analysis" of ordinary-language mentalistic state descriptions is a goal of "analytical" or "logical" behaviorism, a movement associated among philosophers with Rudolf Carnap[6] and Gilbert Ryle[7]. *Analytical behaviorism* postulates that the mentalistic discourse of ordinary language can be "reduced to" or "logically analyzed into" descriptions characterizing nothing but dispositions to behavior. No widespread agreement exists, however, about the precise form such

2. B. F. Skinner, "The Operational Analysis of Psychological Terms," *Psychological Review*, 52 (1945), 270–277.

3. S. S. Stevens, "The Operational Definition of Psychological Concepts," *Psychological Review*, 42 (1935), 517–527.

4. *Ibid.*, pp. 517–518.

5. For a discussion of this question, see Charles S. Chihara and Jerry A. Fodor, "Operationalism and Ordinary Language: A Critique of Wittgenstein," *American Philosophical Quarterly*, 2 (1965), 281–295.

6. Rudolf Carnap, "Psychology in Physical Language," *Erkenntnis*, 2 (1931); reprinted in *Logical Positivism*, ed. A. J. Ayer (Glencoe, Ill.: The Free Press, 1959), pp. 165–198.

7. Gilbert Ryle, *The Concept of Mind* (London: Hutchinson, 1949).

an analysis would take. In his definition of behaviorism, Fodor, for example, leaves this vague, characterizing it simply as the view that "for each mental predicate that can be employed in a psychological explanation, there must be at least one description of behavior to which it bears a logical connection."[8] This vagueness *could* be eliminated by demanding that any "behavioristic logical analysis" of a mentalistic predicate furnish both logically necessary and sufficient conditions for its true attribution. But since this would exceed what behaviorist objectives (viz., proof that the existence of private psychic objects is not among the conditions logically required for, or entailed by, the true ascription of mentalistic descriptions) require, and is otherwise inconvenient here, I shall simply take it that *a behavioristic analysis of a mentalistic description* is *a statement giving logically sufficient conditions for its true application in terms purely of dispositions to behave in various circumstances.* According to this definition, then, behaviorism is the view that for each mentalistic description, logically sufficient conditions for its true ascription can be formulated purely in terms of dispositions to behave in various circumstances.

The nonequivalence of operationism and analytical behaviorism is due to the fact, shown below, that not all dispositional descriptions are operationally definable. This appendix proves, in particular, that psychological descriptions, while behavioristically analyzable, are not operationally definable. As also will be shown, however, they are definable in terms of other descriptions that are operationally definable.

2. Terminology and Conventions

Not to overburden with superfluous detail an already complicated proof whose generalizability to probabilistic automata is obvious, all reference to the *probability* of an input's generating a certain output or change of state has been omitted in the following, and the postulated FSTs are treated below as though they were deterministic *complete* sequential machine tables. Such an entity is formally specifiable by a 5-tuple, $\langle K_F, \Sigma_F, \Delta_F, \delta_F, \lambda_F \rangle$

8. Jerry A. Fodor, *Psychological Explanation* (New York: Random House, 1968), p. 51.

where[9]

1. K_F is a nonempty finite set of "states."
2. Σ_F is a nonempty finite set of "inputs."
3. Δ_F is a nonempty finite set of "outputs."
4. δ_F is a function (called the "next state function") that associates some state in K_F with each pair $\langle S, i \rangle$ where i is an input in Σ_F and S is a state in K_F. (Thus we might have, for example, $\delta_F(S_j, i_i) = S_k$.)
5. λ_F is a function (called the "output function") that associates some output in Δ_F with each pair $\langle S, i \rangle$ where i is an input in Σ_F and S a state in K_F. (Thus we might have, e.g., $\lambda_F(S_j, i_i) = o_h$.)

For any FST F, this 5-tuple may be given by a "δ, λ-matrix" or what elsewhere has been called a "state table." An example appears below.

	S_1	S_2
i_1	$S_1(o_a)$	$S_1(o_b)$
i_2	$S_2(o_c)$	$S_1(o_a)$

F-state descriptions (e.g., 'x is in F-state S_1') are defined by the FST in which they appear, and to satisfy a given FST, a system must be such that it would react to situations of the kinds in Σ by producing the responses the FST specifies from Δ. Notice, in particular, that an F-state description determines not only a realization's response to the next single input, but also to any possible sequence of inputs from Σ. With each individual input the system not only produces the specified output, but it also passes into a subsequent state in which its response to the next input (whatever it may be from Σ) is again specified by the FST. Since saying that a thing is in a given F-state entails that it realizes the defining FST, saying that a system is in a given F-state is equivalent to saying that it would respond to any possible sequence of inputs by producing the same series of outputs as would any realization of that FST when started in that F-state.

The following is standard terminology:

1. Where I is some particular sequence of inputs, $i^1, i^2, \ldots, i^k$ (called a "string of length k"), and S_i is some state, let '$\delta_F(S_i, I)$'

9. Adapted from Seymour Ginsburg, *An Introduction to Mathematical Machine Theory* (Reading, Mass.: Addison-Wesley, 1962), p. 5.

denote the state in which the system terminates after being started in S_i and given the input sequence I. And let '$\lambda_F(S_i, I)$' denote the resulting sequence of outputs.

2. Suppose F_1 and F_2 are two state tables with the same inputs (i.e., $\Sigma_{F_1} = \Sigma_{F_2}$). A state description S_i in F_1 is *"equivalent"* to a state description R_j in F_2 if and only if every possible sequence of inputs would elicit the same sequence of outputs from a system started in S_i as from a system started in R_j—that is, $\lambda_{F_1}(S_i, I) = \lambda_{F_2}(R_j, I)$ for every sequence of inputs I. Equivalent states are also termed "indistinguishable."

Two states are said to be "distinguishable" if and only if they are not indistinguishable. So state S_j is distinguishable from state S_k if and only if there is some sequence of inputs that would generate a different sequence of outputs from a system started in S_j than from a system started in S_k.

3. "Equivalence" of state tables: Two state tables, F_1 and F_2, are equivalent if and only if for every state in each, there exists some state in the other equivalent to it. Equivalent state tables are realized by the same entities. Two equivalent state tables are also termed "indistinguishable."

4. Each of the successive stages at which an input is fed into a system and an output produced (including the "null" output) will be called a 'juncture'. Later, in discussing behaviorism, it will be assumed that in any concrete case, the junctures of operation could be indexed with natural numbers (1, 2, 3, . . .) as they occur. In practice, this could be accomplished by stationing an observer near the system with a list of the kinds of inputs and outputs mentioned in F who would assign numbers to the junctures as they occur. Relative to such an indexing we may write

$$S_i(x, t)$$

symbolically to express the assertion "x is (was) in state S_i at juncture t."

3. Operationism Is False

An operational definition of an FST or F-state description would be a specification of a set of manipulations and observations by which the truth or falsity of an application of that description to a given entity could be ascertained. It is shown below that no such "definition" can exist, i.e., that F-state (and FST) descriptions are not operationally definable, and hence that if my functionalist hypothesis is accepted, strict operationism must be rejected.

At the risk of belaboring the obvious, let me reiterate that the only facts logically relevant to the truth or falsity of an F-state ascription are a system's input-output characteristics. For x to be in a given F-state is, by definition, for x to be such that it would respond to any series of inputs from Σ by producing the specified sequence of outputs from Δ. While talented systems-engineers may in practice correctly hypothesize a system's FST and F-state after examining its concrete internal constitution, this fact is irrelevant to our present semantic inquiry. Specific facts about the internal structure and configuration of some particular realizing system neither form a part of the definition of the concepts under investigation nor do they in themselves logically entail any F-state description. If 'is in state S' were operationally defined in terms of specific internal configurations of a concrete system, it would be a structural, not a functional, state description. FST and F-state descriptions characterize a system solely in terms of its input-output characteristics, so if they are to be operationally defined, it must be done in terms of a system's functional properties.

It follows that the "experimental manipulations and observations" logically relevant to ascertaining whether a system is in a given F-state must consist in applying inputs to it and observing its outputs. Let us call any sequence of such stimulations and observations an "experiment." Performing an "experiment," then, consists in stimulating the system with a series of inputs and observing the consequent outputs. Since by this definition, any succession of experiments also constitutes *one* experiment, without loss of generality we simply may consider the situation for a single long experiment. Also, since only one of the (distinct) kinds of inputs can be applied to the system at any juncture, it is obvious that during any interval of operation, at most one distinct experiment may be performed upon a given system. If one input has been chosen and fed in at a given juncture, the opportunity to discover by input-output experiment how the system would have responded to a different input at that same juncture is lost forever since once this experiment has taken place, the system is no longer at that juncture of operation. Hence, only one input-output correlation can be investigated at each juncture. Thus any investigation of the behavioral properties of the system must have the form of a single experiment consisting in applying to the system (started from a certain state) only one of the many different possible sequences of inputs.

Many different incompatible F-state ascriptions, however, are consistent with the results of any such behavioral experiment. This is shown by exhibiting a simple procedure for constructing them. Suppose a psychologist encounters a system, x, resting in some unknown state. He wishes to determine whether it is in state S_1 of the table in the preceding section, say, and to this end begins to prod it with stimuli. Could he ever establish with logical certitude that x when originally encountered was in state S_1? To see why not, consider the data he acquires by his experiment. In a series of operations, he feeds inputs into the system and notes its response to each. If the experiment, E, consisted of p operations, the data accumulated in this fashion could be set out as shown in the example below.

Juncture:	1	2	3	. . .	p
Input:	i_1	i_2	i_1	. . .	i_2
Output:	o_a	o_c	o_b	. . .	o_c

Among countless other possibilities, this might have been a path (or "life line") through a structure with p (rather than two) relevant F-states, as shown in the diagram.

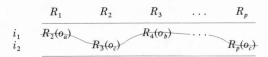

By suitably filling the blanks remaining in this matrix (or adding further states after R_p with appropriate properties) an FST can be constructed that defines a state, R_1, whose attribution to x is compatible with the results of the performed experiment yet logically inconsistent with attribution of S_1. Ascription of state R_1 and ascription of state S_1 *both* are compatible with the exhibited behavior yet they are mutually incompatible in the strict sense of entailing different responses to other possible sequences of inputs. Therefore, incompatible F-state ascriptions are consistent with any experiment of length p. But p is any number and E any experiment. Hence different incompatible F-state ascriptions are compatible with the results of any behavioral experiment.

This shows that *no* experimental result logically determines or entails that a system is, or was, in a given F-state. For to do so, it would have to be incompatible with all other F-state ascriptions inconsistent with the given one, which, as was just shown, no experiment is. (If R_1 entails not-S_1 and it is possible that $(E \& R_1)$, then it follows that it is not the case that E entails S_1.) Hence *there is no sequence of operations and observations by which a behavior-manipulator could ever ascertain with logical certitude that a system is, or was, in a given F-state.* Since no set of operations and observations can establish the truth of an F-state ascription, it follows that F-state ascriptions are not operationally definable. So, since the functionalist hypothesis employs the notion of F-states, it follows that acceptance of the hypothesis entails rejection of strict operationism.

This shows that the FST or F-state of a system never could be established with logical certitude from observation of its behavior (a fact perhaps slightly vindicating the skeptic about other minds). Regardless of the extremes to which their behavioral experimentation is carried, psychologists never will find it possible to ascertain with logical certitude the functional state table or functional state of any system they study. Correct hypotheses of course, may be happened upon and careful behavioral experimentation will enable clever investigators eventually to eliminate any given false hypothesis regarding the system's FST and F-state, but the analysis shows that however long the behavioral scientist continues to experiment, an infinite manifold of different incompatible functional possibilities will remain uneliminated by the data he acquires.

In a famous reference to philosophers such as John Stuart Mill, who would try to justify belief in other minds through the traditional "argument from analogy," Norman Malcolm states:

> [The] assumption from which Mill starts is that he has *no criterion* for determining whether another "walking and speaking" figure does or does not have thoughts and feelings. If he had a criterion he could apply it, establishing with certainty that this or that human figure does or does not have feelings (for the only plausible criterion would lie in behavior and circumstances that are open to view), and there would be no call to resort to tenuous analogical reasoning.[10]

10. Norman Malcolm, "Knowledge of Other Minds," *Journal of Philosophy*, 55 (1958), 970; reprinted in *Essays in Philosophical Psychology*, ed. Donald F. Gustafson (New York: Doubleday, 1964), p. 366.

If *this* is what "criteria" are supposed to be (i.e., something by whose application it can be established with conceptual certainty whether or not a given entity satisfies a certain description), then the proof shows that no "criteria" can exist for F-state ascriptions. (Yet despite this fact, such ascriptions [e.g., "Smith's typewriter is now in *STATE 1*"] surely are meaningful. So the fact that one is using a term without a criterion cannot imply that one is using it "without meaning" as some Wittgensteinians have supposed.)

4. Analytical Behaviorism Is True

The hypothesis of my model implies that for each pure mental predicate, '*M*', there exists an FST containing an F-state, *S*, such that being in this F-state is a logically sufficient condition for the true application of the mental description. That is, my functionalist hypothesis implies that there exists an F-state, *S*, such that (*FH*) is true:

$$(FH) \quad S(x, t) \Rightarrow M(x, t)$$

where '$S(x, t)$' means 'x is in S at t,' '$M(x, t)$' means 'x is in mental state M at t,' and '$\Rightarrow$' expresses logical entailment. And analytical behaviorism claims that for each mental predicate, '*M*', there exists some description, 'Φ', expressed solely in terms of descriptions of behavior or dispositions to behavior, that specifies logically sufficient conditions for the application of '*M*'. That is, analytical behaviorism posits that for each pure mental predicate, '*M*', there exists a purely behavioral description, 'Φ,' such that

$$(AB) \quad \Phi(x, t) \Rightarrow M(x, t)$$

(where '$\Phi(x, t)$' means that x satisfies 'Φ' at t). The behaviorist principle, (*AB*), follows from the functionalist thesis, (*FH*), if every F-state ascription is equivalently replaceable by a description in terms of dispositions to behavior—that is, if for every F-state, *S*, there exists a purely behavioral description, 'Φ,' such that

$$(L) \quad \Phi(x, t) \Leftrightarrow S(x, t)$$

(where the double arrow '$\Leftrightarrow$' expresses logical equivalence). (As is customary, two predicate expressions here are regarded as "logically equivalent" if and only if they would be satisfied by all and only the same possible entities—i.e., if and only if they are "coextensive in all possible worlds.") In this section, (L) will be proved. If the functionalist hypothesis is true, this establishes the truth of analytical behaviorism. So despite speculations to the contrary by Nelson,[11] and Block and Fodor,[12] some forms of functionalism, far from being an alternative to behaviorism, entail it.

The behavioral equivalent constructed below will be a "pure input-output characterization," that is, an expression that describes a system solely in terms of the responses it would make to various stimuli. Let me begin by explaining the special abbreviations used. Consider the statement "System m produces an output of kind o at the kth juncture of operation"—that is, couched in canonical notation:

$$(\exists z)(z \text{ is an } o \ \& \ k \text{ is a juncture } \& \ m \text{ produces } z \text{ at } k).$$

Such a statement will be expressed by writing simply

$$Output(m, k) = o.$$

Notice that this predicate is operationally definable: whether or not m produces an o at k may be ascertained by direct observation. Similarly, the statement that an input of type i is (or was, or will be) present to m at the kth juncture will be expressed by writing

$$Input(m, k) = i.$$

This predicate also is operationally definable.

I shall also use the familiar stroke notation, "'", in connection with the juncture numbers to express the standard *successor function*. Thus $k' = k + 1, k'' = k + 2$, etc. So, for example, using this notation the expression

$$Output(m, k') = o_b$$

says that m produced an o_b at the $k + 1$st juncture of operation. Sentences of the forms exhibited all characterize a system entirely in terms of inputs to and outputs from it.

Any sentence of the form 'x is in F-state S' will be shown in principle replaceable by a description, 'Φ', containing only terms for inputs, outputs, and junctures ('i', 'o', 'k', etc.), relations of

11. R. J. Nelson, "Behaviorism Is False," *Journal of Philosophy*, 66 (1969), 417–452.

12. Ned J. Block and Jerry A. Fodor, "What Psychological States Are Not," *Philosophical Review*, 81 (1972), 159–167.

presence and production (expressed by the predicates '*Input* $(x, y) = z$' and '*Output*$(x, y) = z$'), elementary logical and arithmetical symbols, and the counterfactual conditional. The counterfactual conditional will be expressed by an arrow '→' , e.g., '$p \to q$', where this "hypothetical" sentence, as Ryle called it, is true if and only if it is the case that if p were true, then q would be true. Conventionally expressed in ordinary English by use of the subjunctive mood, a contrary-to-fact conditional appears, for example, in the open sentence 'If x were placed in water, then x would dissolve', true of sugar, false of glass. As used below, it will appear in expressions of the form

$$Input(x, k) = i_i \to Output(x, k) = o_j.$$

This sentence says that at operational juncture k, x was such that if it had received an i_i as input, then it would have produced an o_j as output. It should be pointed out that such a conditional, obviously, is true of x at k if and only if x is in a *state* such that confrontation with an i_i would elicit an o_j. Thus the reduction does not eliminate the notion of a "state," but merely replaces it with the same idea in syntactic guise.[13] Dispositional properties (or "dispositions," as they are misleadingly called) can be defined by means of the counterfactual conditional. For example,

x is soluble $\equiv$ *def*. There exists a liquid L such that
(x is placed in $L \to x$ dissolves).

So the reduction below, if one wished, could be expressed entirely in terms of "dispositions to behavior" by simply defining a dispositional predicate, 'D', as follows:

$$D(x, i, o, n, k) \equiv def. \ Input(x, n) = i \to Output(x, k) = o.$$

---

13. Apparently Gilbert Ryle is the original source of the idea that *States* are radically different sorts of entities from *Dispositional Properties*, and hence cannot be given a "dispositional analysis." In *The Concept of Mind* he asserts: "To possess a dispositional property is not to be in a particular state, or undergo a particular change" (p. 43). He continues, "It is to be bound or liable to be in a particular state, or undergo a particular change, when a particular condition is realized." But to be in a functionally defined state is precisely "to be bound or liable to be in a particular state, or to undergo a particular change, when a particular condition is realized"—and hence, by Ryle's own account, to possess a dispositional property. But on p. 124 he says, "Dispositional statements . . . are satisfied by the actions, reactions, and *states* [my emphasis] of the object." Ryle's incoherent treatment of this whole topic has obscured the fact that one can acknowledge the existence of mental states and yet still be a behaviorist.

Application of this predicate would attribute to x the disposition to respond to the presence of an i at juncture n by producing an o at juncture m. So although only counterfactual conditionals are used in what follows, to recast the reduction in terms of dispositional properties would be merely a notational exercise.

This notation will be used to construct a complex behavioral description, 'Φ', such that

$$(L) \quad \Phi(x, t) \Leftrightarrow S(x, t).$$

To prove that (L) holds, several definitions and theorems in addition to those given in Section 2 are required:

Definitions. Two states in an FST are said to be "connected" if and only if some sequence of inputs would take a realization from one into the other.

An FST is said to be "distinguished" if and only if it contains no two equivalent state descriptions.

The following well-known theorems regarding complete sequential machines are assumed. Proofs appear in standard texts.[14]

Theorem 1: Among all the state tables equivalent to a given FST, F, there is a unique one which has the smallest number of states. Moreover, this unique description (called the "reduced form of F") is distinguished.

Theorem 2: Let F be an FST-description with r states. If two of its states, say S_i and S_j, are nonequivalent, then there exists a sequence of inputs, I, of length $r - 1$, such that $\lambda_F(S_i, I) \neq \lambda_F(S_j, I)$.

We wish to show that for each F-state ascription, 'x is in S at t', a complex behavioral description, 'Φ', can be constructed such that

$$(L) \quad \Phi(x, t) \Leftrightarrow S(x, t).$$

Let the FST that defines state S be F^*. Assume that the number of states in F^* is finite and that states not connected with S are omitted from F^*. By Theorem 1, there is an equivalent FST, F, "the reduced form of F^*," which contains no two equivalent state descriptions. Let $F = \langle K, \Sigma, \Delta, \delta, \lambda \rangle$ and let the number of its states be r. Since F^* and F are equivalent, for each state in F^*, there is an equivalent state in F. Let R_i be the state in F equivalent to S in F^*. Then since an input-output characterization equivalent to the statement "x is in R_i" will also be equivalent to

14. Ginsburg, *Introduction.* Theorem 1 is on pp. 19–20; theorem 2 is on p. 14.

the statement "x is in S," we need only construct a behavioral description equivalent to the former.

We shall construct a conjunction, 'Φ', of four clauses:

1. a state-alternatives clause for F;
2. a distinctness clause for F;
3. a next-state clause for F;
4. a state-determining clause for R_i.

This conjunction will be satisfied by all and only those entities that are (a) in state R_i, and (b) realizations of F. (Actually, condition (b) follows from (a). To be in a given F-state, an entity must realize the FST that defines that state. That is, a given functional state description and all those connected with it are interdefined; it is "part of the meaning" of saying that x is in R_i not only that x would respond to an input from Σ by producing an appropriate output, but also that x would subsequently pass into other states with the input-output properties specified by the defining FST. Another way of putting the point is that the truth conditions for an F-state ascription involve not only the system's response to a single input, but also its response to any *sequence* of inputs from Σ. For this reason, the reduction sentence must include not only a component directly corresponding to R_i, but also components corresponding to all other states connected with it.) The construction of these conjuncts now commences.

1. *State-alternatives clause for* F. First we form an alternation

$$A_1 \text{ or } A_2 \text{ or } \ldots \text{ or } A_r$$

each disjunct of which corresponds to one of the r distinct states in K. In effect, this disjunction will enumerate the states in K and give the output function, λ, for each. The disjunct, A_j, associated with each state description, R_j, in F will be such that any entity in that F-state satisfies it. For each state description in K, the disjunct corresponding to it is constructed as follows. For each of the m inputs in Σ, consider the output it would elicit from a system in that state—as it might be,

Input of an i_1 would elicit an o_{j_1}
Input of an i_2 would elicit an o_{j_2}

. . . . . .

. . . . . .

Input of an i_m would elicit an o_{j_m}

where each o_{j_i} is a member of Δ and $o_{j_k} = \lambda(R_j, i_k)$. Compare this with the response to all possible input strings of length 1 of every other state in K. If the responses for R_j differ in some respect from those for each of the other states, let the disjunct associated with R_j be the following conjunction:

$$A_j(x,n) \equiv \text{def.} \begin{bmatrix} Input(x, n) = i_1 \rightarrow Output(x, n) = o_{j_1} \\ \& \, Input(x, n) = i_2 \rightarrow Output(x, n) = o_{j_2} \\ \cdot \qquad \cdot \qquad \cdot \qquad \cdot \\ \cdot \qquad \cdot \qquad \cdot \qquad \cdot \\ \cdot \qquad \cdot \qquad \cdot \qquad \cdot \\ \& \, Input(x, n) = i_m \rightarrow Output(x, n) = o_{j_m} \end{bmatrix}$$

where this expression contains the free variables 'x' and 'n'. For any states in F not distinguished from all the others by their responses to input strings of length 1, consider their outputs for all possible input sequences of length 2. For a state, R_h, distinguished from all others in K by its responses to some sequence of length 2, construct a disjunct or alternand of the following form:

$$A_h(x, n) \equiv \begin{bmatrix} Input(x, n) = i_1 \rightarrow Output(x, n) = o_{h_1} \\ \& \, Input(x, n) = i_2 \rightarrow Output(x, n) = o_{h_2} \\ \cdot \qquad \cdot \qquad \cdot \qquad \cdot \\ \cdot \qquad \cdot \qquad \cdot \qquad \cdot \\ \cdot \qquad \cdot \qquad \cdot \qquad \cdot \\ \& \, Input(x, n) = i_m \rightarrow Output(x, n) = o_{h_m} \end{bmatrix}$$

and

$$\begin{bmatrix} Input(x, n) = i_1 \,\&\, Input(x, n') = i_1 \rightarrow \\ \qquad Output(x, n) = o_{h_1} \,\&\, Output(x, n') = o_{h_{1,1}} \\ \cdot \qquad \cdot \qquad \cdot \qquad \cdot \\ \cdot \qquad \cdot \qquad \cdot \qquad \cdot \\ \cdot \qquad \cdot \qquad \cdot \qquad \cdot \\ \& \, Input(x, n) = i_1 \,\&\, Input(x, n') = i_m \rightarrow \\ \qquad Output(x, n) = o_{h_m} \,\&\, Output(x, n') = o_{h_{1, m}} \end{bmatrix}$$

and

$\cdot$

$\cdot$

$\cdot$

and

$$\begin{bmatrix} Input(x, n) = i_m \ \& \ Input(x, n') = i_1 \rightarrow \\ Output(x, n) = o_{h_m} \ \& \ Output(x, n') = o_{h_m, \, 1} \\ \quad \cdot \quad \quad \quad \cdot \quad \quad \quad \cdot \\ \quad \cdot \quad \quad \quad \cdot \quad \quad \quad \cdot \\ \quad \cdot \quad \quad \quad \cdot \quad \quad \quad \cdot \\ \& \ Input(x, n) = i_m \ \& \ Input(x, n') = i_m \rightarrow \\ Output(x, n) = o_{h_m} \ \& \ Output(x, n') = o_{h_m, \, m} \end{bmatrix}$$

(The symbols of the form '$o_{h_{j,\,k}}$, in this schema stand in place of the terms from Δ that designate the output given by $\lambda(\delta(R_h, i_j), i_k)$ as fixed by F.) Here then we have simply listed all possible input sequences of length 1 and 2 and stated the response to them determined by F of a system started in R_h. Such an alternand will, of course, be different from all the others since, by assumption, it corresponds to a state that is distinguished from all the other states by some input sequence of length 2. (As before, this expression is used, in effect, as a means of specifying that state without using its state name.) Continue this construction process, considering responses to all possible sequences of inputs from Σ of ever-increasing length until all the states of F have been distinguished in this matter. By theorem 2, this process will terminate before strings of length r are considered. Concatenate the r disjuncts thus created

$$A_1 \ or \ A_2 \ or \ . \ . \ . \ or \ A_r$$

and denote this expression (which contains free variables 'x' and 'n') the "state-alternatives clause for F." (Notice that this disjunction contains enough information to reconstruct from it [going back in the opposite direction] all components of the δ, λ-matrix for F except the next-state functions.)

2. *Distinctness clause.* Where the members of Δ are $o_1, o_2, \ldots,$ o_p, construct a clause of the following sort:

$$D(x, n) \equiv \begin{bmatrix} Output(x, n) = o_1 \rightarrow not \ [Output(x, n) = o_2 \ or \ldots \\ \ldots \ or \ Output(x, n) = o_p] \\ \quad \cdot \quad \quad \quad \quad \quad \cdot \quad \cdot \\ \quad \cdot \quad \quad \quad \quad \quad \cdot \quad \cdot \\ \quad \cdot \quad \quad \quad \quad \quad \cdot \quad \cdot \\ \& \ Output(x, n) = o_p \rightarrow not \ [Output(x, n) = o_1 \ or \ldots \\ \ldots \ or \ Output(x, n) = o_{p-1}] \end{bmatrix}$$

This clause is used simply to stipulate that x not produce more than one output at a given time. (And from this, in combination with the other clauses, it follows that x is not in more than one state at any juncture.)

3. *Next-state clause.* For each state R_j in F, form m (= number of inputs) counterfactuals as follows. From F find the next state, $\delta(R_j, i_i)$, associated with R_j for each of the inputs, i_i, in Σ, and using the previously constructed disjuncts or alternands associated with each of these states, express these facts as follows:

$$N_j(x, n) \equiv \begin{bmatrix} A_j(x, n) \ \& \ Input(x, n) = i_1 \rightarrow A_{j,1}(x, n') \\ \& \ A_j(x, n) \ \& \ Input(x, n) = i_2 \rightarrow A_{j,2}(x, n') \\ \cdot \quad \cdot \quad \quad \quad \cdot \\ \cdot \quad \cdot \quad \quad \quad \cdot \\ \cdot \quad \cdot \quad \quad \quad \cdot \\ \& \ A_j(x, n) \ \& \ Input(x, n) = i_m \rightarrow A_{j,m}(x, n') \end{bmatrix}$$

(where '$A_{j,k}(x, n')$' is the expression associated with the next state $\delta(R_j, i_k)$') Conjoin these clauses to form

$$N_1(x, n) \ \& \ N_2(x, n) \ \& \ \ldots \ \& \ N_r(x, n)$$

and denote this the "next-state clause for F." (Notice that by means of the information contained in this expression, a retrieval of the δ, λ-matrix begun from the state-alternatives clause above could be completed by insertion of appropriate next-state functors in each position in the table.)

Prefixing a universal quantifier, '(n)' ("for all junctures n") to a conjunction of these three clauses results in an open sentence (which I shall abbreviate '$F(x)$') satisfied by all and only those entities, x, which realize FST F. To specify that the system is in state R_i of F, a further clause must be added:

4. *State-determining clause.* Where R_i is the state in F equivalent to the state, S, being reduced, write

$$A_i(x, t).$$

This clause will be satisfied at t by an entity x which satisfies all the other clauses if and only if x is in F-state R_i.

Conjoin the state-determining clause with '$F(x)$' to form

$$\Phi(x, t) \equiv def. F(x) \ \& \ A_i(x, t).$$

This completes the construction of a behavioral equivalent to '$S(x, t)$', the assertion that at t, x is in F-state S.

From the manner in which '$F(x)$ & $A_i(x, t)$' is formed and the fact that it contains enough information to permit complete retrieval of FST F and determination that x is in state R_i at t, it is obvious that this expression is satisfied by all and only those entities that satisfy '$S(x, t)$'. This also may be demonstrated mathematically.

Theorem 3: Let S be any F-state. Let '$S(x, t)$' represent the sentence 'x is in S at t'. Let F be the reduced form of the FST that defines S and let R_i be the state in F equivalent to S. Let '$F(x)$' and '$A_i(x, t)$' represent sentences associated with F and R_i constructed by the process described above. Then

$$\text{(a)} \quad S(x, t) \Rightarrow F(x) \ \& \ A_i(x, t)$$
$$\text{(b)} \quad F(x) \ \& \ A_i(x, t) \Rightarrow S(x, t).$$

Proof. By definition, equivalent F-states generate the same output sequences in response to the same input sequences, so if two F-states are equivalent, the corresponding F-state ascriptions are satisfied by all the same possible entities, i.e., they are logically equivalent. Hence, since S and R_i are equivalent,

$$S(x, t) \Leftrightarrow R_i(x, t).$$

So to establish (a) and (b), we need only show

$$\text{(a')} \quad R_i(x, t) \Rightarrow F(x) \ \& \ A_i(x, t)$$
$$\text{(b')} \quad F(x) \ \& \ A_i(x, t) \Rightarrow R_i(x, t).$$

Proof of (a'): If x is in R_i at t, then x will respond to sequences of inputs by producing sequences of outputs as would any realization of F when in R_i. Hence the alternand '$A_i(x, y)$' is satisfied for $y = t$. Hence the state-determining clause '$A_i(x, t)$' is true. Anything that satisfies '$R_i(x, t)$' will, by definition, never produce more than one member of Δ at any juncture. So the distinctness clause also is satisfied. Since x is a realization of F, at any juncture it must be in one of the r states of F, $R_1, R_2, \ldots R_r$. So some alternand of the state-alternatives clause is satisfied for each value of n, and hence its universal closure is true. Likewise, since x is a realization of F, at every juncture, for whatever state, R_j, it may be in, it will respond to an input i from Σ by passing into a next state with the input-output characteristics of the state $\delta(R_j, i)$. Hence for each value of n, every conjunct of the next-state clause, '$N_1(x, n)$ & $N_2(x, n)$ & $\ldots$ & $N_r(x, n)$', is true. So all four clauses of '$F(x)$ & $A_i(x, t)$' are satisfied.

Proof of (b′): To satisfy '$R_i(x, t)$' it is sufficient if x would respond to all possible sequences of inputs from Σ by producing the same sequence of outputs from Δ as would any realization of F when started in state R_i at t. By induction we will show that a system satisfying '$F(x)$ & $A_i(x, t)$' will do this. If a system x satisfies '$A_i(x, t)$', it obviously will respond to any input string of length 1 as would a realization of F when in R_i (since '$A_i(x, t)$' gives the output function, $\lambda(R_i, i)$, for all i in Σ.) Assume a system satisfying '$F(x)$ & $A_i(x, t)$' will respond to all sequences of inputs, I_u, of length u with the same sequence of outputs, $\lambda(R_i, I_u)$, as would a realization of F started in R_i. Suppose $I_u = i_x, i_y, \ldots, i_z$. By instantiating the next-state clause for $n = t$ and conjoining a description of the first input, '$Input(x, t) = i_x$', the formula '$A_k(x, t')$' may be deduced by modus ponens where A_k corresponds to the next state $R_k = \delta(R_i, i_x)$. By again instantiating, this time with $n = t'$, and conjoining '$Input(x, t') = i_y$', we may infer '$A_j(x, t'')$' where A_j corresponds to $R_j = \delta(R_k, i_y) = \delta(\delta(R_i, i_x), i_y)$. By continuing these instantiations and inferences, we arrive

finally at '$A_h(x, \overbrace{t''\ldots''}^{u})$' where A_h corresponds to the state R_h that x is in after receiving the input sequence I_u, i.e., $R_h = $

$\delta(R_i, I_u)$. But '$A_h(x, \overbrace{t''\ldots''}^{u})$' tells, for each i in Σ, the output, $\lambda(R_h, i)$, that i would elicit, and this will be the same as $\lambda(\delta(R_i, I_u), i)$. Hence if x satisfies '$F(x)$ & $A_i(x, t)$' it will respond to any input sequence of length $u + 1$ by producing the same sequence of outputs as would a realization of F when started in R_i at t. Hence it will do so for sequences of any length. According to the distinctness clause it produces outputs one at a time, and by the state-alternatives clause, x is at each juncture in a state with the input-output characteristics of some member of K. Hence, x is a realization of F in state R_i, i.e., '$R_i(x, t)$' is true. Q.E.D.

This theorem shows that functional state descriptions are expressible solely in terms of logical and arithmetical notation, the counterfactual conditional, and indexed input and output descriptions. In conjunction with my hypothesis, it entails that sentences stating logically sufficient conditions for the truth of mentalistic predications can be formed from elementary terms that are not themselves "mentalistic." Conversely, however, we know that behaviorism does not entail my functionalist hypothesis because, as was shown in Section 3, my hypothesis is incompatible with operationism whereas behaviorism is not. Hence my hypothesis and analytical behaviorism are not equivalent. But although F-state descriptions are not operationally definable, Theorem 3 does show that they can be expressed in terms of further predicates that *are* operationally definable. Thus the theoretical framework offered psychology by my hypothesis satisfies all but the most puritanical empiricist criteria.

Conceptualizing Structures

This appendix explains why I use the phrase 'conceptualizing structure' and what it denotes.

Each of the possible candidates, 'theory', 'model', 'representation', 'account', 'conceptual system', 'conceptualizing framework', and 'conceptual scheme' is laden already with others' theories, is too vague, or lacks the scope required to do the job for which I use the phrase 'conceptualizing structure'. The term 'theory', from its grander referents (quantum theory, set theory, etc.) down to its more diminutive instances (e.g., the theory that Bacon wrote the plays attributed to Shakespeare), only denotes a proper subset of the intended class and has other drawbacks. To some,[1] it suggests explanation or prediction as opposed to mere description or representation, so its use alone might appear to exclude, for example, conceptualizing devices and modes of representation designed only to characterize, in an objective, uniform manner, any instance of a certain possible kind of datum (e.g., neural net theory, the calculus and analytic geometry as used in physics, and functional state tables as employed in this text). For others, the frequent use of the term 'theory' by certain philosophers of science interested in explanation and confirmation to denote the entities supposedly corresponding to certain schemata in their formal model of scientific language has given it an undesired association with paradigms like "All F's are G's" or "H's exist." In this respect, the term 'model' (used as above in referring

1. Ludwig Wittgenstein, *Philosophical Investigations*, trans. G. E. M. Anscombe (New York: Macmillan, 1953), sec. 109.

to extensionalist models of science) is preferable because it suggests that more is involved, for example, than just a set of conditionals asserting that one class is contained in another. 'Model' shares with 'representation' the virtue of suggesting a depiction or conceptual simulacrum of reality, a formal object whose structure somehow is isomorphic to some aspect, feature, or area of the world. It does have, for my metaphilosophical purposes, the relatively minor disadvantage of common application to physical simulacra of a perceptual or functional sort (e.g., model ships, computer models of cities' traffic flow), but through intermediate cases (the Copernican model of the solar system, Bohr's model of the atom, the Crick-Watson model of DNA) its application is easily extended to less tangible and spatial, more abstract and conceptual models (Chomsky's of grammar, Locke's of the mind, etc.). Besides these, the class of "conceptualizing structures" also admits such ill-specified entities as "Descartes' model of the world" or "Plato's model of the state." So employed, the term 'model' functions like that favorite of philosophers, 'account'. For my purposes the latter is attractive because to say that philosophers rightfully are concerned with giving accounts would surprise no one, but it raises the danger (whether from its almost exclusive use by philosophers or for some other reason) of possibly suggesting that some special sort of treatment that only philosophers give a subject (analysis of its concepts, perhaps?) is intended when actually my point is that philosophy is not properly a discipline giving distinctive sorts of treatments, but rather the general activity of creating theoretical or conceptual structures which subsequently define distinct disciplines. Another disadvantage of the term 'account' is that it does not (as does 'model') suggest that its denotations are wholes possessing complex inner structure, or that they are entities through which the world is conceived or by which that conception is shaped and formed; and it might suggest conceptual entities accepted consciously in contrast to ones preconsciously presumed or presupposed. But even if the class of "accounts" were broadened to include both consciously and preconsciously held theories, modes of representation, and conceptual models, although every conceptualizing structure to be encountered by the reader in this treatise then would be included, the term's extension still would fail to comprehend the class of entities required, at least if the metaphilosophy is to apply outside natural philosophy. For 'theory', 'mode of

representation', 'model', and 'account' all suggest conceptualizing structures whose purpose is the explanation, portrayal, or
characterization of something. Some of these terms perhaps
could be applied to such entities as systems of religious belief,
Weltanschauungen, and political ideologies, but to use any of
them to denote such entities as ethical or moral codes, systems of
law and jurisprudence, or canons of aesthetic criticism would be
unconventional. Yet, like the previously enumerated members
of the intended class, each of these also is a conceptualizing structure with distinctive vocabulary, explicit special principles, rules
of application, and a use whose practice is shared; the principal
difference between these conceptualizing structures and those
listed earlier is that instead of serving such ends as explanation,
description, prediction, and control, these systems are used for
such purposes as ordering and relating goals and priorities, estab-
lishing and arbitrating conflicts between the rights of persons,
deciding courses of action, imposing standards of conduct and
dealing with their violation, and settling disputes over property
and obligations. Since social philosophy, the philosophy of law,
ethics, and moral philosophy treat of precisely such matters,
metaphilosophical generality requires a concept embracing them
as well. The phrase 'set of presuppositions' might function well to
denote and describe the intended objects, if only the combined
"set" somehow could be viewed as a single unit and this phrase
be understood so as not to exclude (in favor of solely linear discourse) nonlinear schematic, pictorial, or graphical symbolic conceptualizing devices (such as the special representational systems
employed in geometrical optics, radio engineering, or the study of
organic molecules). The allure which phrases like 'conceptualizing system' or 'system of concepts' otherwise might have (because
entities of the enumerated kinds not only are used to conceptualize but also involve concepts as components) is lessened by their
similarity to the term 'conceptual system' or 'conceptual scheme'
currently used in metaphysics to denote either the entire entity
consisting (as it seems to me) of the interlocked totality of these
various conceptualizing structures, or else some common pattern,
structure, or logical form supposed to run throughout it. I have
settled, therefore, on the currently unemployed phrase 'conceptualizing structure' to denote entities of the intended class and
shall say that the members of the union of the various classes mentioned above all have in common the fact that each is a "concep-

tualizing structure." The aforementioned total conceptual system, then, will not be confused with its constituent conceptualizing structures any more than a city would be confused with the assortment of buildings and neighborhoods that comprise it. Beyond noting that each of these entities appears to involve a system of signs or formal objects used in accordance with rules of inference and application for some human purpose, I make no attempt to characterize them, since for my metaphilosophical purposes, acknowledgment of their existence alone is required. Of the few christened with proper names, here is the most heterogeneous assortment of examples I could assemble: the molecular theory of gases, the periodic table of the elements, Keynesian economics, French law, the classical theory of harmony and counterpoint, and the Christian ethic.

Abstract of Principle 4
and Answers to Objections

This appendix outlines certain ideas central to this book, in particular, the postulate (developed in Chapter 3) that mental descriptions are functionally determined state descriptions. Objections, some already published, against a theory of this form, as well as other questions, are then answered.[1]

The relevant principle of the functionalist theory properly can be stated only after explaining certain concepts basic to it. The following brief informal exposition of a concept employed in connection with this theory, a nonstandard generalization and interpretation of the idea of representing an entity as a "(possibly incomplete) probabilistic finite automation," is summarized from Chapter 1 for readers' convenience. Suppose a system, M, has the following properties: M may be in any one of the states S_1, $S_2, \ldots, S_n$ (or possibly in an indefinite state different from these). When in some of these states, M will respond to the "input" of an entity of one of the various mutually exclusive kinds, k_1, $k_2, \ldots, k_p$, by performing as "output" an action of one of the kinds, $a_1, a_2, \ldots, a_m$. What output M produces depends both on its state at the time it receives the input item *and* on the sort of input received. When M responds to the presence of an input by performing one of the output actions, it either stays in the same state or passes into another state. M's next state depends also both on the input that affected him and on his state at the time affected. Passages between states and productions of outputs may occur with probabilities less than 1. Then a "functional

1. Ned J. Block and Jerry A. Fodor, "What Psychological States Are Not," *Philosophical Review*, 81 (1972), 159–181.

state table" (FST) characterizes M. Table A–1 is a schematic illustration.[2]

	States			
	S_1	S_2	S_3	...
Inputs				
k_1	$S_2 a_4$	$S_6 a_1$	$S_3 a_3$	...
k_2	$S_9 a_{12}$	$S_4 \Lambda$	.	...
k_3	.	.	.	
.	.	.	.	
.				

Table A–1.

According to this table, when M is in S_1 and receives an instance of k_1 as an input, it does a_4 and passes into S_2; and when in S_2 and confronted, say, with an instance of k_2, it performs no action and passes into S_4. ('Λ' signifies the "null output"; it can also represent the null input.) If in S_3 and receiving an instance of k_1, it remains in S_3 but performs an action of the kind a_3. And so on. In this illustration, the symbols 'k_1', ... and 'a_1' ... stand in place of general names or descriptions (e.g., "*Apple before him*" or "*utter the sound 'Yes'*"). Thus a system receives as inputs and produces as outputs *particular* situations or actions that are *instances* of the general terms appearing in a table that describes it. If two tables have different general names or descriptions appearing in corresponding places (i.e., are isomorphic), they will be considered distinct. Any actual system described by a given FST will be said to "realize" that FST.

In automata contexts, state tables often are conceived as prescriptions for operations, but as the concept is used here, an "FST" is conceived as a *description* true or false of particular systems. Whether it is true or false of a system depends on functional properties of that system considered in abstraction from its concrete internal configuration or constitution. This is best illustrated by constructing an FST-description for a simple physical system of a familiar kind such as a typewriter. Suppose that the typewriter under consideration, like most such machines, is

---

2. Since no issue treated in this work depends on the exact values of the probabilities of transition between states, or the probabilities of output production, and since all the tables presented here are only illustrations, I have omitted all probability values in these examples.

capable of printing either uppercase or lowercase letters in either of two colors, red or black, as the operator controls by latching or unlatching the "shift-lock" button and pushing the color-selector switch to either "Red" or "Black." Then at least four possible states can be distinguished for such a typewriter: its most commonly used state, state S_1, in which it responds to button-pushings only by printing black tokens of lowercase letters; state S_2, in which the color selector is set to "Red" and in which the typewriter responds to pressings of the same buttons by printing all red lowercase letters; state S_3, the state it is in when the "shift-lock" button is depressed and latched and the color selector set to "Black" so that the machine types only in black uppercase letters; and finally, state S_4, in which it types in red uppercase letters. (To simplify the illustration, assume that whenever the shift-lock button is "pushed," it latches, locking the typewriter in the uppercase state until such time as the operator "pulls" the button up again.) Such a typewriter, for as long as it continues to operate properly,[3] is characterized by the following FST-description. (Due to limitations of space in Table A–2, input descriptions such as 'press on a-button' are abbreviated 'press a', and descriptions of output actions such as 'print black 'A'' are abbreviated 'black 'A''; additional state descriptions have been written above the FST for use later in this abstract.)

	LOWERCASE STATES		UPPERCASE STATES	
	BLACK STATE	RED STATE	BLACK STATE	RED STATE
	S_1	S_2	S_3	S_4
press a	S_1 (*black 'a'*)	S_2 (*red 'a'*)	S_3 (*black 'A'*)	S_4 (*red 'A'*)
press b	S_1 (*black 'b'*)	S_2 (*red 'b'*)	S_3 (*black 'B'*)	S_4 (*red 'B'*)
·	·	·	·	·
·	·	·	·	·
·	·	·	·	·
push Red	$S_2(\Lambda)$	$S_2(\Lambda)$	$S_4(\Lambda)$	$S_4(\Lambda)$
push Black	$S_1(\Lambda)$	$S_1(\Lambda)$	$S_3(\Lambda)$	$S_3(\Lambda)$
push shift	$S_3(\Lambda)$	$S_4(\Lambda)$	$S_3(\Lambda)$	$S_4(\Lambda)$
pull shift	$S_1(\Lambda)$	$S_2(\Lambda)$	$S_1(\Lambda)$	$S_2(\Lambda)$

Table A–2.

3. If it operates "improperly" there exists another, different FST-description characterizing its behavior.

This table shows, for example, that when in state S_1 the typewriter prints black lowercase letters. When in this state, moreover, pushing the "Red" switch causes the machine to pass into state S_2, in which it outputs red lowercase letters when the key-buttons are pushed; on the other hand, when in state S_1, pushing the "shift-lock" button causes it to pass into state S_3 where it prints only capital black letters. In fact, by manipulating the color and shift-lock buttons, the machine can be caused to pass from any given state to any other state in the FST. For example, by pushing "Black" and pulling "shift" (in either order) the machine can be transferred from state S_4 to state S_1. The reader can easily verify that this FST also describes the rest of the operations of such a system.

This simple example illustrates several important facts about the logic of "FSTs." First, notice that the table *describes the functioning of the system in abstraction from its internal concrete constitution or arrangement.* That is, the applicability of the FST-description to the system depends logically only on its overall operational properties. Two typewriters, one manual, the other electric, with entirely dissimilar internal physical arrangements and operating in accordance with completely different physical principles, both could satisfy the above FST-description. All that is required is that both respond to inputs of the same kinds with outputs of the same kinds. As in this illustration, so in general, a multitude of different physical systems all can be realizations of the same FST.[4] That is, as the concept is defined and used in this work, an FST is an abstract description satisfied by any system possessing the input-output properties it characterizes.

Second, the state descriptions (e.g., 'S_1', 'S_2') in an FST *are defined solely by the table*; they have no definition outside that given by the table. In the illustration above, for example, to *"be in state S_1"* is just to be in a state that has the properties given by the table for this state. Any realization of this FST that would react to any of the listed inputs with the responses indicated for state S_1 (including changes into other states with the properties described by the table) is, by definition, *"in state S_1."* Thus, an electric and a manual typewriter both could be in state S_1 even

---

4. Of course, even when there is one FST-description that two concrete systems, M_1 and M_2, both satisfy, there also may be *other* FST-descriptions that only one of the two systems satisfies.

though each is in a different internal structural state. This is because these state descriptions operate in functional abstraction from the system's internal physical configuration. Such states are called *"abstract functional states,"* or just *"F-states"* for short. The same F-state, then, can have different physical realizations in different systems when in that state. For example, the structural correlate of state S_1 in a manual typewriter could be a certain configuration of its type-panel, levers, springs, and ribbon-holder while the correlate of the same F-state in an electric typewriter might involve different component parts (e.g., a type-ball instead of a type-panel) plus electrical potentials, currents, and magnetic fields.

Like typewriters, persons also can be described by FSTs. Of the various possible ways of doing this, only one will concern us. In it, the "inputs" are taken to be external environmental objects or situations (which can affect the person through his sense organs[5]), and the "outputs" include physical bodily movements. In the terminology of psychology, the inputs are external "stimulus objects," the outputs are "responses." An "input," for example, might be a red apple against a white background, or a spoken utterance; an output might be an elevating of the arm, a wrinkling of the brow, or a vocalization. It is assumed that for each human, FST-descriptions exist characterizing his responses (depending on his state) to such inputs.[6] In itself, this assumption prejudges no theory of mind: it would hold whether a person were a randomly operating mechanism or a body activated by a Cartesian soul. Every actually existing system is characterizable (even if only trivially) by FST-descriptions, and humans are no exception.

5. As the notion of an "FST" is used here, the requirement is not in general stipulated that these external situations actually activate his sense organs. The sense organs (e.g., eyes) are part of the system being characterized, and the interface between system and inputs lies on the distal side of the sense organs. If the system is such that certain external situations do not affect it (e.g., if the subject's eyes are closed), this fact will be expressed in the description of the state (e.g., if his eyes are closed, he will be in a state in which, as the table will show, changes in the external visible scene would produce no change in him and no outputs). So as this mode of description is used here, we need not additionally require that the "inputs" *do* affect him; when required, the assumption is implicit in the FST-description.

6. To avoid misunderstandings, I repeat that an "FST," in the sense used here, is a description true or false of the subject depending on whether he operates as it predicts, and *not* something to which he makes recourse in planning or executing his actions.

To give a simple example, suppose a subject is placed in a room, told to watch two light bulbs, one red, the other green, and to press the button before him when one of the lights flashes if and only if it is the same color as the one that flashed previously. Then as long as he obeys this instruction, he will be characterized by the FST-description in Table A–3.

	States		
	S_I	S_R	S_G
red light $\geq$ *100 milliseconds*	$S_R(\Lambda)$	S_R *(press button)*	$S_R(\Lambda)$
green light $\geq$ *100 milliseconds*	$S_G(\Lambda)$	$S_G(\Lambda)$	S_G *(press button)*

Table A–3.

(S_I is the "initial state," i.e., the state of the subject as he begins the experiment.) This example is rather unexciting, but it suffices to show that humans can be characterized by FST-descriptions. It also shows that to qualify as an "FST," the state table need not be complete—i.e., it need not show what the system would do for every possible input. (In fact, it is doubtful whether FSTs that are "complete" in this sense exist.) To realize an FST for a period of time a system need only, for that period of time, be such that it would respond to any of the inputs listed in the FST, and any sequence of these, with outputs of the sort the FST indicates. Although for any person, there are many simple FSTs (such as the one above) describing him at a given time, the FSTs that interest the functionalist are not simple. As will be seen, they describe highly complex sets of rational procedures and patterns of behavior, and realizations of them will, on the thesis stated below, be capable of speaking the language, engaging in reasoning, perceiving, thinking, making judgments, feeling emotions, etc.

One fact must be clarified before stating this thesis. The theory does not construe mentalistic substantives like 'sensation(s)', 'feeling(s)', 'thought(s)', etc., as in themselves designating anything. Rather than interpreting these terms as designators of separate substantial entities (e.g., "pains"), it views them as linguistic constituents of complex predicate expressions like 'has-an-unbearable-pain' or 'has-a-pain-in-the-toe'. These predicates, in turn, the theory treats as true or false of humans (as well as, for some of these predicates, other systems, e.g., animals), and assumes that the only independent concrete substantial entity involved is the system to which these predicates are ascribed.[7] So the theory does not quantify over "pains," "feelings," "thoughts," etc.; it talks about psychological states or state descriptions of a mentalistic sort applicable to humans and tries to characterize the nature of the truth conditions for their attribution.

Principle 4 of my theory postulates that there exists a class of FST-descriptions with the following property: for each predicate expressing a pure[8] mentalistic state description, there exists, in the postulated class, an FST containing an F-state (or sequence of F-states) such that being in this F-state (or passing through this sequence of F-states) is a logically sufficient condition for the applicability of that mental predicate. In other words, according to the principle, necessarily if something is in this postulated F-state (or states), it is in the given mental state. As an example, consider the psychological description 'has a pain in the toe'. According to the hypothesis, there exists at least one FST, say F_i, containing at least one F-state, say S_j, such that necessarily, 'has a pain in the toe' is true of any realization of this FST when in F-state S_j. Diagrammatically, the postulated situation can be represented as in Table A–4.

$$\overbrace{\phantom{\text{'has a pain in the toe'}}}^{\text{'has a pain in the toe'}}$$

| $FST\ F_i:$ | S_1 | S_2 | ... | S_j | ... |

Inputs

Table A–4.

(The placement of the predicate 'has a pain in the toe' above 'S_j' in the diagram represents the fact that when a realization of this FST is in the F-state S_j, the psychological description 'has a pain in the toe' is true of it.) Block and Fodor refer to such an FST as

7. A similar idea is developed by Peter Strawson, *Individuals* (London: Methuen, 1959), chap.3.
8. I.e., nonrelational.

the abstract functionalist's postulated "best description."[9] (It is not, however, "unique," as they claim.)

Several points deserve amplification. First, this principle does not assert that any particular individual (say John Smith) who has a pain is a realization of any of the postulated FSTs. The hypothesis only entails that necessarily, any realization of the postulated FST, when in a certain F-state of it, would have a pain in the toe. Of course, FST-descriptions probably will be true of John Smith that contain F-states such that any realization of these FSTs (e.g., John Smith) when in this F-state will also, ipso facto, be in a state of having a pain in his toe. But this claim is not made by Principle 4.

Second, this is only one postulate of the theory. Its full axiomatization has many implications not developed in this appendix. Among other consequences, the full theory is incompatible both with behavioristic operationalism and with central state materialism. It offers a new way of conceiving of psychological states and their relationship to physical processes (in particular, neural processes), it permits an account of the epistemic relationship between a subject and his own mental phenomena (including what he does to report them and why his "introspective" reports seem privileged and incorrigible) that avoids the difficulties generated by traditional accounts of self-knowledge, and it provides a conceptualizing structure in which various theoretical problems in action theory, the psychology of perception, psycholinguistics, and neuropsychology can be solved. N.B.: This functionalist postulate is part of an account of the nature of *mental states in general*; it does not purport to specify the defining characteristics of any particular subclass of these states!

Third, note that the hypothesis does *not* assert that the postulated F-states are *identical* with the given mental states. Indeed, the relation between mental states and F-states is not even necessarily one-to-one. In the first place, for each given psychological predicate, there may be (and in general will be) many different FSTs each containing many different F-states in which that predicate is true of the system. Moreover, each of these F-states may constitute a sufficient condition for the application of other mental predicates as well. The situation anticipated here is diagrammatically illustrated in Table A–5.

9. Block and Fodor, p. 165.

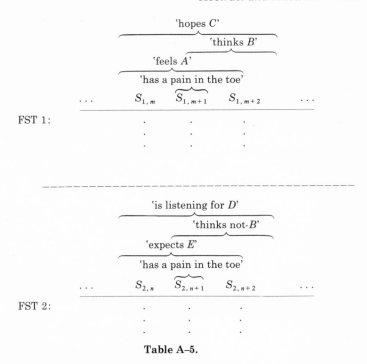

FST 1:

FST 2:

Table A–5.

Suppose that FST 1, FST 2, etc., are some of the members of the postulated class of FSTs. When in state $S_{1,m+1}$ of FST 1, for example, the psychological predicates 'has a pain in the toe', 'feels A', 'thinks B', and 'hopes C' (as well, perhaps, as indefinitely many others not shown) are all true of a realization of FST 1. When in state $S_{1,m}$, on the other hand, the predicates 'feels A' and 'hopes C' are true of it, but not 'has a pain in the toe' or 'thinks B' (assuming these do not appear higher up in the part of the stack not shown). Notice that the same psychological predicate (e.g., 'hopes C') may be true of the system when it is in a variety of different F-states. Notice too that a state in one FST (e.g., state $S_{1,m+1}$ in FST 1) *also* may be correlated with some of the *same* psychological state descriptions (e.g., 'has a pain in the toe') as another state in an entirely different FST (e.g., state $S_{2,n+1}$ in FST 2).

On this point the theory criticized by Block and Fodor differs from mine. They attribute to the abstract functionalist the claim that organism "O is in such and such a type of psychological state at time t if and only if O is in such and such a type of machine table state at time t.''[10] But, in fact, Principle 4 only asserts sufficient conditions, not necessary and sufficient conditions. Expressed in their terminology, the claim is of the form, "If O is in such and such machine table state(s), then O is in such and such a psychological state." Many of the objections Block and Fodor raise apply only to their improperly stated version of the theory. One such is the following:

> The set of states which constitute the machine table of a probabilistic automaton is, by definition, a list. But the set of mental states of at least some organisms (namely, persons) is, in point of empirical fact, productive. In particular, abstracting from theoretically irrelevant limitations imposed by memory and mortality, there are infinitely many type-distinct, nomologically possible psychological states of any given person. The simplest demonstration that this is true is that, on the assumption that there are infinitely many non-equivalent declarative sentences, one can generate definite descriptions of such states by replacing S with sentences in the schemata A: "the belief (thought, desire, hope, and so forth) that S."[11]

This argument shows that the psychological states of an organism cannot be placed in one-to-one correspondence with the states in an FST describing that organism. But this is compatible with Principle 4. For, as has been seen, it does not assert a one-to-one correspondence between psychological states and F-states. Indefinitely many different mental state descriptions may be simultaneously predicable of the system when it is in a given F-state. As illustrated in the previous diagram, the mental state descriptions may be thought of as stacked up, infinitely far if need be, above the state descriptions in the FST. So the fact that psychological states cannot be put into one-to-one correspondence with F-states does not refute my theory.

A related objection is the following:

> Two machine table states of a deterministic automaton are distinct if they differ either in their associated outputs or in their associated successor state. Analogously, two machine table states of probabilistic automata differ if they differ in their range of outputs, or in their range of successor states, or in the probability distributions associated with either of these ranges.

10. *Ibid.*
11. *Ibid.*, pp. 175–176. (Objection 5.)

If, however, we transfer this convention for distinguishing machine table states to the type identification of psychological states, we get identity conditions which are, as it were, too fine-grained. Thus, for example, if you and I differ *only* in the respect that your most probable response to the pain is to say "damn" and mine is to say "darn," it follows that the pain you have when you stub your toe is type-distinct from the pain I have when I stub my toe.[12]

This conclusion does not follow from Principle 4. To be sure, if my response to stubbing my toe is different from yours to stubbing your toe, then some FST-description of me is different from some FST-description of you. And in relation to these FST-descriptions, you and I are in different F-states. But from this its does not follow, by my functionalist thesis, that your state of pain is different from my state of pain. In fact, the very opposite is true. Supposing that these FSTs were in the postulated class and that the mental description 'has a pain in the toe' is determined by states in these two FSTs, Principle 4 entails that we *both* are in a "state of having a pain in the toe" even though each of us is in a different F-state. The situation is like that portrayed in Table A–5. Suppose FST 1 describes you and FST 2 describes me, and that on some occasion, your stubbing your toe causes you to pass into $S_{1,m+1}$ and my stubbing my toe causes me to pass into $S_{2,n+1}$. Then, according to the hypothesis, each of us would be in a state of having a pain in the toe. We both are in the *same psychological* state although our F-states are different.

It also might be objected that such a thesis is incompatible with the distinction between dispositional psychological states (beliefs, desires, inclinations, and so on) and occurrent psychological states (sensations, transient thoughts, feelings, and so on).[13] This objection, too, is mistaken. As was already shown, a variety of different psychological state descriptions all may be predicable of a person when he is in a given F-state. Some of these may be "dispositional," others "occurrent." A system may pass into or out of some of these psychological states while remaining continuously in others. For example, referring again to Table A–5, by passing from $S_{1,m+1}$ to $S_{1,m+2}$ a realization of FST 1 would pass out of a state of pain while retaining his hope for C. This accords with the fact that, for example, a person may cease to feel a pain

12. *Ibid.*, p. 174 (Objection 4.)
13. *Ibid.*, p. 168. (Objection 1.)

without undergoing changes in many of his beliefs, hopes, etc. The primary difference between so-called "occurrent" and so-called "dispositional" states is simply one of duration. (In fact, the difference is not even sharp. The having of transient sensations appears as "occurrent" when contrasted, e.g., with the having of a belief, because the latter is generally more long-lasting. But relative to something even more enduring such as the ability to speak the language, beliefs may appear "occurrent" since they come and go in time.) If one were to choose some segment of a person's life history and rewrite the names of his F-states in the order in which he actually passed through them, the result might look like Table A–6.

			'has a pain'						
			'desires *X*'						
					'believes *Y*'				
...	S_6	S_8	S_3	S_4	S_5	S_1	S_7	S_2	...

Table A–6.

Throughout this short interval of his life, the subject retained his desire for *X*. During a short period (when he was in S_3 and S_4) he had a pain. And at a certain point in time (state S_5) he acquired the belief *Y*. Some of his psychological states ("dispositional" states, such as desire) persisted for a greater length of time than others ("occurrent" states, such as pain). So the account obviously is compatible with the distinction between "occurrent" and "dispositional" states, and indeed reflects some of its basis.

Some mentalistic attributions, such as 'speaks English', seem located so far to one extreme of the occurrent-dispositional spectrum as not to refer to psychological states at all. Intuitively, the ability to speak English seems best categorizable not as a "mental state," but instead perhaps as an "intellectual capacity." The model also captures this distinction. If true of a system, a predicate such as 'speaks English' is true of it simply in virtue of the system's *realizing an FST* of a certain kind. That is, there are FSTs in the postulated class of which any realization will be able to speak English, and the mentalistic description 'speaks English' is, ipso facto, true of any realization of such an FST regardless of his state in it. To be able to speak English, in other words, is simply to be a realization of a certain sort of FST. Hence the description 'speaks English' is different from mental state descriptions that differentially depend on the F-state of the subject. Thus the model reflects the distinction between mental states on the one hand, and intellectual capacities on the other.

Block and Fodor also object that a theory of this kind provides no way of accounting for "interactions" among simultaneously existing psychological states.

> It is empirically immensely likely . . . that there are *two* kinds of behaviorally efficacious interactions between psychological states, and *FSIT* provides for a natural model for only one of them.
>
> On one hand, behavior can be the product of a *series* of psychological states, and the *FSIT* account shows how this could be true, and how some of the states occurring in such a series may not themselves have behavioral expressions. But, on the other hand, behavior can be the result of interaction between *simultaneous* mental states. For example, prima facie, what an organism does at t may be a function of what it is feeling at t and what it is thinking at t. But *FSIT* provides no conceptual machinery for representing this state of affairs.[14]

Part of this objection is correct. My theory not only provides no account of causal *interactions* among simultaneous psychological states; I deny that such interactions take place. In so doing, I oppose faculty psychology, that tendency in behavioral explanation to account for human action as resulting from the causal interaction of various mental forces or influences. Mental states, as such, are abstract entities, and they interact neither with each other nor with the concrete system that realizes them. The only particulars causally interacting to produce behavior are the concrete components of the realizing system. The relationship between a person's mental states and his behavior is the same as the relationship between a typewriter's abstract functional states and its behavior. (Presumably, no one would assert that the abstract state, e.g., of "readiness to type in uppercase letters" interacts with, or exerts an influence on, a typewriter's keys causing them to act as they do.) Denying that mental states can *interact* causally with anything, of course, does not preclude their figuring in other ways in causal explanations.

My theory does not, however, imply that *no* relations exist among various mental states, or between mental states and

14. *Ibid.*, p. 170. (Objection 2.) *"FSIT"* refers to the "functional state identity theory"; here as elsewhere I respond as if my theory were the intended referent. Block and Fodor mistakenly attribute *FSIT* to Hilary Putnam.

behavior. Instead of causal interactions, other relations are postulated of the following general sort. First, the relationship hypothesized between mind and body is already clear. There is no causal interaction between mind and body. Rather, the relationship between mind and body is like the relationship between a universal and a concrete particular falling under it. The body is a physical system that realizes a certain FST and hence *has* mental states. Second, the theory postulates logical relationships among the various abstract states, and between these states and descriptions of behavior. To say that a system is in a certain F-state entails that it will respond to various particular environmental situations in ways specified by the defining FST. In cases of interest to psychophysics, for a system to be in a certain F-state also logically implies that it is in certain mental states. Formal relations of the sort investigated in automata theory also can exist among the various F-states in the FST. Logical relationships likewise can exist among various *mental* state descriptions. Some logical relationship clearly exists between the psychological state that one is in if he believes that *P*, for example, and the psychological state that he is in if he believes that $P \& Q$;[15] similarly for the relationship between being depressed and being unhappy. By linking mental states to F-states, my functionalist thesis provides a means for investigating the actual logical interrelationships among psychological states. In itself, the thesis, of course, does not detail the particular logical relationships between specific mental state descriptions, or their defining characteristics, but this is no criticism of it.[16] To detail these would be a monumental undertaking which the theory does not purport to have accomplished, although it shows in general how such a project might be carried out. If one possessed FST-descriptions of the postulated kind, studying them might reveal the features of each F-state (including its relationships with its neighbors) that are responsible for the applicability of each of the various mental predicates stacked up above it.[17] For example, in this way one might see

15. *Ibid.*, p. 178. (Objection 6.)

16. Some work has been done on this problem by ordinary-language philosophers. Here, too, Grician analysis might play a role.

17. General procedures for separating out the components of an F-state specifically relevant to each of the various simultaneously applicable mental descriptions—or fusing two separate FST-descriptions of a system (e.g., a visual perception FST and a language FST) into one FST—to my knowledge have not been worked out yet. This is called "the factoring problem."

why some specific conjoined set of mentalistic attributions entails a certain further mentalistic attribution, or why two other mental predicates never are simultaneously applicable.

(Although none is postulated by the theory itself, there also may exist *contingent* correlations between mental states. For example, there might be two psychological states, *State X* and *State Y*, such that although a system logically could be in both simultaneously, in fact no organism occurring in nature ever is. On my theory, such empirical psychological generalizations imply that certain FSTs in the postulated class are actualized nowhere.)

More important here are the relations between mental descriptions and behavioral descriptions. In the objection quoted above, Block and Fodor observe that "what an organism does at t may be a function of what it is feeling at t and what it is thinking at t" and claim that functionalism "provides no machinery for representing this state of affairs." This claim is mistaken. Mental states (and F-states generally) can enter as values of variables in functions that describe behavior, and my theory provides a clear account of the nature of such functions. To begin with a simple illustration, let us return to the typewriter in Table A–2. Suppose we call 'is ready to type in red' and 'is ready to type in black' descriptions of the system's "*color state.*" And let us call 'is ready to type in lowercase' and 'is ready to type in uppercase' descriptions of the typewriter's "*case state.*" Then what a typewriter does at t is a function of what its color state is at t and what its case state is at t. For example, when it is in the "red" color state and the "capital" case state, it will respond to a pushing of the b-button by outputting a token of a red capital 'B'. This fact is explicitly expressible by a function

$$f(press\ b\text{-}button,\ RED,\ CAPITAL) = red\ uppercase\ 'B'$$

where the function f is defined by the FST plus the correlated functionally determined states (designated here by 'RED' and '$CAPITAL$'). There clearly is no problem about this. Analogously, psychological states can appear as values for variables in functions that describe organisms' behavior. For example, what a given organism does at a given time might be a function of what it is feeling at that time and what it is thinking at that time (plus the external situation in which it finds itself). To illustrate, using the example of FST 1 in Table A–5, the value of the function

$$F_1(input\ x,\ feels\ A,\ thinks\ B) = output\ y$$

is given, for each value of x, in the state column under '$S_{1, m+1}$'. (This illustration assumes that 'feels A' and 'thinks B' do not overlap elsewhere in the FST.) The function F_1 is defined here by FST 1 plus the associated mental state descriptions. So my theory not only provides general conceptual machinery for representing functional relationships between simultaneously occurring mental states and behavior, but it also shows the general form of the function.[18]

A standard traditional argument against any form of mechanism is that it can provide no account of the so-called "sensory *qualia*" (i.e., the qualities of color, sound, taste, smell, pain, and so on, as subjectively experienced).[19] After all, if the only concrete existent is a functionally organized body, where are the subjective sensory qualities (colors, pain, etc.) located? Presumably not in this bodily entity since it is just a mechanical system composed of various physical parts (which indeed may have various colors and tastes but generally not the colors and tastes appearing in the subject's experience). Nor, apparently, in some separate incorporeal entity called "the mind," since physicalistic functionalists deny the existence of any such thing. Yet we experience such qualities. Where, then, do they fit into the scheme? As applied to my functionalist theory, the objection would be that it cannot accommodate at least one critical determining feature of some

18. I should remark that I do not urge the use of ordinary-language mental descriptions in scientific behavioral explanation. They are used in this example only to show that the theory accommodates functional relationships between mental states; similar functions can be defined for other, more precisely defined abstract state descriptions. For the most part, ordinary-language mental descriptions are so imprecise that little use can be made of them in many rigorous psychological investigations except as general indicator words. Nor is there any guarantee that the ordinary-language mental descriptions will pick out the theoretically significant states of an organism. The general thrust of my functionalist thesis is to replace ordinary-language mental state descriptions with more precisely defined state descriptions (in particular, the rigorously defined F-state descriptions) in psychological explanation. It justifies this replacement by showing that nothing will be lost by it. For the theory assures investigators interested in mental phenomena that they can gain access to everything relevant to a subject's mental states by restricting their attention to states in certain machine tables. Since, according to the theory, FSTs of the postulated sort leave nothing relevant to a subject's "mental life" uncharacterized, psychologists and physiologists can confine themselves to studying F-states, their interrelationships, their behavioral consequences, and their underlying neurological realizations, confident that they are not thereby overlooking some aspect of mentality.

19. This argument was used, e.g., by C. D. Broad in *The Mind and Its Place in Nature* (London: Routledge & Kegan Paul, 1925), pp. 46–52.

mental states, namely, the fact that they involve sensory *qualia*:

> It does not, for example, seem entirely unreasonable to suggest
> that nothing would be a token of the type "pain state" unless it
> felt like a pain, and that this would be true even if it were con-
> nected to all the other psychological states of the organism in
> whatever way pains are. Moreover, it seems to us that the stan-
> dard verificationist counterarguments against the view that the
> "inverted spectrum" hypothesis is conceptually coherent are
> not persuasive. If this is correct, it looks as though the possi-
> bility of qualia inversion poses a serious prima-facie argument
> against functionalist accounts of the criteria for type identity
> of psychological states.[20]

My answer to this objection is that, however "reasonable" its
claims may appear, they are false. There are various states of one's
body and nervous system (states that realize the FST-determined
description 'is in pain') such that, when one's body is in any of
them, one will be in a state of pain. Correspondingly, according
to the thesis, there are FSTs containing F-states in which the
predicate 'feels pain' is true. A realization of such an FST when
in one of these F-states will show all the signs of pain (both in
explicit actions and nonactions and in alterations in other mental
states and dispositions), and he himself will claim that he feels a
pain, and he will be correct in what he says. So, contrary to the
objection, when in a state "connected to all other psychological
states and behavior of the organism in whatever way pains are,"
according to my theory, a subject *will* be in a state *with the full
qualitative content of pain*. Similarly for the "inverted spectrum
hypothesis." Strange as it may seem to philosophers who maintain that it is possible, for example, that I always experience
"green" when viewing objects that cause others to experience
what they (if they could have my experience) would call "red"
(but that we both have learned to apply the same color words to
the same objects and that all of our other behaviors and dispositions to behave in relationship to colored external objects are
the same),[21] the functionalist denies this possibility. (His denial,
moreover, is independent of any verificationist arguments.) If
some stimulus object puts both of us into all the same F-states,

---

20. Block and Fodor, p. 172. (Objection 3.)
21. E.g. Hilary Putnam, "Reds, Greens, and Logical Analysis," *Philosophical Review*, 65 (1956), 211.

then we both will have the same color sensations. Qualia inversion (unmanifested in behavior or dispositions to behavior) is not possible according to the thesis, a theoretical implication that has received indirect empirical confirmation,[22] or so it appears.

Block and Fodor are correct in saying that accounting for "sensory *qualia*" (and indeed, sense perception generally, the larger topic of which sensory *qualia* constitute a subtopic) poses a deeper problem for functionalism than any of the other objections considered.[23] Can sense *qualia* be explained consistently with the theory, and if so, how? Certainly, no presently available alternative theory satisfactorily accounts for these phenomena, and whether they can be explained in detail within the general functionalist theoretical framework remains to be discovered. Since I do not know the answer to this question, I will confine myself to a few general remarks indicating the approach that functionalists may take.

Traditionally, sensory *qualia* generally were conceived as qualities or properties possessed by mentalistic entities (called "sensations," "impressions," "percepts," "subjective sense-data," or some such thing) with which the subject (or the "Self" or "Ego") who possessed them was supposedly in direct cognitive contact. This "direct cognitive contact" usually was conceived as some sort of quasi-perceptual relationship. It was supposed, for example, that a "patch" or "area in the subjective visual field" might have "red *quale*" or red quality, and that this is what the subject senses or experiences. Similarly, a certain "sensation" might or might not possess "pain quality" (the quality that makes pains unpleasant). But since my version of functionalism (through its other postulates) rejects the model of mental phenomena as possible objects of inner awareness, it cannot follow the traditional approach of analyzing sense *qualia* as qualities of inwardly apprehended mentalistic entities.

Before functionalism's probable alternative approach is discussed, the confusions existing in this area necessitate some antecedent terminological clarification. In ordinary language, one sometimes correctly may say that a strawberry or a boiled lobster "is red." Following this linguistic convention, let us take, e.g., 'is red' to be a predicate sometimes true of such physical

22. This is discussed in Chapter 4, Section 2.
23. Block and Fodor, p. 173.

objects. Correspondingly, when this predicate is true of some object, we also may say, speaking platonistically, that it *has the quality or property* of "redness." Second, in ordinary language one sometimes can say of a person in relation to some physical object, e.g., "He sees the strawberry." Following this terminology, let us take, e.g., 'sees', as a two-place predicate or term expressing a relation that sometimes holds between a perceiving subject and a physical object or situation. (Explaining or analyzing this relation is the task of a theory of perception.) Finally, whenever this relation obtains (i.e., whenever someone sees something), the subject is in a certain sensory state. (He also may be in this sensory state when he does not see anything, for example, when hallucinating.) Accordingly, certain state descriptions truly are predicable of him. When someone sees a strawberry, for instance, it is normally true to say of him, "He is now having the sense impression of something red" or "He is now experiencing red visual impressions." In the following discussion, the various mentalistic predicates 'is having the sense impression of something red', 'is experiencing red visual impressions', 'is seeming to see something red', 'is sensing redly', etc., are used interchangeably when describing the subject's sensory state.

Turning now to the relationship between so-called "sensory *qualia*" and the subject's sensory states, it scarcely needs pointing out that the appearance of the *word* 'red' in the linguistic expression of these mentalistic predicates hardly implies that the *predicate* 'is red' is a logical constituent of them (i.e., it does not imply that something of which the predicate 'is red' is true is itself a constituent of the situation described by application of the predicate 'is-having-a-red-sensory-impression'). Or putting the point in the material mode, the fact that a subject is having a sensory impression of redness does not imply that something that is red or has the quality of redness is itself a part of the subject or inside the subject. This is important to my hypothesis because according to it, a complete and adequate account of the nature of these sensory *states*, showing in what they consist and how they come about, will constitute a satisfactory account of sensory *qualia*. The ultimate phenomenon to be explained, then, is taken to be not "sensory *qualia*" themselves, but rather the property of *having-an-experience-of-such-and-such-sensory-quale*. "Sensory *qualia*" themselves, conceived as (qualities of) directly or inwardly apprehended mentalistic entities, the theory rejects.

The problem now is to characterize (e.g., in terms of physics) a structural state that could realize, say, the sensory state of experiencing red visual impressions and explain how it could do so. The task, in other words, is to explain in general how a system of components could possess visual sensory consciousness. This problem might be approached along the following lines. One might try to describe, at least in general outlines, an FST containing F-states such that, when in these F-states, a system will have all the functional characteristics of someone in the psychological state of "experiencing a sense impression of redness." When in such a state, not only will a realization of this FST respond to red objects in its environment in all the ways appropriate to this predication (including, of course, reporting that it sees, or seems to see, something red, as well as possessing the image memory latency of visual perception), but also all its other states of consciousness (beliefs, desires, thoughts, and so on) will be appropriately modified. If my hypothesis is true, when in such a state, a realization of such an FST actually will have-the-experience-of-red-sensory-*qualia*, an experience in every way similar to ours when we see something red.

The plausibility of the claim that such an FST's realizations would be capable of sensory states similar to ours is not supposed to rest solely on my functionalist thesis. Technology, for one, may provide support. As such FSTs are constructed, engineers may be able to develop artificial realizations of them (devices called "perceptrons") whose sensory and other capabilities are indistinguishable from those of humans to whom sensory awareness unhesitatingly is attributed. This strongly would substantiate the theory. Of course, just as it still would be possible in principle for someone even today to maintain a phlogiston theory of heat, it probably would be possible even at this projected time for someone who still maintained a private-inner-object model of mental phenomena to claim that such systems did not really possess sensory consciousness, but only exhibited the relevant behavior. As these devices become better, however, skeptics may find that they can doubt that such systems have sensory experience only if they genuinely extend this doubt to every person besides themselves. As auxiliary substantiation to satisfy such pyrrhonists should come a special additional philosophic construction: a theoretical analysis mapping between the perceptual situation as experienced from the first-person standpoint and the perceptual situation as described by the functionalist from the third-person standpoint.[24] That is, to be fully convinced of the correctness of the theory, a point-by-point correlation may be required of every feature or aspect of (a) a subject's perceptual experience as he seems to view it or would describe it from a phenomenological standpoint with (b) his perceptual state as described from an objective external standpoint. To express the demand still another way, one will want to be shown and have explained in detail how a person's total present conscious awareness of a sensory field can be the FST-determined macrolevel outcome of a large number of microlevel processes that lack such properties. This supplementary piece of philosophy presumably can be developed only after (or at best, simultaneously with) the construction of a special theory of sensory states, a task yet unaccomplished.[25]

Another *objection* the theory may encounter is the following:

It is an empirical fact that certain neurological dysfunctions can result in a subject who is incapable of any output motor behavior but in whom at least some mental processes still continue. For example, when afflicted with the muscle-paralyzing agent curare, a person is completely immobilized, incapable of producing any bodily movement or overt response to outside sensory influences. Yet when (and if) the effects of the drug pass, he is capable of reporting events that took place around him, sights and sounds he saw and heard, as well as thoughts he had, while paralyzed. So it seems reasonable to say that he had thoughts and experiences while paralyzed. Now suppose this same patient never recovered his output capabilities but remained paralyzed until death. Surely a *subsequent* event, such as the recovery or nonrecovery of motor ability, cannot affect the truth value of mentalistic statements made about him at an *earlier* time. So it remains true to say of him that he had thoughts, experiences, and so on; we simply were unable to find out what they were.

24. In this connection see Thomas Nagel, "What Is It Like to Be a Bat?" *Philosophical Review*, 83 (1974), 449f.

25. A little progress has been made, however. Chapter 2 shows how psychological phenomena involving the apparent perception of mentalistic entities (e.g., afterimages, dreams, pains) can be treated as degenerate versions of full-blown perception of external objects. An analysis of one famous sensory *quale*, "pain quality," also is given, an analysis delineating a set of functional disabilities that are plausibly such that a system possessing them would experience, or begin to experience, "pain quality," showing thereby, at least in broad outline, how some sensory *qualia* can be accounted for along my functionalist lines.

But according to your hypothesis, mental descriptions can be linked with FST-descriptions, and these, in turn, depend on the input-output characteristics of the subject. But if there were no output responses from him, an FST-description could not be applied to the subject, for without outputs, no F-states of the postulated kind could be distinguished for him.

Reply: This objection is easily answered. No fact it cites is incompatible with my hypothesis. Principle 4 states that FSTs exist that determine mental state descriptions; it does not assert that every subject of a mental state is a realization of one of these FSTs.

My theory shows the nature of mental state descriptions by characterizing their truth conditions in a certain set of paradigmatic situations; abnormal situations also may arise. The earlier typewriter example can be used to model the curare situation. If the ribbon were removed from the machine, we still could understand someone who said, "The typewriter is in a lowercase state" even though it no longer could print letters. Nor would we take this possibility as showing that the meaning of this state description is unrelated to the ability to print letters. Likewise, the fact that the curare-poisoned man can be said truly to be in various mental states even though part of the mechanism by which these are expressed in behavior is disconnected does not show that mental state descriptions are definable independently of behavior.[26] Probably the best way to think of the curare situation physically is in terms of serial subcomponents of the physical realization. The physical system realizing the subject can be divided theoretically into two components, an afferent-and-central system unaffected by the drug, and in serial connection, a peripheral motor system that is rendered inoperative or functionally disconnected from the former by the drug. After injection of curare, the afferent-and-central system continues to operate by itself in somewhat its normal way (except that events in it do not lead to motor behavior and there is no motor feedback), while parts of the peripheral motor system become inoperative. Inside the paralyzed subject are occurring, therefore, the same events that formerly occurred in him when he was normal and having

26. See also Lawrence H. Davis, "Disembodied Brains," *Australian Journal of Philosophy*, 52 (1974), 121–132.

thoughts and experiences; they just do not express themselves in behavior because part of the necessary mechanism has been disconnected. But if his peripheral motor output component were reattached, the appropriate behavior again would be observed.

Objection: Whatever may be its relation to the truth conditions of mental descriptions, the conceptual machinery of FST-descriptions cannot be applied to human beings because, unlike machines, humans grow and learn and change over time. An infant, a toddler, an adolescent, and a young adult each would have different FSTs. So a different FST-description would be required to characterize a human being at each of these stages of development as well as at each intermediate phase. But people change and develop *continuously* throughout their lives. Therefore, nothing less than an infinity of FST-descriptions, each true of him for only an instant, would be required to characterize a human being.

Reply: Contrary to what this objection assumes, the model is fully dynamical. In particular, the fact that people constantly change and learn does not imply that they cannot be characterized by a unitary FST- description. Certainly, for some purposes in theoretical psychology, learning might be represented as a change from one FST to another FST. On such a model, the task of learning theory would be to describe these successive FSTs and find functions that predict the actual transitions from FST to FST. But these successive FSTs also could be welded together into one large FST whose different subparts characterize the organism at different stages in its development. Such an FST would show the F-states of the system initially (e.g., in its infancy) together with various external stimuli (food, punishments, imitable actions, or whatever) that cause the system to pass into other F-states in which it behaves differently. On this model, learning would be represented as passing from F-states of one kind to F-states of another kind in the same FST-description.[27] (Such a unitary FST-description, of course, presumably would not be "strongly connected," that is, it would not always be possible to

27. Certain special internal states in the system (e.g., pain) also could play a special role in learning transitions. For an excellent theoretical analysis of the mechanisms by which the changes of state involved in learning may occur, see W. Ross Ashby, *Design for a Brain* (New York: John Wiley & Sons, 1960).

get from any state in it to any other state by some sequence of external inputs; some changes from state to state would be irreversible by any series of inputs listed in the FST.)

"Given a computer simulation of a person experiencing an emotion, when can we say the computer also *experiences* the emotion, and when can we say it only *simulates* the experiencing of the emotion?" Since my hypothesis provides no necessary condition for having or experiencing emotion, it gives no sufficient condition for saying that something does *not* experience an emotion. But it does give sufficient conditions for having an emotion. The hypothesis entails that any concrete system ("computer" or otherwise) can experience a given emotion if it does nothing more than realize a suitable FST. (One must always remember, of course, that satisfying such an FST will require the system to be capable of responding to perceivable physical environments by actually exhibiting the same patterns of motor behavior as do naturally occurring organic realizations.) This sufficiency claim is substantiated by the evidence adduced for my hypothesis in Chapters 3 and 4 of the text. (If, however, by the phrase "when can we say . . ." the question asks not for logically sufficient conditions for the computer's experiencing an emotion, but rather for some performable series of (input-output) operations and observations by which the fact that a computer experiences an emotion could be established with logical certitude, then as Section 3 of Appendix II proves, none exists if my theory is true.)

The following objection challenges the account of pains as apparent objects:

In your analysis of pain, in one special case at least, the pain was *identified*, e.g., with an apparent hurtfully embedded thorn. To the subject it seemed that there was something in his body affecting him hurtfully, and it is this, you claim, that he calls a pain. This identification was supported by noting that a subject who is asked to focus attention on his pain will do subjectively the same as he would if, in the case of a real thorn in his finger, he focused attention on the thorn in his finger. But this is mistaken. Told to focus his attention on *the thorn hurting him*, one might discover and say that it is brown, it has a jagged end, it is sharp and small, a rose thorn, etc. Or if the object is the *thorn's being there*, he may say it is unfortunate, painful, doesn't hurt a bit, has caused a puffiness, is likely to result in an infection, etc. None of these describes a pain. On the other hand, the features that might characterize a pain, the features a person might note and mention upon being asked to focus on his pain, will not well characterize a thorn, or a thorn's presence in the finger: it is unbearable, dull, throbbing, intense, intermittent, somehow "ticklish" or "tingly," apt to go away if a drug is administered, etc. It may well be, as you claim, that in at least some cases of pain, the subject seems to himself to be aware of the presence of something in his body affecting him hurtfully. But to claim that he calls *this* object a pain, that the apparent object is *identical* with the pain, is wrong.

Reply: Even in the case where there actually exists a thorn in his finger hurting him, if the subject closes his eyes and, focusing his attention, goes by feeling alone, as we are supposing, how could he tell that it was "brown" or "a rose thorn"? To recognize something's *color* by sense, normally one must see it; and even experienced gardeners cannot tell the origin or variety of embedded thorns by their feel alone. Likewise, due to its small size, a victim probably could not tell by feel that the thorn's point is jagged. Going by feeling alone, the most that he probably could discriminate is (as the objection mentions) that the perceived entity is "sharp and small," but this description is also truly applicable to the pain: "It's a small, sharp pain" (assuming we are to continue speaking in this reprehensible manner as if apparent objects were logically proper subjects of predication). And contrary to the objection's claim, the descriptions 'unfortunate' and 'painful' *can* describe a pain. ("This pain is [an] unfortunate [occurrence]," and the redundant but true, "This pain is painful.") By hypothesis, in the case imagined, the thorn's being there *did* hurt, so 'doesn't hurt a bit' is true neither of the thorn nor of the pain. I agree that the descriptions 'has caused a certain puffiness' and 'is likely to result in an infection' are not true of the pain itself, but neither do they characterize or express felt qualities of a thorn in the fingertip, or consequently, of an *apparent* thorn, the "entity" whose identity with "the pain" is at issue. (The properties of an "apparent thorn," it must be remembered, are just its apparent properties; the apparent thorn's properties are only the sensory qualities of which it seems to the subject he is aware in his state of truncated awareness.) Again, contrary to what the objection assumes, the descriptions 'unbearable' (meaning presumably something like "It very much bothers me and I wish it would go away"), 'intense[ly felt, intensely unpleasant, whatever is meant]', 'tick-lish'(?), 'tingly', and 'apt to go away if a drug is administered' can truly characterize an apparent hurtful thorn in one's fingertip. So none of these predicates distinguishes or separates "the pain" from "the apparent thorn" in the present case.

Objection: Thomas's theory is *trivial*. Even if his so-called axioms or principles are true, they say nothing significant or important about mental phenomena, for the philosophy of mind or otherwise.[28]

Reply: This line of attack recalls the logical positivists' (prob-ably correct) assaults on the metaphysical systems of some tradi-tional philosophers (e.g., Aristotle, Leibniz) as "pseudo-theories" that lack bona fide cognitive content, convey no genuine informa-tion, and are devoid of significant or important consequences. The fact that unlike "scientific" theories, these philosophical theories entailed no experimentally testable consequences or predictions allegedly showed their cognitive emptiness. To dis-tinguish empirically meaningful scientific theories from such vacuous pseudo-scientific "metaphysical" theories (pejoratively called "a priori chemistry"), the positivists proposed their famous *verifiability criterion of meaningfulness*. The following conse-quence was a common aim of the varying statements of this crite-rion: A statement that is not "analytic" or a logical truth is cognitively meaningful or significant if and only if empirical experiments or observations can confirm or disconfirm it. Thus, by this criterion so formulated, a statement or theory has genuine cognitive content if it entails even one empirically testable conse-quence. Indeed, even less suffices. If, in conjunction with further "auxiliary hypotheses," a theory is demonstrated to entail empiri-cally testable predictions that are not implied by these auxiliary hypotheses alone, this demonstration shows the nonvacuousness of the theory. In the ensuing decades, many philosophers have protested that this criterion is excessively stringent and demand-ing (since it apparently would preclude as significant language normative judgments, moral discourse, and aesthetic criticism, among other notables), but to my knowledge, *no one* ever has

28. According to David Keyt in 1975, this objection was raised by Charles Marks, Marc Cohen, Kenneth Clatterbaugh, and Karl Potter, among others.

suggested that this criterion is not strict enough. Without endorsing the positivists' presuppositions, the verifiability criterion is recalled simply to point out that my hypothesis passes this strict test with flying colors. For the hypothesis implies empirically testable experimental consequences or predictions (as James Meiss says in the science abstract, the theory "entails physical results"). For example, it implies that fully adapted blind subjects using an operating TVSS will have *visual* sensory subjective experience (i.e., they will actually seem to *see* their surrounding environment). Another specific empirical implication is the possible experimental separability of the "two ways of knowing" positions and movements of one's own bodily parts (as confirmed by William James's psychological observations); another is that fully adapted wearers of inverting spectacles will ipso facto again return to "seeing things rightside up." Any one of these entailments singly, by itself, suffices to prove the cognitive nontriviality of my theory. Furthermore, as has been demonstrated elsewhere in this treatise, this theory (either in isolation or in conjunction with auxiliary hypotheses that do not by themselves imply these consequences) entails a number of important theoretical consequences: the rejection of any "introspectionist" (i.e., transitional) model of psychological self-knowledge, the affirmation of a nontransitional model of mental self-knowledge together with a directly realistic theory of perception, the denial of "private inner object" conceptions of mental phenomena, an explanation of the so-called "incorrigibility" of sincere beliefs or reports about one's own mental state, the truth of analytical behaviorism (with all that is entailed by this), the falsity of supplemented (or "logical") dualism, the likely falsity of "contingent" dualism, an explanation of how purely material physical systems could have mental states, an explanation of how one subject can occupy a unique and intrinsically privileged epistemological position vis-à-vis an event occurring in a certain location in physical space, the falsity of operationism, and the falsity of central state materialism. (Figure A–1 diagrammatically summarizes some of these implications.) Furthermore, it might be added that the majority of modern philosophical constructions, from Descartes to Ayer, are based on epistemologies that foundationally assume a direct acquaintance model of the cognitive relationship between a subject and his own mental phenomena, constructions that all fall if the rejection of Application I of the

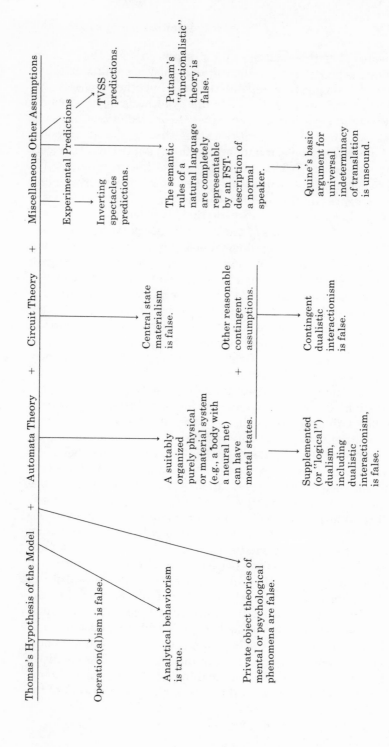

Figure A-1. Informal diagram of some logical consequences of the hypothesis

Transition Model stands. So the hypothesis is logically well bastioned and secure against any attack on grounds that it is "trivial" or a "vacuous pseudo-theory." If true, the theory's truth is clearly far from "trivial." (Indeed, relative to the present context where the theory includes, along with its statement, many purported logical deductions of significant theoretical and experimental consequences from it, the charge of "triviality" is not even in proper logical order unless accompanied by specific refutations of each of these alleged deductions, since the correctness of even one of them refutes the objection.)

In short, then, the reply to the objection is this: calling a theory "trivial" implies that it logically entails no important consequences. Accordingly, this charge is refuted conclusively by valid logical deductions of important consequences from that theory. Such deductions from the hypothesis of my model have been exhibited in the body of this text. Therefore, it has been shown to be nontrivial.

The next *objection* falls somewhat outside the theory of mind:

The functionalist thesis entails that any realization of one of the postulated FSTs will have mental states. Since, according to the theory, mental descriptions are abstract functional descriptions, it does not matter how these abstract states are concretely realized. A realization need not be built from organic tissue such as neurons and muscles, but, in principle, could be built entirely from wires, switches, and other mechanical parts. What matters is form, not substance. So the theory entails that if they were suitably organized, inorganic mechanical artifacts, "machines," could have states of mind or consciousness.

But mental predicates carry ethical and other implications. To apply certain sets of mental predicates to something entails that it is a moral agent and merits special considerations which we do not accord to machines. However, *we* might not relate to artificial realizations of FSTs in the same way we do to naturally occurring ones. We might, for example, "enslave" them. We might refuse to count them as "persons" or to apply ordinary mentalistic predicates to them because we might not want to accord them the rights and privileges that go with those attributions. So realizing a certain FST-description is not a sufficient condition for the application of these mental predicates.

Reply: I think something is right in this claim:[29] the way we act toward entities we call "machines" certainly differs from the way we act toward entities we call "persons" (although whether such a difference *ought* to exist is another question). And the matter surely bears theoretical inquiry. Although I am uncertain how best to respond to it, I fail to see that this objection poses a serious difficulty for the functionalist theory of mind per se. The thesis is intended as a pure theory in the foundations of psychology and neuropsychology, and I cannot see that its task is to describe the moral or social import of states of consciousness. If it is true that mental descriptions indeed carry these implications, and that inorganic systems cannot be moral agents, then the thesis must be modified to imply only that inorganic machines can have states similar to the states of consciousness of humans in every respect except perhaps their moral or social significance.

29. Putnam discusses this in "Robots: Machines or Artificially Created Life?" *Journal of Philosophy*, 61 (November 1964), 676–687.

Science Abstract

BY JAMES MEISS

The Formal Mechanics of Mind begins with a "metaphilosophical apology" that attemps to set the book in its proper place in the context of philosophy itself. Ideas of Wittgenstein, Carnap, and Kuhn are amended and combined in an effort to explain how philosophical problems (cf. Kuhn's "extraordinary science") are actually difficulties within a conceptualizing structure (cf. Kuhn's "paradigm"). To solve such a problem, the author claims, it is necessary to modify that conceptualizing structure. This viewpoint differs from that of Wittgenstein who believed that philosophical problems are linguistic in origin and that a proper solution "leaves everything as it is." To replace an old conceptualizing structure with a new one may be equivalent to constructing a new scientific theory, and such a solution may entail empirically confirmable physical results. This work is conceived by its author as an attempt to construct a new conceptualizing structure to solve the traditional mind-body problem.

The old model postulated such phenomena as private objects and introspections; the new conceptualizing structure involves primarily behavioral predicates. The mentalistic descriptions of ordinary language are postulated by the new theory to be entailed by states in a table of stimulus inputs and behavioral outputs. The mode of representation used is that of a functional state table (FST). An FST is a generalization of the concept of a Turing Machine. Formally it is represented by (1) a set of states, (2) a set of inputs, (3) a set of outputs, (4) a next-state function, and (5) an output function. A system that "realizes" or "implements" an FST has certain states that determine what output will be produced upon a given input. Inputs not only cause an output to be produced (depending upon the F-state the system is in), but also cause the system to change states. The next-state function and the output function are, in general, probabilistic functions.

The author states that the assumption that any system is represented by an FST is philosophically neutral. He attempts to support this claim by showing how introspectionist and psychological behaviorist models of the mind both can be represented using a state table. These models (surprising that both are similar) both involve what is called "transitional self-description"; that is, in order to produce a mentalistic self-description the subject observes what is being described (in one case, he observes private objects in his mind, in the other case, he is assumed to observe his own behavior, and thereby report—as any outside person would—his own mental state).

The new theory, on the contrary, postulates that mentalistic self-descriptions are not produced by observation of anything, but instead are produced "nontransitionally." This idea is illustrated with the example of an imagined specially modified typewriter that can produce reports of its inner states without self-observation. When in the state of "being ready to produce capital letters," this typewriter will, upon someone's hitting the proper key, print 'I am in the state of being ready to produce capitals'. Such a system, involving no internal sensing elements to observe its own state, is shown easy to conceive. Such a system can produce self-descriptions reporting its states simply because it is constructed in a certain manner. The author hypothesizes that through natural learning processes, people become so constituted that they likewise can report the state they are in as just part of being in that state. Thus, for example, a subject can report whether his arms are moving even if he is not observing them; in fact, his arm can be completely without feeling and the subject still can report its actions without looking at it (experimental data).

A major effort is made in this book to formulate a distinction that will set mentalistic states apart from all other states. One traditional way in which this has been done is by postulating that psychological states are characterized by the "principle of incorrigibility" (if a person knows the language and speaks sincerely, he cannot make a mistake in judging or ascertaining his mental state). The author replaces this with a concept that is alleged to eliminate some of the objections to incorrigibility. He postulates that mentalistic states are "functionally determined" states. They are such that it is a sufficient condition for a person to be in a certain mental state if he is in a given state in a given FST. In terms of the typewriter analogue, the state of "being ready to type capitals" is functionally determined, but the state of "having a lowered type-panel" is not. Typewriters could be constructed in many different ways (e.g., with a ball instead of a type-panel), but the input-output characteristics, hence the FST, and hence the functional state, would be the same.

The author hypothesizes that "the mind" (or better: each mental property) is totally determined by a system's input-output characteristics in a totality of possible situations. Mental states are abstract functional states of a system, a means of indexing its input-output characteristics to give it functional form.

This model leads to what is called a "modest incorrigibility." It follows that a person who is a realization of a particular FST will, when in certain states of it, never produce a mental self-description that is false. (He could, however, produce a false self-description when in a state of "intending to lie" or when he has been hypnotized into having a false belief, or under other circumstances.)

The author's model is logically compatible with a type of mind-body dualism that would posit a nonphysical "soul" that is part of the concrete realization of the person's FST. Since anything can be represented by an FST, an immaterial soul is no exception. The author also presents an argument to show that any function mediated by such a "soul" also could be mediated by a neural network, and that this latter way of realizing the FST is much less problematic. A proof is presented to show that the model also entails "analytical behaviorism" (which is understood as the view that logically sufficient conditions for any mental state can be expressed in purely behavioral terms).

For a psychologist, actually enumerating the FST representing a person would be a tremendous task. One can consider a partial FST, however—one characterizing only the responses to certain stimulus inputs when a person is in certain states—as a true description of that person. (The author appears to believe that all FSTs are "partial" in this sense.) In actual practice, there will be many coapplicable FSTs of varying degrees of detail. One task is to build up such FST descriptions, obtaining finer and finer distinctions between different states and inputs.

The author claims that his version of a functionalist theory can be used to give clean accounts of many types of mental phenomena. Hallucinations, dreams, and afterimages are characterized by a model of "truncated awareness," which views these phenomena as occurring when a person is in a mental state similar to that in a real perceptual relationship, but caused by something other than the apparently perceived phenomenon. The experience of pain is analyzed as having two different components: a sensation at a certain location and the suffering or attitude of aversion to it. An analysis of the inverting spectacles experiments is given. Subjects who have worn the spectacles for a period of time have their FSTs reprogrammed so that given the same input as before from the outside world, the subject automatically produces the same output response as before. This reprogramming occurs because as the subject moves through what appeared at first to be an inverted world, he was forced to learn how to react to inputs so as to avoid running into things, etc. After learning again to make the proper responses to various inputs, the subject returns to something like the original FST and consequently again perceives the world as rightside up. The theory also leads to interesting predictions about the outcome of experiments with a "tactile vision substitution system" prosthetic eye.

Index